THE EASTERN QVESTION

The Eastern Question
A Geopolitical History
in 108 Maps & Drawings by Ted Danforth

OMNES MVNDI THEATRVM

ANEKDOTA

VISIT OUR WEBSITE

www.easternquestion.com

FOR GLOSSARY AND UPDATES

Cataloging-in-Publication Data
Danforth, Ted.
The Eastern question: a geopolitical history in 108 maps & drawings/Ted Danforth.
pages cm
ISBN 978-0-692-30840-0
1. Eastern question. 2. Eastern question (Balkan). 3. Geopolitics—Middle East.
4. History and Geopolitical Divisions. I. Title
956—dc23   2015904488

© 2015 Ted Danforth

PRINTED AND BOUND BY
ELEGANCE PRINTING & BOOK BINDING CO. LTD.

Published by
ANEKDOTA
AN IMPRINT OF TOWNSHEND HOUSE

ANEKDOTA

PRINTED AND BOUND IN CHINA

PRO SUA NAN SINE QUIS NON

CONTENTS

Prologue   1
    Byzantine/Ottoman Empire
    Cockpit of Conflict
    Persians, Alexander, Romans
    House of Rome
    Old War/Cold War/New War

On Reading History   12
    The Library
    Streams of History
    A Museum of History
    Geopolitical Dynamics
    Commedia della storia
    The Historian's Colors

I. The Geopolitical Dynamics of History

Geopolitics   26
    Mackinder's World Island
    Desert & Sown: The World Egg
    East & West: Climatologic Zones
    Order & Fragmentation: Ibn Khaldûn

Desert & Sown   34
    Nomads
    Horses, Camels, Ships
    Mongol's-Eye View
    Attila Playing Pool
    Good Stuff Comes from the East
    Silk Road

East & West: The East   46
    Ecumene, or Known World
    Six Geopolitical Zones
    Persian/Alexander's Empire/Caliphate of Baghdad
    Sunni and Shia
    Great Mosque of Damascus

The True East: Turks, Mongols, Russians   56
    Selçuks and Crusaders
    Mongols
    Russian Façade
    Succession of States

East & West: The West   64
    Cross and Crescent
    Two Great *Jihads*
    Holy Roman Empire
    Peninsularity of Europe
    Eastern Borders of Europe

The West: A Mighty Fortress   74
    Ein Feste Burg
    Two-Fronted Wars
    Hapsburg Military Frontier

Empire: Order & Fragmentation   80
    The World Egg Broken
    Act One: Empire Divided, AD 395
    Act Two: Empire Divided, 1292

Act Three: Empire Divided, 1699
Intermission: Analysis of the Plot
Act Four: The Red Apple
Act Five: Zagros Mountains
A Geopolitical Fable

II. The Eastern Empire

The Legacy of the Eastern Empire   100
    A Virtual Tour of the Former Ottoman Empire
    The Petri Dish
    Battle of Issus
    Voyages of Saul of Tarsus
    Epic as History
    Greek Letters Encircle the Mediterranean
    Religion as Politics
    Jerusalem the Golden
    Intersection of Three Major Language Groups
    Persian Letters
    Rumi's Tomb
    Architecture, East and West
    Time and Space in Church and Mosque

The Ottoman Empire   126
    The Ottoman Rhinoceros
    Topkapi Palace
    Three Extraordinary Institutions
    Ertoğrul Gazi Turbesi

III. The Eastern Question Is Asked

The Rise of the West — 136
    Great 'C' of Reconquista and Conquista
    Passing of Greek Manuscripts
    Capital Flows
    The Turning Point
    European Conquest of the World
    Fall of Dar al' Islam

The Eastern Question, Per Se — 148
    Catherine and Potemkin at Kherson, 1787
    Russian Bear
    Gates of India
    Afghanistan

The Eastern Question Full-Blown — 156
    Political Football
    Sandbox of Empire
    Full Steam Ahead!
    Origin of the War
    What Was the Cause?
    Butcher Block of Empires
    Breaking of Sèvres
    Mighty Caesar's Heirs

The Cold War — 172
    Years Between the Wars
    Russia and the United States: Geopolitically
    Russia and the United States: Politically
    Passing of the Baton
    A Delicate Balance Upset
    Fate Power Vacuums the Dusty Old Oriental

IV. New Conflicts, Old Questions

The East Strikes Back   186
    Revolt of Islam
    Oil Farm
    World Traders and Raiders
    Killing the Golden Goose

The Eastern Question, Again   194
    Geopolitics
    Desert & Sown
    East & West
    Order & Fragmentation

Imperia Irredenta   202
    Persia/Iran
    Syria/Isis/Israel
    Ukraine, 2014
    A Geopolitical Theater in the Round
    Dreams from My Fathers
    Oxbows in Time

A CHRONOLOGY   214
NOTES   216
ACKNOWLEDGMENTS   247

TO THE READER

This book is the result of my inquiries into the geopolitical dynamics of history, illustrated with maps and drawings in dialogue with texts, corroborated and elaborated with notes, arranged thematically, but chronologically within themes.

There are three ways to read this book. Read it first as a story, flipping through the drawings, glancing at the first text paragraphs, which serve as captions. Then later, read the rest of the text, even read the notes—but first, flip through it. Read it fast. You could even read it backwards.

Take a peek at the end. Don't worry about spoiling the story. You already know how it turns out.

—T.D.

THE EASTERN QUESTION

Are they assigned, or can the countries pick their colors?
—What suits the character or the native waters best.
Topography displays no favorites; North's as near as West.
More delicate than the historians' are the map-makers' colors.

—ELIZABETH BISHOP

The Maps in this book are metaphorical and are not to be used for navigational purposes.

THE EASTERN QUESTION

PROLOGUE

LIKE BEN FRANKLIN, I am a printer by trade. At the time of 9/11, I had a shop in downtown Manhattan, not far from the World Trade Center. Being so close, the attacks made a big impression on me. Like most Americans, I wondered 'why.' Then, a month later, I got a clue when I read what Osama bin Laden had said in one of his pronouncements, in classical Arabic: that the attacks were revenge for what had happened 80 years before, and 'the subsequent humiliation and disgrace' that Islam has suffered at the hands of the West. That comment gave me a vision of history and our place in it. This book is my attempt to convey that vision.

I am not only a printer but a 'scholar-printer,' one who works in the trade but also studies printing history, which begins in the Renaissance. From that perspective, I realized the significance of the Fall—or Conquest—of Constantinople in 1453, when the Ottoman Turks dealt a fatal blow to the last remnants of the Greek-speaking eastern half of the classical world, which the Renaissance was trying to revive. That blow was the culmination of an 800-year advance by Islam, a historical process that, with the rise of the West over the succeeding 400 years, was slowly reversed, leading 80 years ago to another fall—or conquest.

I saw that what might seem to be the multitudinous and arbitrary events of history, its apparent 'buzzin' jammin' confusion,' are manifestations of dynamics that go back to the beginning of recorded time. Every time you read the international news you find history—like an old man repeating himself—flowing on in endless dynamics of opposition played out upon the stage of geopolitics: between *Desert & Sown*, between *East & West*, and between *Order & Fragmentation*.

Byzantine/ Ottoman Empire

It occurred to me that Osama bin Laden was most likely referring to the fall of the Ottoman Empire at the end of the First World War. This was the first insight that led to the writing of this book. Well, of course: if we are talking about the Ottoman Empire, then we are talking about the long struggle of Dar al' Islam and Christendom, an opposition older than either religion, one that reflects the great underlying geopolitical dynamic of East and West. The attack of 9/11 was not an isolated event but a continuation of patterns woven into the warp of historical time.

The Ottoman Empire was the successor state of the Byzantine Empire—itself the successor of the Eastern Roman Empire—shown here in the upper drawing at its greatest extent under the reign of Emperor Justinian, who died in 565. Culminating with the Conquest of Constantinople by Sultan Mehmet II in May 1453, it was conquered by the armies of Islam, and its Greek culture overlaid first by an Arabic and then a Turkish one. The Turkish Ottoman Empire reached its height in 1565 with the death of Sultan Suleyman, exactly a millennium after the death of Justinian. The succession of empires in the same place demonstrates that this Eastern Empire is a natural geopolitical zone.

For the West, the Eastern Empire is like an amputated limb that can still be felt. It is the lost half of Christendom, the birthplace of Western civilization, the *fons et origen* of its culture, its two religions, its intellectual inheritance. It is why Western tourists travel to Turkey, Syria, Jordan, Libya, and Tunisia, looking at Greek and Roman ruins. It is why Greeks and Turks don't get along. It is why the West long dreamed of retaking the holy city of Jerusalem, which it did in December 1917—and why now it will not give it up.

The conquest of the Ottoman Empire some notional 80 years ago represents the complete reversal of 1453, a reversal for which Osama bin Laden and the *jihadi* sought revenge—historically the principal *casus belli*, or cause of war—in September 2001.

Ocean Sea
Gothic Kingdoms
Ravenna
42 BC
Philippi
Constantinople
168 BC
Pydna
31 BC
Actium
Antioch
Byzantine Sea
Pirates
BYZANTINE
EMPIRE
A.D. 565
Babylon
Alexandria
Jerusalem
Persia

Atlantic Ocean
Christendom
Mohácz
Belgrade
Bucharest
Kosovo
1389
Constantinople
1453
Adrianople
Rome
Gallipoli
Ankara
Lepanto
1571
Malta 1565
Pirates
Ottoman Sea
OTTOMAN
EMPIRE
A.D. 1565
Alexandria
Baghdad
1537
Jerusalem
1517
Persia

Cockpit of Conflict

The Ottoman Empire was the last regime to bring order—and hence stability—to the Middle East. Both it and its predecessor, the Byzantine Empire, were ultimately the heirs of the earliest empires in the world, those of the 'Fertile Crescent.'* Here in the lands between the Tigris and Euphrates rivers (Mesopotamia), and along the banks of the Nile in Egypt, man first settled in cities, or *civis*, in Latin. Here men ceased to be hunter-gatherers, planting crops, erecting public buildings, and keeping written records, thus creating the world of the sown—outside of which was the desert, where nomads roamed beyond the control of cities.

For this reason, the Fertile Crescent has been called the cradle of civilization, but we might also call it a cockpit of conflict. No sooner were cities erected than the struggle to control other cities and thus to create empires began. Indeed, the origin of the state is instinct with struggle. States are created by struggle and maintained by struggle; and their fragmentation engenders yet more struggle, when people once more 'cry "Havoc," and let slip the dogs of war.'*

For some three millennia*—more than the time that has passed since then—from Sargon to Cyrus, empires rose and fell in the Fertile Crescent. Chaldeans, Babylonians, Egyptians, Hittites, Assyrians, and then Persians succeeding one another as lords of all or large parts of this 'well-watered land' (Iraq). Cyrus welded the Persians and the Medes into a nation and founded the first world empire, commanding the juncture of three continents. By 550 BC, his empire stretched from Libya and the Balkans to the Indus River. His nephew Darius was as accomplished an administrator as his uncle had been a conqueror. Darius introduced sound fiscal policy, accurate weights and measures—and toleration, that sine qua non of any great empire. Even though it has been overrun several times since then by invaders, it always reverts to being Persia.

With the rise of Persia, and then the later rise of the Roman Empire and then the Ottoman Empire, the Fertile Crescent was no longer the center and became a borderland between empires, a place where battles necessarily are fought.

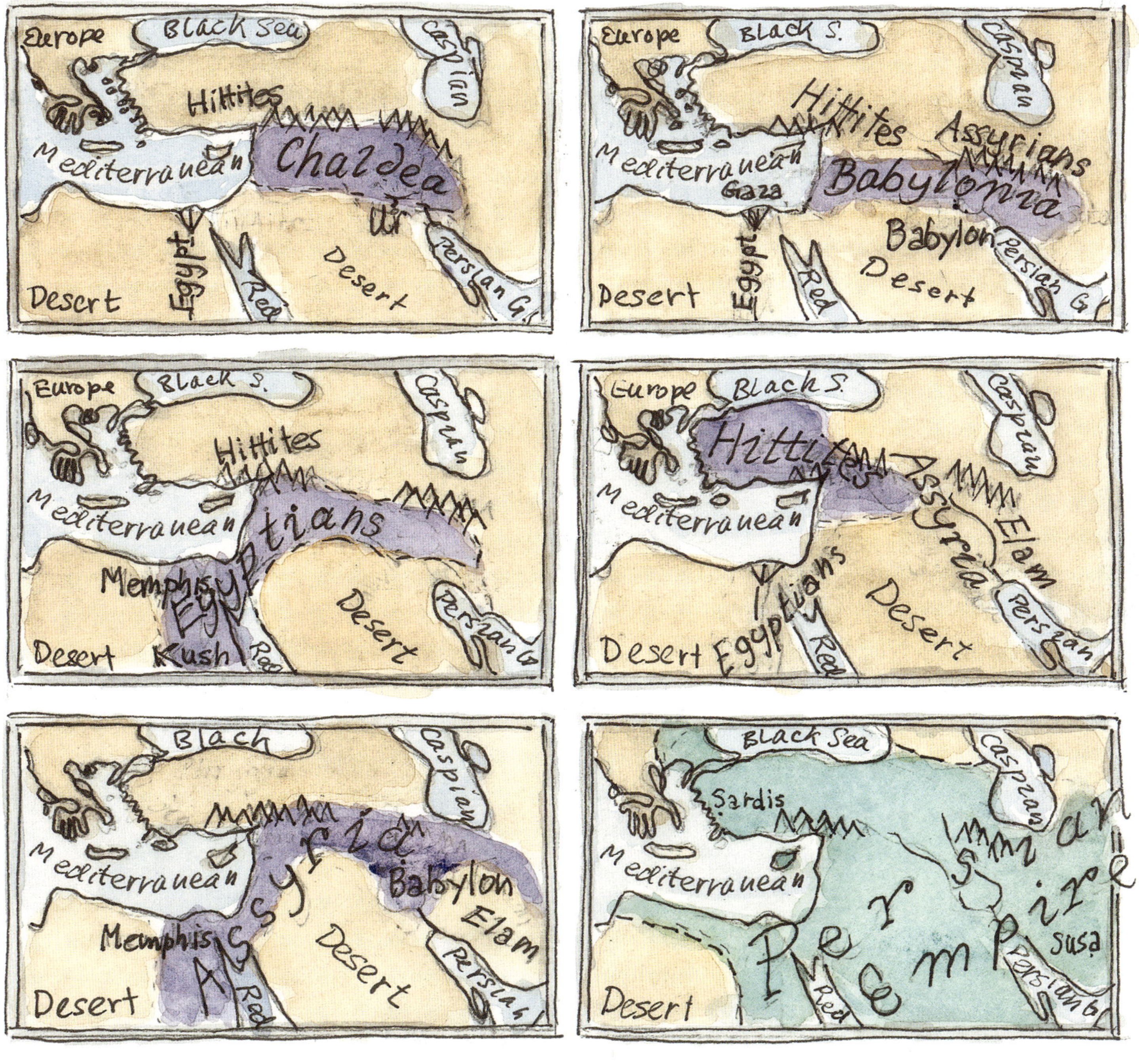

Europe
Black Sea
Caspian
Hittites
Mediterranean
Chaldea
Ur
Egypt
Red
Desert
Desert
Persian G.
Europe
Black S.
Caspian
Hittites
Assyrians
Mediterranean
Gaza
Babylonia
Babylon
Egypt
Red
Desert
Desert
Persian G.
Europe
Black S.
Caspian
Hittites
Mediterranean
Egyptians
Memphis
Kush
Red
Desert
Desert
Persian G
Europe
Black S.
Caspian
Hittites
Assyria
Elam
Mediterranean
Egyptians
Red
Desert
Desert
Persian
Black
Caspian
Mediterranean
Assyria
Babylon
Elam
Memphis
Red
Desert
Desert
Persian
Black Sea
Caspian
Sardis
Mediterranean
Persian Empire
Susa
Red
Desert
Persian G

Persians, Alexander, Romans

These three drawings show the strikes, counterstrikes, and encirclings that were the birth pains of the West, the Middle East, and Persia (Iran). The first attack of East on West was the Persian assault on Greece* described by Herodotus in the first Western book of history. Herodotus gave the capital letters to East and West, making it the struggle of the little guy (Greeks) versus the big bad empire (Persians), of freedom versus tyranny.* Here are the origins of the struggle of East and West before the rise of the Arabs, when this struggle became that of Dar al' Islam and Christendom.

The first counterstrike of the West against the East was Alexander's conquest of Persia, when he defeated Darius III at the battle of Issus in 333 BC. In doing so, Alexander and his successors (his former generals, the Diadochi) founded the Greek-speaking Hellenistic kingdoms, the lands that came to be known under the Romans as the Eastern Empire. One of Alexander's successor dynasties, that of the Seleucids, held on to Persia for some time, but, in one of the periodic revivals of Persian history, it reverted to its distinctly Persian identity and never became Greek-speaking.

The Romans were the next to bring order to these lands. In 189 BC, they conquered the Seleucid kingdom of Antiochus III. Circling to the west of the Mediterranean, Rome then conquered Carthage in 146 BC. The circle of conquest* was completed with Cleopatra's death in 30 BC. She was the last of the Ptolemys, descendants of another of Alexander's generals. Spurning her advances, Octavian (later Augustus) preferred to complete the Roman Empire than be a third Roman leader—after Caesar and Antony—in her bed, so that nations might insensibly melt* into Rome's embrace.

Christianity and Roman imperialism were born together in the same cradle. Three decades after Cleopatra's death, Jesus was born in nearby Palestine as Octavian was transforming the old Roman republic* into a world empire. Three centuries later, in an attempt to forestall its fragmentation, Constantine arranged the marriage of the dying empire to the budding bride of the Christian Church.

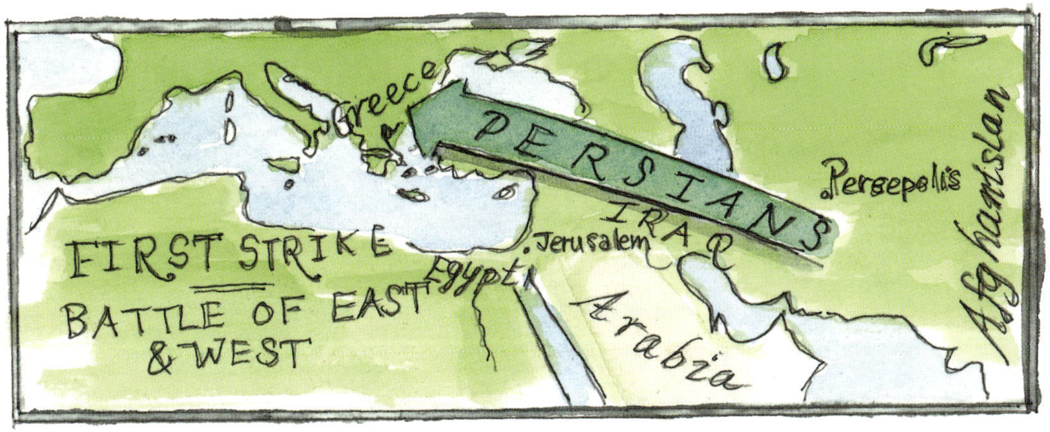
Greece
PERSIANS
Persepolis
IRAQ
Jerusalem
Egypt
Arabia
Afghanistan
FIRST STRIKE
BATTLE OF EAST & WEST

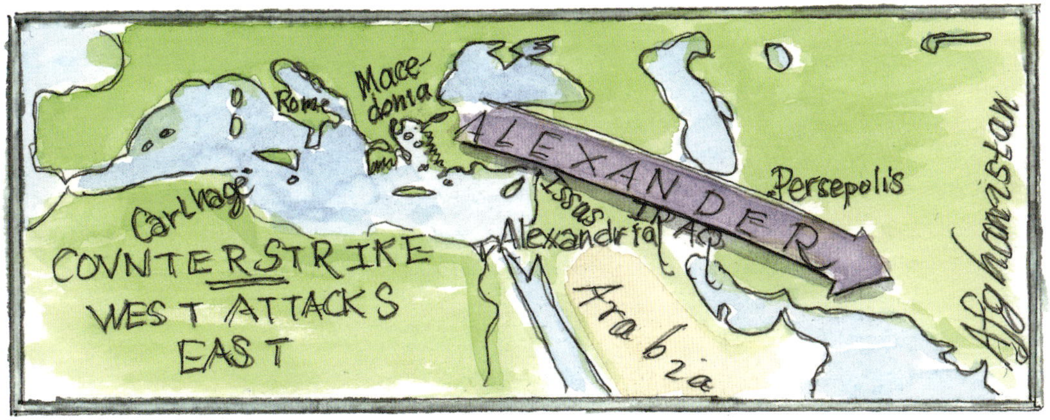
Rome
Macedonia
ALEXANDER
Persepolis
Issus
IRAQ
Alexandria
Carthage
Arabia
Afghanistan
COUNTERSTRIKE
WEST ATTACKS EAST

SCIPIOS
POMPEY·JULIUS·OCTAVIAN
Rome
Actium
Carthage
Alexandria
IRAQ
Parthians
Sassanid Persians
Arabia
Afghanistan
ROME CLOSES THE CIRCLE OF MED., BUT FAILS TO TAKE PERSIA

House of Rome

Imagine the Roman Empire as a house built around a courtyard with a pool in the middle. The pool is the Mediterranean Sea, or Middle Earth Sea. The Romans called it *Mare Nostrum*, Our Sea. It was a *mare clausum*, or 'closed sea,' and the Romans completely controlled the trade across it, primarily grain from a then fertile Africa.

Constantine began the process by which the empire became Christian. He built a new Eastern, Christian capital, Constantinople. Rome was then too identified with the old pagan state religion. Later, in AD 495, the empire was divided in halves: an Eastern, Greek-speaking (later the Byzantine, or Lower) empire—shown here in purple—and a Western, Latin-speaking empire, shown here in red. Less than a century and a half later, in 632, with the death of Mohammad and the rise of Islam—shown here in green—most of the Eastern Empire, and the African territories of the Western, were conquered by the Arab armies, which brought about the end of the Western Empire more effectively than the so-called barbarian northern Germanic invasions.

No wonder Islam and Christendom came to clash: two religions, each claiming to have the final revelation of God to man, trying to live together in the same house with a third, which had had the first revelation.

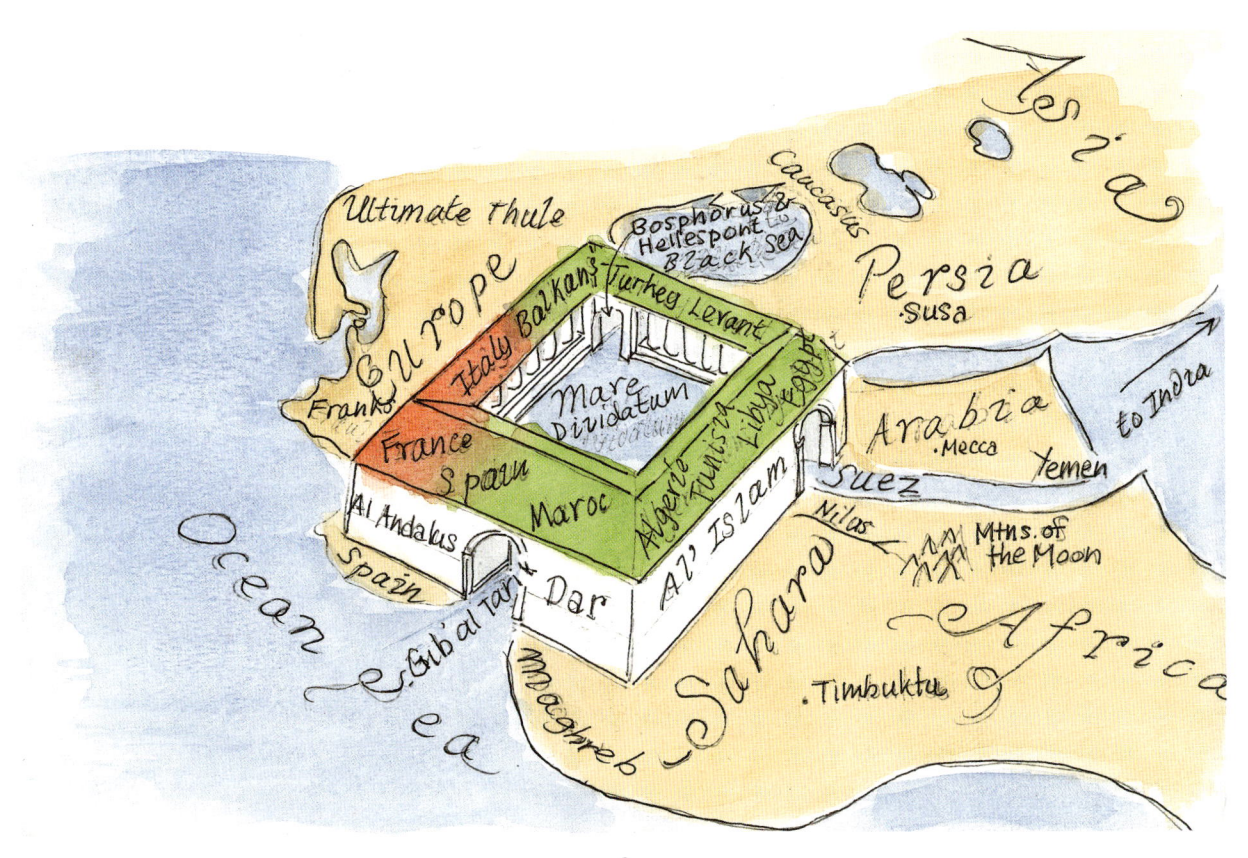

***Old War/
Cold War/
New War***

The division of the Roman Empire was 'a revolution that will ever be felt by the nations of the earth,' wrote Edward Gibbon, the historian of its decline and fall. This division is the great drama of history. Here is one way to diagram its narrative.

The Eastern and Western empires were two very distinct places, divided not only by geography, but also by language and religion. The Eastern Empire was Greek-speaking, and the Western Latin-speaking. 'While the Romans may have conquered, they never succeeded in imposing their language on the Eastern Empire.'* That linguistic failure increasingly pushed them apart, and in 1064, the Great Schism* split them definitively. In spite of repeated efforts, the breach has never been healed.

The rise of the Arabs in the 7th century led to the eventual political extinction of the Eastern Empire and to what might be called the Old, or Long, War between Dar al' Islam and Western Christendom, ultimately fought between the Ottoman Empire and the Hapsburg Empire (F.H.E.) of Spain, Italy, and Austria. This Old War lasted more than a thousand years, from the death of Mohammad in 632 until the last Turkish assault on Vienna was turned back in 1683.

From that point on, with the decline of both the Hapsburg and Ottoman empires, bankrupted by wars and the inflation of the 16th century, the struggle between East and West shifted north to a struggle between the land power of Russia, the heir of the Eastern Empire, and the Western European sea powers, heirs of the Western Empire and also of the German tribes. Eventually the struggle became one for the remains of the Ottoman Empire, the last colonial prize left, and it exploded into world war in 1914. After the Second World War, the struggle of East and West became one between the 'Eastern Bloc' and the 'Free World,' a struggle that seemingly ended with the collapse of the Former Soviet Union (F.S.U.), brought down in part by its defeat in the mountain passes of Afghanistan. In the power vacuum left by the absence of an Eastern Empire, a New War has erupted between the sole remaining 'superpower' and the remnants of the Former Ottoman Empire (F.O.E.).

COLD WAR
1945-1989

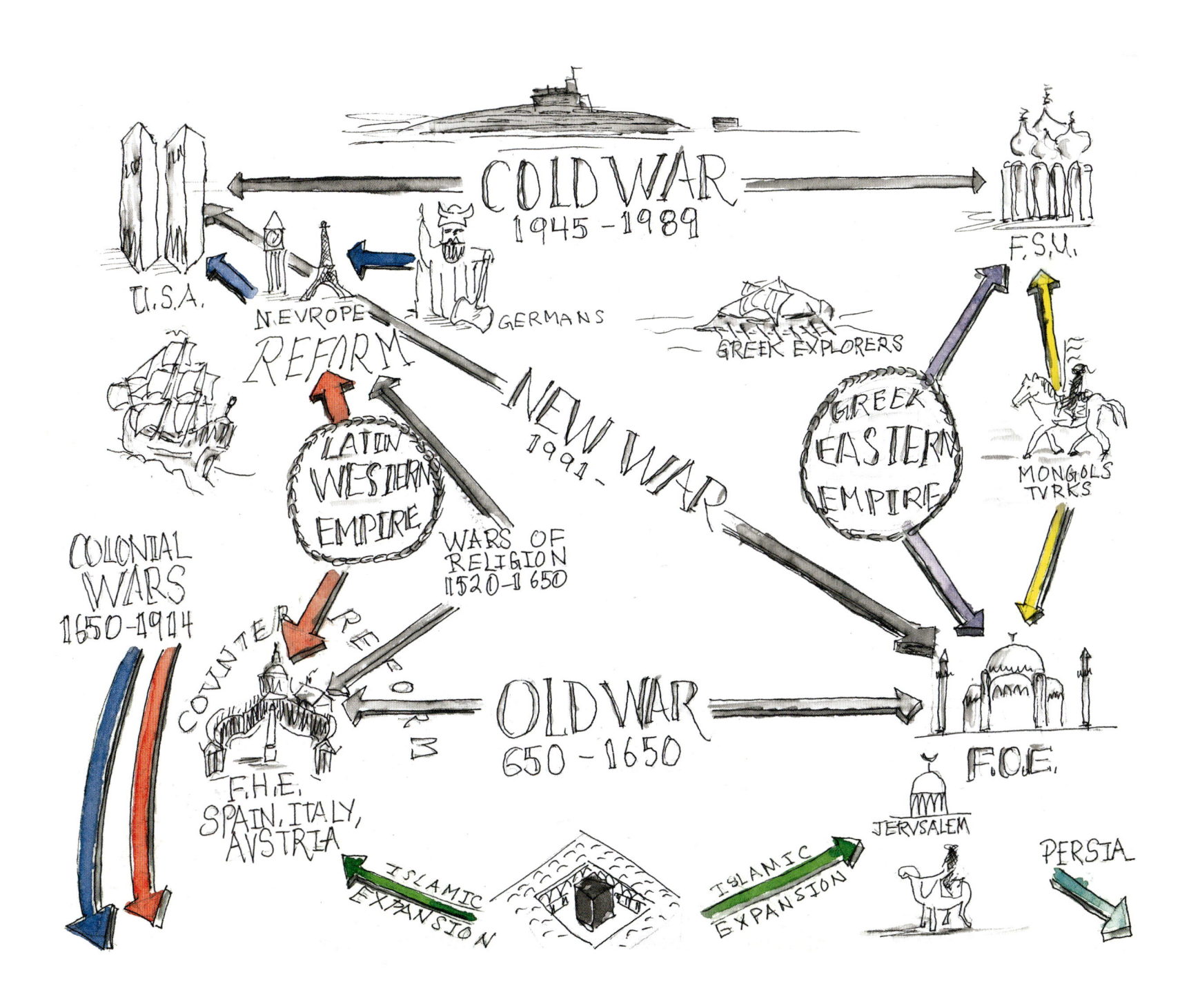

U.S.A. — N. EUROPE — GERMANS — GREEK EXPLORERS — F.S.U.

REFORM

LATIN WESTERN EMPIRE

GREEK EASTERN EMPIRE

MONGOLS TURKS

NEW WAR
1991-

WARS OF RELIGION 1520-1650

COUNTER REFORM

COLONIAL WARS
1650-1914

F.H.E. SPAIN, ITALY, AUSTRIA

OLD WAR
650-1650

F.O.E.

ISLAMIC EXPANSION — JERUSALEM — ISLAMIC EXPANSION — PERSIA

ON READING HISTORY

The Library

Sometime after 9/11, I began to see history graphically. In the library of our printing shop, I began making maps and drawings,* in dialogue with texts so that the drawing ideally would illustrate the text as much as the text would explain the drawing.

Making the drawings sensitized my historical antennae. I began to notice things, the trail of little clues that history litters after itself, like the spoor of a beast that a stealthy barefoot hunter tracks. We had some old newspapers in frames hanging on the wall of the shop. My eye was caught by a headline in one of them, the first edition of the Paris *Herald Tribune**: 'The Eastern Question, Again.' At the foot of the column is a small piece that reads: 'The recent cession by the Border Commission of territory in Afghanistan to the Russians really gives them the key to Herat and Kandahar,' calling it a 'blunder.' The dateline might have been the 1980s, not the 1880s.

The term 'The Eastern Question' refers to the problem that the slow dissolution of the Ottoman Empire posed to the Great Powers between the 1770s and 1921. In 19th-century diplomatic history, this mostly meant Austrian, British, and French opposition to the perceived threat of Russian expansion into the Balkans, the Middle East, Persia, and Afghanistan. But it will be used here in a more extended sense, because for the West, the East has always been a question: it's where trouble comes from, such as Huns, Goths, Arabs, Mongols, Turks, Russians… and now *jihadi*.

Nowadays, newspapers use the term 'the West,' but where did 'the East' go—at least an East with a capital E? During the late, lamented Cold War, it was clear what the East was. It was the Eastern Bloc. Now, post-9/11, it is more a question.

The histories of these places—Russia, the Ottoman Empire, Persia, and Afghanistan—are all part of various streams of consciousness, streams that braid and rebraid and must remain forever interwoven.

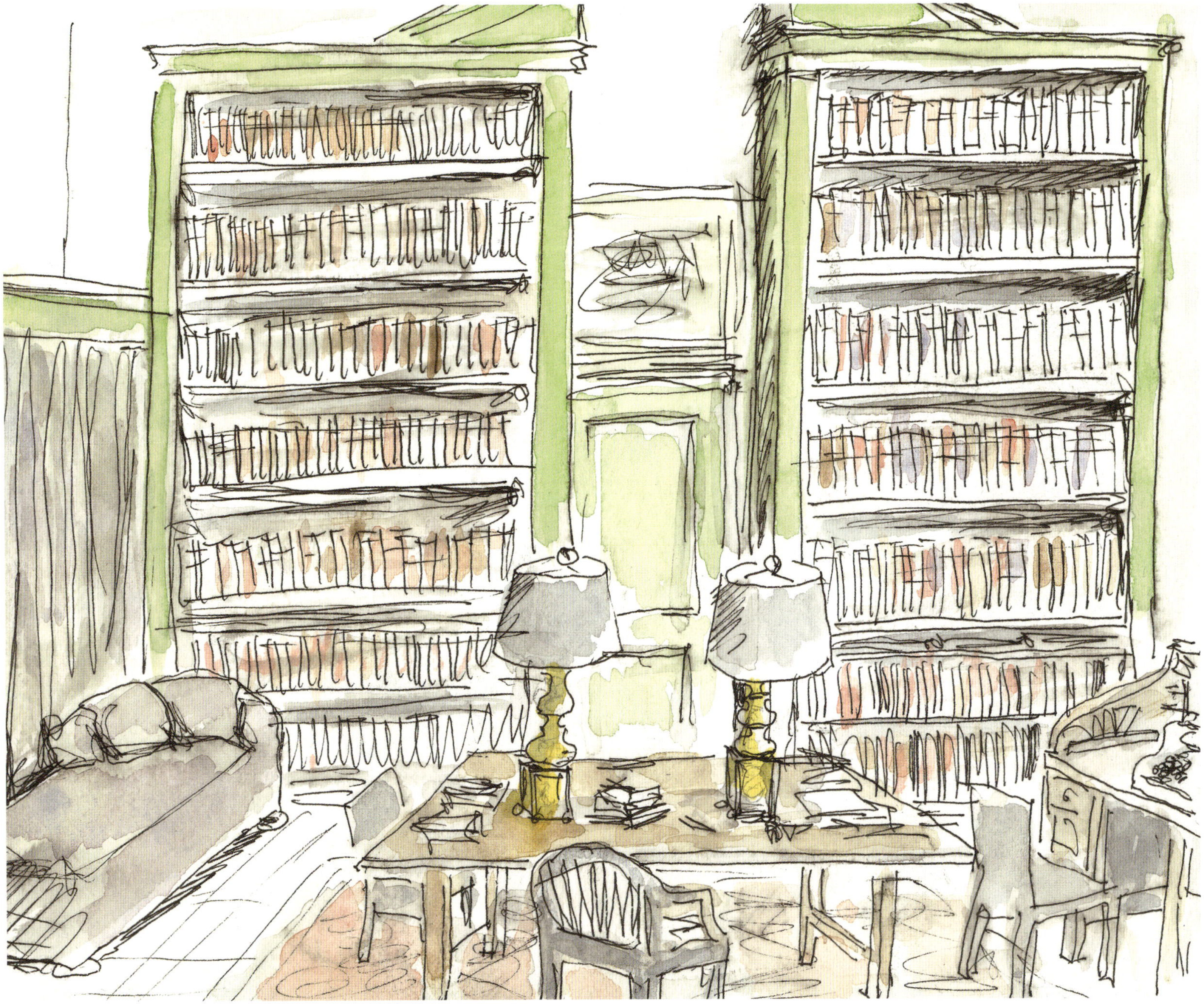

Streams of History

Ages ago, these streams surged up in the East, in Mesopotamia, and flowed toward the West—and the present. Archaeologists usually give the mid-4th millennium BC for the beginning of civilization in Mesopotamia. Coincidentally, the Jewish calendar, the oldest in the world still in use, begins at 9 AM, October 7, 3761 BC. Appropriately, it is called Anno Mundi, the year of the world, or A.M.—as A.D. is the year of the Lord and A.H. the year of the Hegira.

Like the tributaries of the Amazon, the streams of history flow together at great, broad confluences where the muddy white waters meet the clear black waters—and then flow on for hundreds of miles before mixing and flowing on toward another broad confluence.

Several streams combined together to form the Roman Empire, and then—with its division—creating the world we know today, both East and West, both Islam and Christendom. Out of the vast steppes of Asia to the east flowed the horse people; out of the dry deserts of Arabia flowed the camel people; and out onto the wet deserts of the vast oceans sailed the coastal Europeans, the ship people.

These streams have created the world we now live in and will continue to create other worlds in the future—other worlds unimaginable to us today. Sometimes freshets cut unsuspected, unknown channels, such as a new Islamic State.

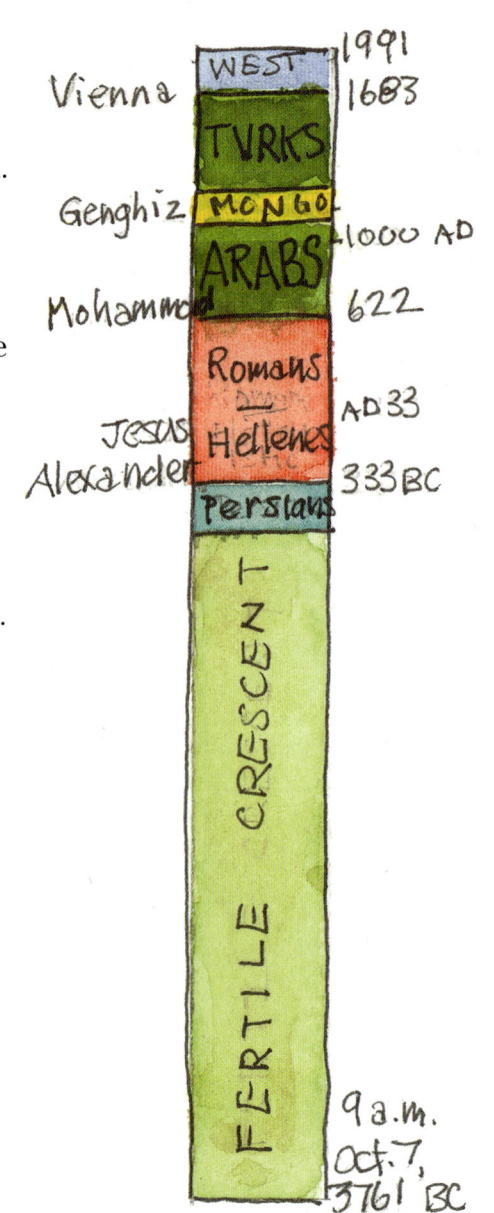

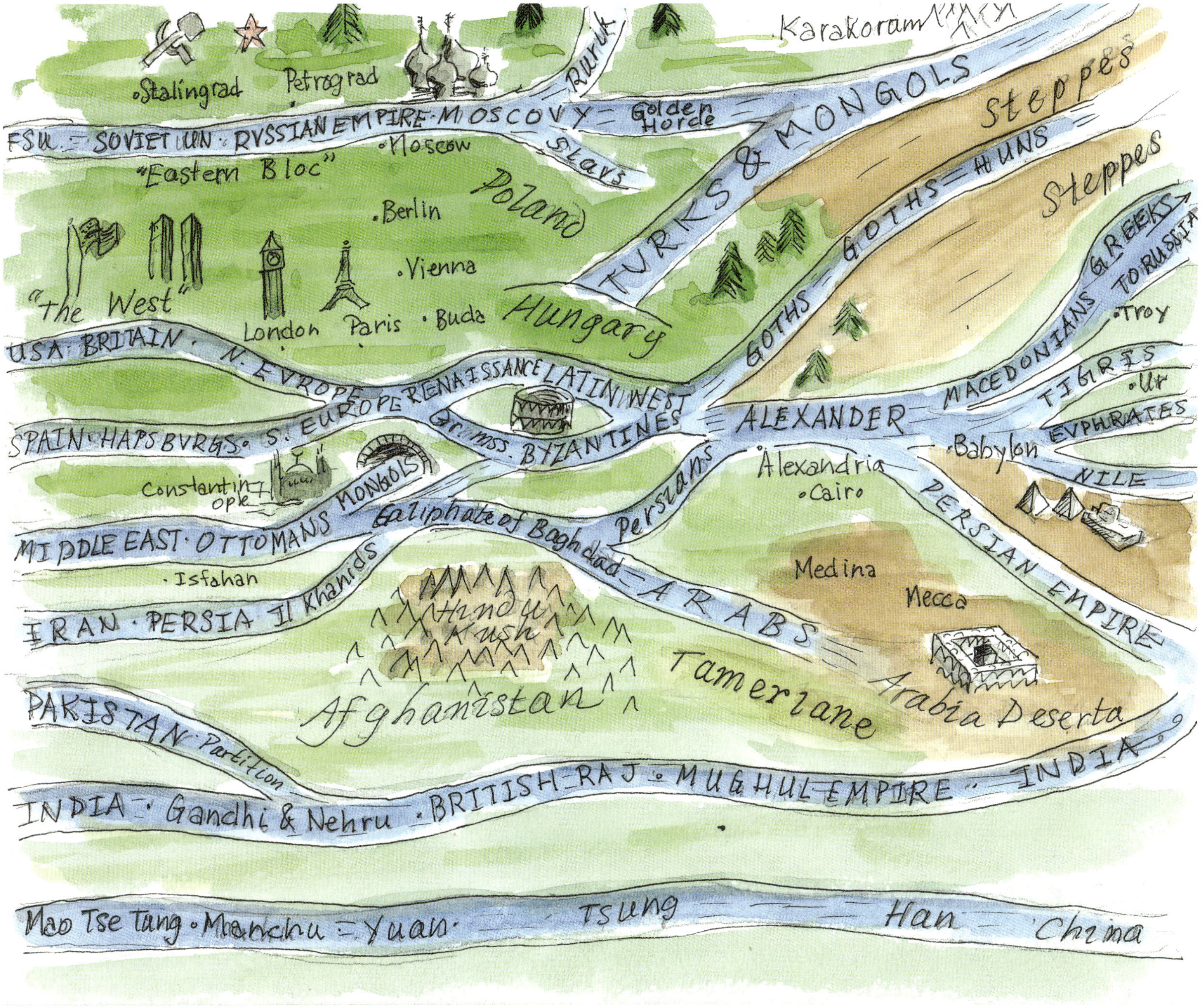

Karakoram
Stalingrad
Petrograd
Rurik
FSU · SOVIET UN · RUSSIAN EMPIRE · MOSCOVY
Golden Horde
Moscow
Slavs
"Eastern Bloc"
TURKS & MONGOLS
Steppes
HUNS
GOTHS
Steppes
Poland
Berlin
Vienna
"The West"
London
Paris
Buda
Hungary
GREEKS
TO RUSSIA
Troy
USA · BRITAIN · N. EUROPE
RENAISSANCE LATIN WEST
GOTHS
MACEDONIANS
TIGRIS
Ur
SPAIN · HAPSBURGS · S. EUROPE
Gr. mss. BYZANTINES
ALEXANDER
EUPHRATES
Babylon
Alexandria
Cairo
NILE
Constantinople
MONGOLS
Persians
PERSIAN EMPIRE
Caliphate of Baghdad
MIDDLE EAST · OTTOMANS
Isfahan
Medina
Mecca
ARABS
IRAN · PERSIA · Il Khanids
Hindu Kush
Tamerlane
Arabia Deserta
Afghanistan
PAKISTAN · Partition
INDIA · Gandhi & Nehru · BRITISH RAJ · MUGHUL EMPIRE · INDIA
Mao Tse Tung · Manchu · Yuan · Tsung
Han
China

A Museum of History

Viewed in a certain way, this story of East and West is neither all that sprawling nor all that complicated. We might imagine history as a palace of memories that has been converted into a major world museum. It consists of period rooms representing the succession of states, leading from one to another, through the *enfilade* of historical time. It is possible to see this museum in a day. Allow me to be the guide as we walk briskly along, looking at some maps and drawings hung like tapestries* along these former corridors of power, looking at history in big graphic chunks.

In the first four rooms, we find the precursors of the Roman empire: Mesopotamia and Greece, with their alternative forms of government, despotism and democracy, followed by the Persian Empire, which was succeeded by Alexander's empire.

Written history begins with the Persian attack on the Greeks—the subject of the first book of history, that of Herodotus. The first counterstrike of the West against the East was Alexander the Great's conquest of Persia, creating the world of the Hellenistic East, the petri dish of Western culture.

In the main room of the museum is the Roman Empire, and in the following rooms its successor states, alternating east and west: the Caliphate of Baghdad, Charlemagne, the Selçuk Turks, the Mongols, the Ottomans, the Italian Renaissance, the Rise of the West, and the World Wars of the 20th century. The Cold War is in an annex, just recently completed.

Churches have been built on the ruins of pagan temples and, in the New World, on those of Aztec pyramids. Mosques have been built on the ruins of churches. The modern nations of Europe were built on the ruins of the Western Roman Empire; and on the ruins of the Eastern Roman Empire was built the Ottoman Empire—on the ruins of which sit unsteadily the modern nations of the Middle East.

> The tradition of countless dead generations is an incubus in the mind of the living.*

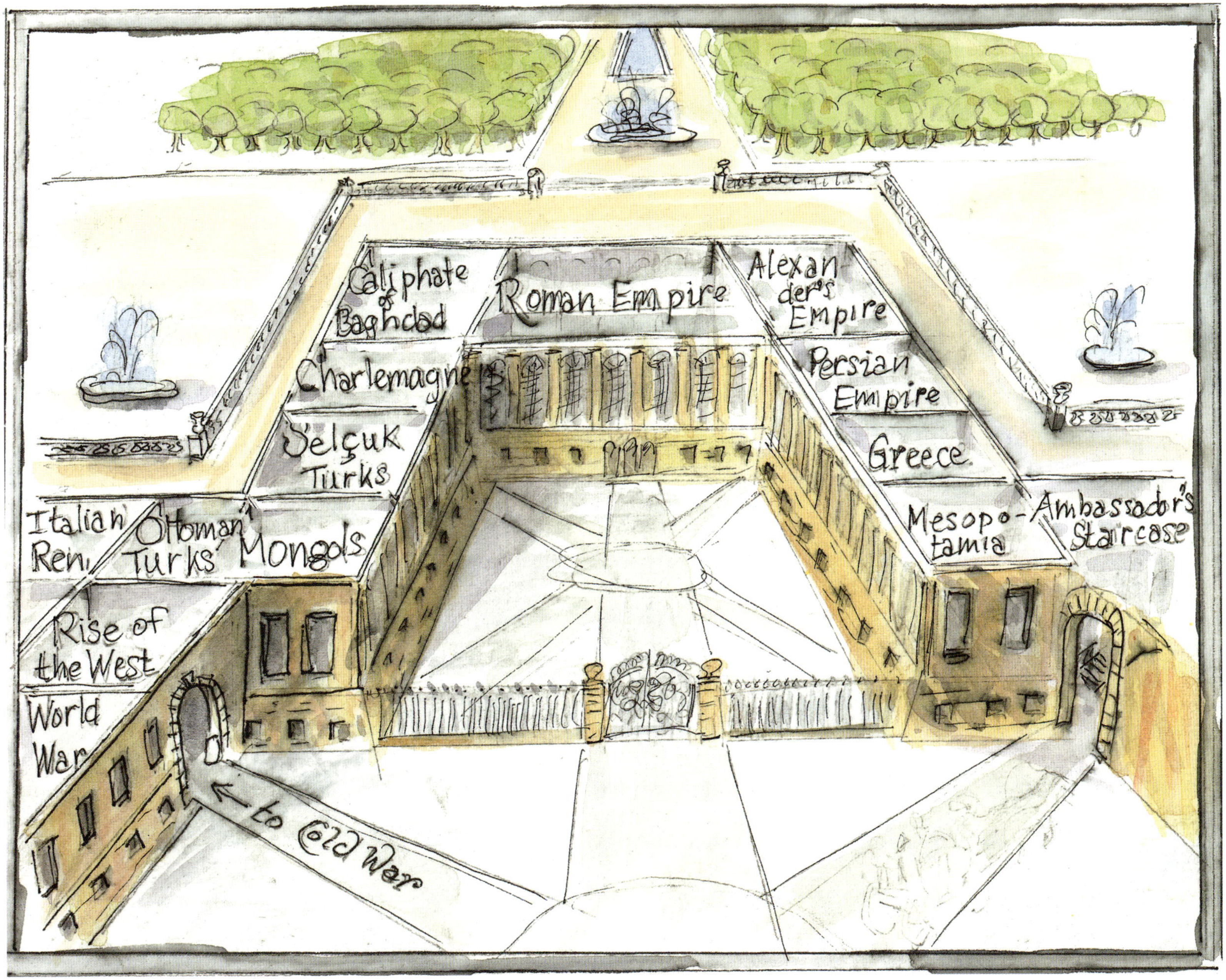

Caliphate of Baghdad
Roman Empire
Alexander's Empire
Charlemagne
Persian Empire
Selçuk Turks
Greece
Italian Ren.
Ottoman Turks
Mongols
Mesopotamia
Ambassador's Staircase
Rise of the West
World War
← to Cold War

Geopolitical Dynamics

For centuries, the struggle of East and West was played out as the advance-and-retreat of the Ottomans in the Balkans, toward and away from Central Europe, as if on a football field—teams advancing and retreating, yard by yard. Games have rules; Nature has laws,* which over time have been seen differently. Where Aristotle saw a pendulum as a stone whose fall is broken by a string, Galileo* saw it as an oscillation between limits. Later, Newton defined three laws which govern physical dynamics.

Geopolitics has its own dynamics, its own laws decreed by the physical surface of the globe effecting the histories and strategies of peoples and nations.

Here are three postulated laws of geopolitical dynamics that will form the argument of this book: three intertwined oscillations between the poles* of desert and sown, East and West, and order and fragmentation.

Desert & Sown Our first dynamic is been between those regions where agriculture can be practiced, and therefore people settle and prosper, which we call the *Sown*; and those other places which we call the *Desert*, where people cannot settle but are forced to move from one grazing area to another in order to live there, often raiding the *Sown*.

East & West A second dynamic is between the twin poles of East and West: between the peoples living in the settled lands of the *Sown*, lying mostly to the *West*, and those living in the *Desert*, or the semideserts of Asia and Arabia, lying mostly to the *East*, who from time to time in great hordes either migrated into or invaded the settled areas of the *West*.

Order & Fragmentation Intertwined with the first two dynamics is a third, between *Order* imposed by a conqueror coming out of the *Desert* into the *Sown*, or an *Order*, or hegemony, established by a power within the *Sown*, which is mutually accepted. If not accepted, then revolution and *Fragmentation* ensue, and the order is overthrown.

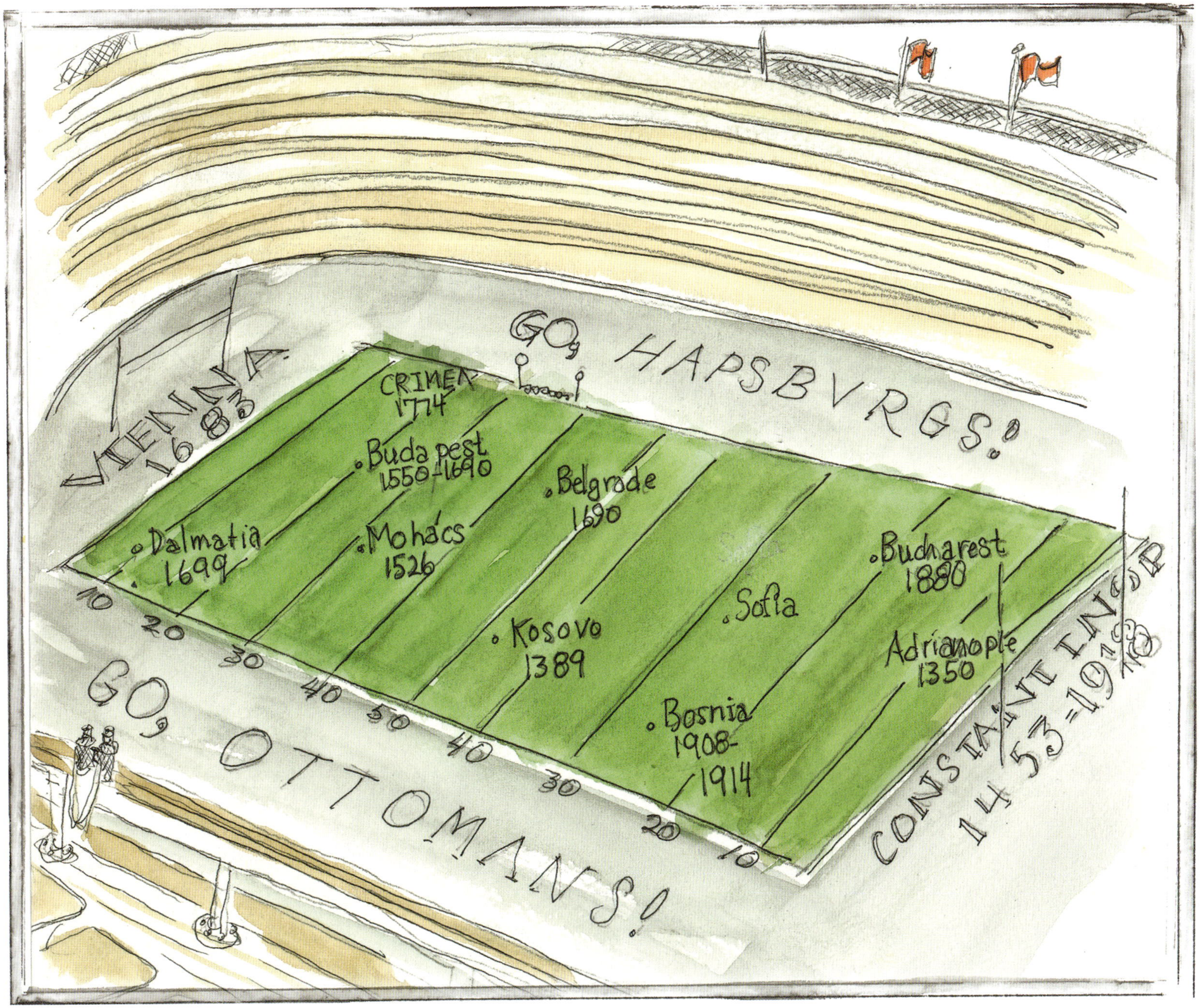
GO, HAPSBVRGS!
VIENNA 1683
CRIMEA 1774
Buda pest 1550-1690
Belgrade 1690
Dalmatia 1699
Mohács 1526
Bucharest 1880
Sofia
Kosovo 1389
Adrianople 1350
Bosnia 1908-1914
CONSTANTINOP
1453-1918
10 20 30 40 50 40 30 20 10
GO, OTTOMANS!

Commedia della storia

The drama of East and West, of Islam and Christendom, is played out today in the Sicilian puppet theater,* in which large and gorgeously dressed puppets alternately fight and dispute with each other, trying to win the other over to the true faith.

The stories are taken from the old French *chansons de geste*, like the *Song of Roland*,* which tell of the struggles between the Saracens of Spain and the French champions, paladins like Roland himself; and of how he is surprised and killed in the narrow pass of Roncesvalles in the Pyrenees. These mountains lie along the present-day border of Spain and France, but in the 9th century marked the frontier between Dar al' Islam and Christendom, Charlemagne's empire. The *chansons* are thought to have originated during the time of the Crusades, along the pilgrim routes leading to Compostella and the shrine of Santiago Matamoros, or Saint James the Moor-killer, patron saint of the Crusaders. With artistic license the Sicilian puppet plays have added Saladin, who took back Jerusalem in 1188. Here he is, that noble and clement Kurd, brandishing an admonitory sword.

The Sicilian puppet plays are part of the old theatrical genre of *commedia dell'arte** with its set plots and stock characters such as Harlequin and Columbine. Geopolitics is a *commedia della storia*, a comedy of history played out on a relief map of the world. It is a drama full of conflict, veering between laughter and tears, a drama 'tragical-comical-historical.'* It is tragical in the sense that people do die, and thrones, dominions, and powers do fall; comical in the sense that in the end life goes on and people marry; and historical in the sense that it is the real true story. The plot has been set by the dynamics of geopolitics.

In the *commedia della storia*, kings and caliphs, prime ministers and presidents are the actors, improvising lines set by the roles history has assigned them. The nations are the audience, all crowded around in rows, watching a drama that has been playing for thousands of years. Revenge is generally the motive, and the curtain never falls.

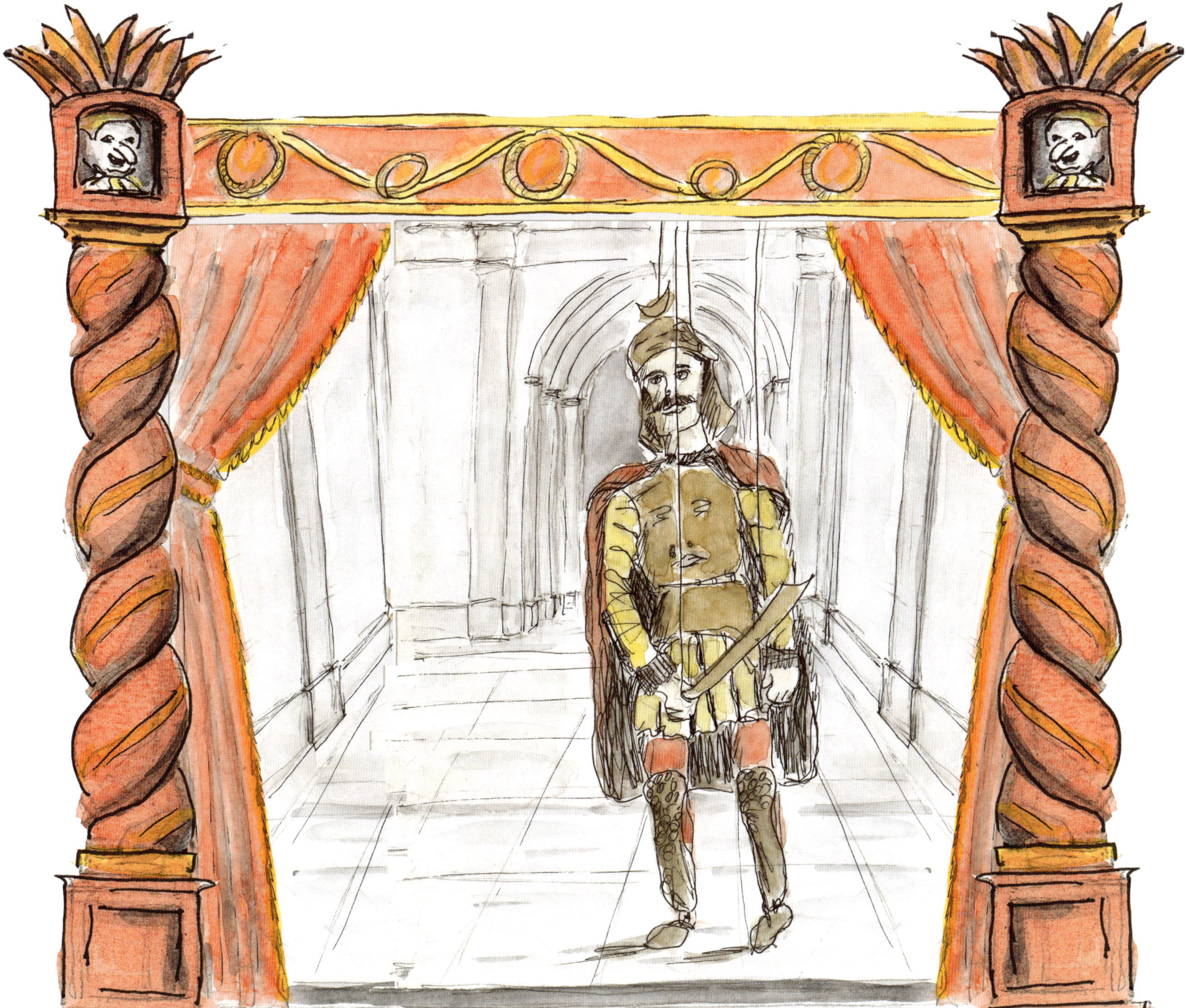

The Historian's Colors

Here we present a drama in which the characters are geopolitical zones, like the tectonic plates that underlie the earth's crust, drifting slowly together or apart. The *characters* are six, represented by six colors. The hero is the Eastern Empire, formerly the Eastern Roman Empire, whose heartland is Anatolia. The *action* is set by our three dynamics. The *scene* is the relief map of the world. The *time* is the present historic. We call this 'tragical-comical-historical' drama *The Eastern Question*.

DRAMATIS PERSONAE

YELLOW for the Mongols, for the Golden Horde, the Mongol khanate that so long held Russia in subjection

RED for the Latin West, a terra-cotta red that reminds one of the clay-tile roofs of southern Europe

IMPERIAL PURPLE for the Eastern Empire, the color of the emperors, 'born in the purple'*

BLUE for the northern Europeans, those blue-tattooed barbarians, who later became Protestants

TURQUOISE for Shia Persia, for the turquoise Peacock Throne of the shahs, the first world empire

GREEN for the Sunnis, the color of Islam

N.B. The mapmaker also uses *green* for the fertile green earth; *brown* for the dry desert of the land (and areas outside the present purview); and *blue* for the wet desert of the sea.

THE HISTORIAN'S COLORS

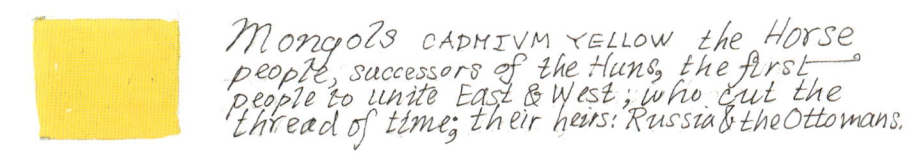

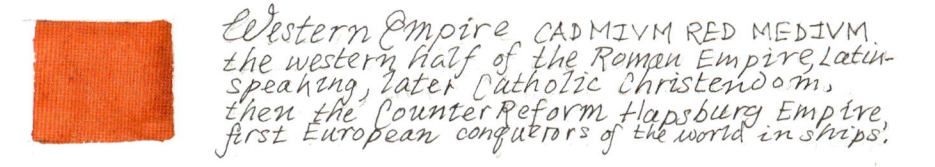

Mongols CADMIUM YELLOW the Horse people, successors of the Huns, the first people to unite East & West; who cut the thread of time; their heirs: Russia & the Ottomans.

Western Empire CADMIUM RED MEDIUM the western half of the Roman Empire, Latin-speaking, later Catholic Christendom, then the Counter Reform Hapsburg Empire, first European conquerors of the world in ships'.

Eastern Empire IMPERIAL PURPLE the Greeks, the first Ship people, Alexander, the Hellenistic Kingdoms of the East then the Byzantines, then Russian Empire.

Northern (Protestant) Europe COBALT BLUE Germanic language, as opposed to Latin, including northern France, the lands of the Reform & Enlightenment, conquerors of the world after the Spanish decline.

Persia (later Shi'a, 1501) TURQUOISE first world empire, the great ancient civilization that lies between the Eastern Mediterranean/Iraq & India, linguistically always distinct from Arab/Turkish Islam.

Sunni Dar al'Islam HOOKER'S GREEN the Camel people, the Muslims, who conquered the eastern empire, first the Arabs, then the Turks who ended the Roman Empire in 1453, survived until 1923 as the Ottoman Empire, now fractured into 22 nations.

I. The Geopolitical Dynamics of History

*[Come] with me along some strip of herbage strown
That just divides the Desert from the Sown...*

—OMAR KHAYYAM

GEOPOLITICS

Mackinder's World Island

IN THIS CHAPTER we will discuss the origin of geopolitics as a study, and in the succeeding three chapters, our three geopolitical dynamics.

The father of geopolitics was Halford Mackinder. His book *Democratic Ideals and Reality* (1919) was written as a guide for British policy makers who were reshaping large parts of the globe after the First World War. Mackinder repeatedly refers to the Fertile Crescent, the land of the earliest empires, as the place of origin of geopolitical struggle. He saw the world in big, distinct chunks. 'When we are talking of large things, we must speak in grand terms.'

Mackinder's fundamental tenet is the distinction between land power and sea power, between the Heartland and the European Coastlands. He feared the power and impregnability of the first and the weakness of the second: '…who rules the Heartland commands the World-Island; who rules the World-Island controls the world.'

The ancients saw the world as an island surrounded by the Stream of Ocean; but as Mackinder points out, it is not an island but a peninsula 'with the ice cap aground on its northern shore.' Because it cannot practically be sailed around, it makes the Heartland inaccessible to naval forces, Britain's principal means of projecting power. Ironically, this was demonstrated when the Russians brought the Baltic Fleet around the entire peninsula—Suez being denied—to disaster in the Tsushima Strait in 1905.

Because sea power could not* penetrate into the Heartland of land power, the Monsoon Coastlands became the battleground between them. In the Cold War, redesignated—along with Africa and Latin America—as the Third World, they became the venue of struggle between the sea power of the First World (NATO) and the land power of the Second World (Warsaw Pact). Through a geopolitical lens, we can see how the struggles of the ancient world and today are connected.

European
Coast Land
Kronstadt
15 Oct. 1904
Heart land
Sahara
Arabia
Monsoon Coast land
Tsushima Strait
27-28 May, 1905
Southern
Heart-
land
RUSSIAN FLEET
HALFORD MACKINDER'S
World
Island

Desert & Sown: The World Egg

The ancients had not read Mackinder. All they knew was the *Ecumene*, or Inhabited World. It was the World Egg in which was imprinted the genetic code of human history.

To the north* are the interminable pine forests and tundra with rivers flowing into ice-choked seas; to the south is the broad river of deserts stretching from Morocco to the Gobi in China which effectively cuts off the *Ecumene*, or Known World, from Africa, India and China.

The 'broad river' of deserts formed a great border: a 'continuous mass to be crossed, rather like linked seas' that could only be traveled by camels. These deserts cleaved the world—cutting it north and south, connecting it east and west.

North of this desert barrier are two worlds. To the west is the World Egg, to the east are the steppes of Asia. From these steppes came danger: invasions and migrations. The dynamic between these two worlds, between *Desert & Sown*, has been called the 'engine of history.' This dynamic began with the retreat of the last of the glaciers of the Ice Age ten thousand years ago, which opened the narrow band stretching between East and West.

By *Sown*, we mean the lands of settled agriculture where civilization arose along the rivers of Mesopotamia and Egypt, the origin of the modern state. This was the Habitable, or Known World: The World Egg. By *Desert*, we mean the lands of the people who lived beyond the areas controlled by cities, hardy people who could make use of land that was otherwise uninhabitable.

Semi-nomadic people living on the edges of the settled lands migrated into the sown. When they arrived in massive waves, they destroyed the current order and forced the emergence of a new order. As settlers, the former became in their turn prey to the next wave of nomads coming out of the desert, or off the steppes, or from the sea.

Sea power's fear of land power is atavistic, based on centuries of invaders coming off the steppes, out of the desert, out of the east, out of the Heartland.

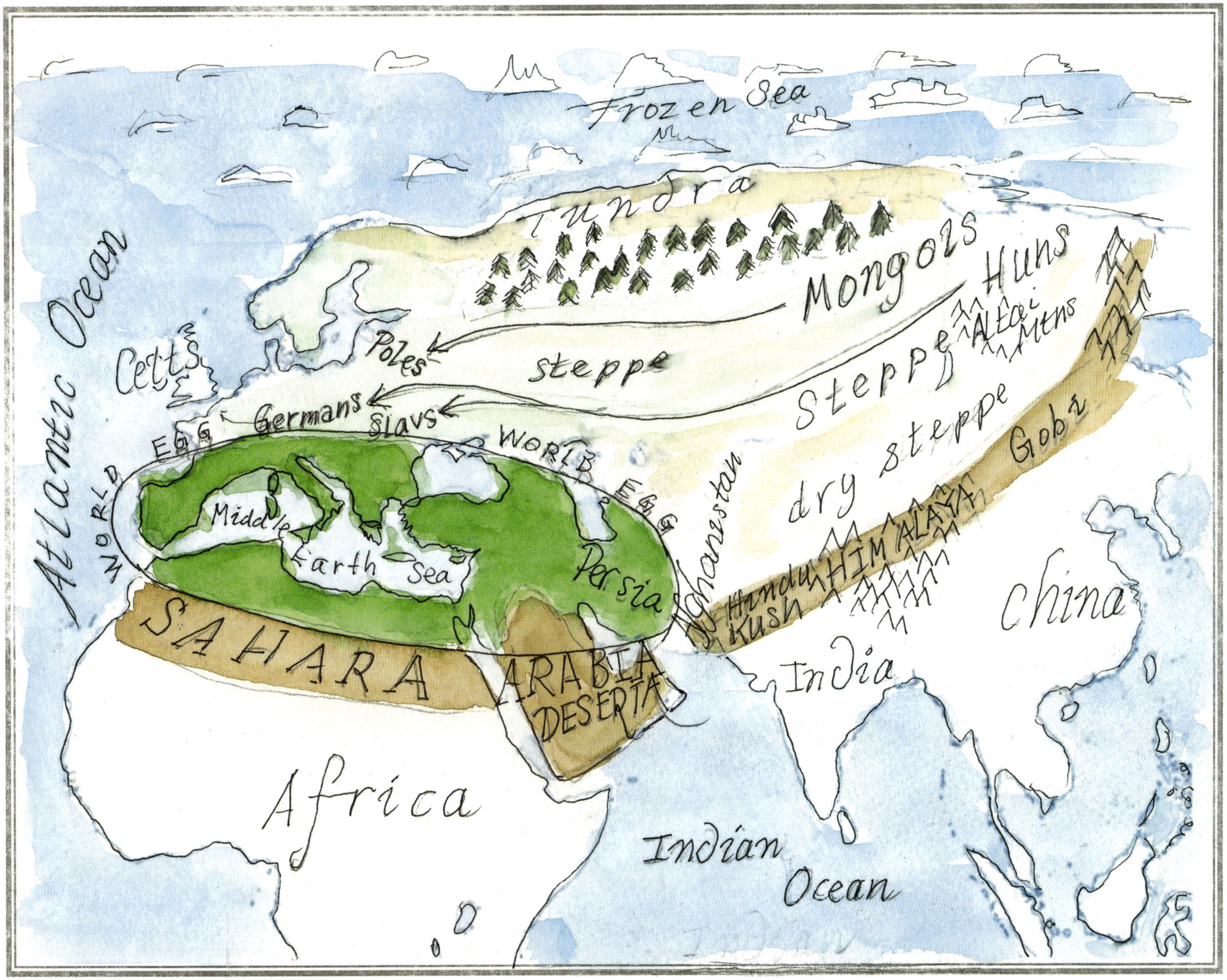

East & West: Climatologic Zones

'History is made in the temperate latitudes of the Northern Hemisphere,' wrote Mackinder's successor, Nicholas Spykman.* These latitudes define a narrow band that girdles the globe, eastward and westward.

The ancients were perfectly aware of this climatologic reality. In the *Dream of Scipio*, Cicero draws a vivid picture of the ancient worldview. He imagines Scipio Africanus, on the eve of the battle that gave Rome victory over Carthage, standing with his grandfather, looking down on the earth from the heavens. Above them are the crystalline spheres set with the jewels of the sun, moon, and stars. The grandfather, the elder Africanus, is speaking.

> Can you not understand* that the earth is totally insignificant? Note how few and minute are the inhabited portions and look upon the vast deserts that divide each one of these patches from the next. Furthermore, you will observe that the earth is girdled by different zones and that the two most widely separated from one another are frigid with icy cold, while the central broadest zone is burnt up with the heat of the sun. Two others, situated between the hot zones and the cold, are habitable. The zone which lies to the south has no connexion with yours; it represents your Antipodes.
>
> As to its northern counterpart where you yourself live, you will realize, if you look, what a diminutive section of this region can be counted as your property. For the territory you occupy is nothing more than a small island, narrow from north to south...

The earth is indeed small in the vast perspective of space, but for us, as for the Romans, it is all we know. Our known world is just a bit more of something very small. Astronomy has evolved beyond the concept of the celestial spheres, and while we once sent men to the moon, we remain confined, by the gravity of the earth, to what astronomers call Lower Earth Orbit. The earth itself is located in a narrow planetary temperate zone neither too close to nor too far from the sun.

Even with rapidly growing populations, especially in the global south, the dynamic of human history is still played out in that narrow band running east to west. It was little more than 500 years ago that Portuguese sailors dared to cross the burning zone and reached the Antipodes, through which were found the only East-to-West sea routes before the Panama and Suez canals were constructed in the late 19th and early 20th centuries. The Greek passion for balance* led Aristotle to posit the existence of a vast southern continent, *Terra Australis Incognita*,* the nonexistence of which was proven only in the late 18th century when Captain Cook circumnavigated at a high southern latitude, and that hemisphere was shown to be mostly ocean, widely separating the smaller land masses there.

East and West are ineluctable. The sun, the moon, and the stars move in this direction. The Latin words for *east* and *west*—*oriens* and *occidens*—mean the rising and setting* of these celestial bodies that mark our hours, days, months and years.

'There are no North* or South winds of any account on this earth… [They] are but small princes in the dynasties that make peace and war upon the sea…. In the polity of the winds, as amongst the tribes of the earth, the real struggle lies between East and West.'

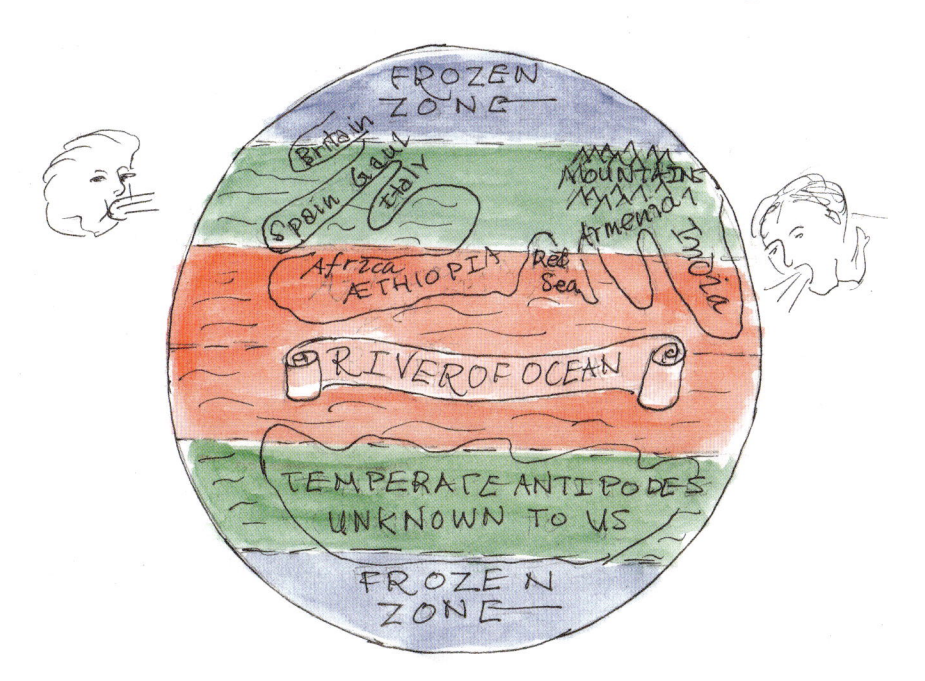

Order & Fragmentation: Ibn Khaldûn

These dynamics of geopolitics would not have been unfamiliar to Mackinder's forerunner, the 14th-century historian 'Abd-ar-Rahman Abu Zayd ibn-Mohammad ibn-Mohammad ibn Khaldûn al-Hadrami, whose *Muqaddimah* has been called* 'the greatest work of its kind that has ever been created by any mind in any time or place.'

He was certainly the first writer to look at history in terms of its underlying dynamics. Surveying the interaction of the settled, or 'sedentary,' peoples with the nomads, or 'Bedouins,'* of the desert, he observed how settled life tends to weaken people, making them dependent on walls and standing armies and the protection of rulers—and eventually prey to the hardier, braver, and hungrier desert dwellers who live by raiding. He showed how this interaction produces a natural succession of dynasties, which have a tendency to decay from one generation to the next—'until their time is up,' as he puts it. He gave many examples from the histories of the Umayyads of Damascus, the Abbasids of Baghdad, and other dynasties. He speculated on what caused independent tribes to submit to a ruler to whom they were not related by blood,* introducing the concept of the legitimacy of power: a three-stranded rope in which are intertwined religious legitimacy, dynastic legitimacy, and *farrh*—the knack for winning battles. When a ruler has this legitimacy, he is able to overcome divisions, unite previously warring tribes, and project tremendous force, as had the Arabs under Mohammad, the Turks under the Selçuk Alp Arslan, the Mongols under Genghis or finally under Tamerlane. He was certainly in a position to observe firsthand the last of these legendary desert conquerors. In January 1401, Tamerlane invited Ibn Khaldûn to his camp outside of Damascus, to which he was then laying siege, to discuss his ideas:

> This King Timur* is one of the greatest and mightiest of Kings. He is highly intelligent and perspicacious, addicted to debate and argumentation about what he knows and also what he does not know.

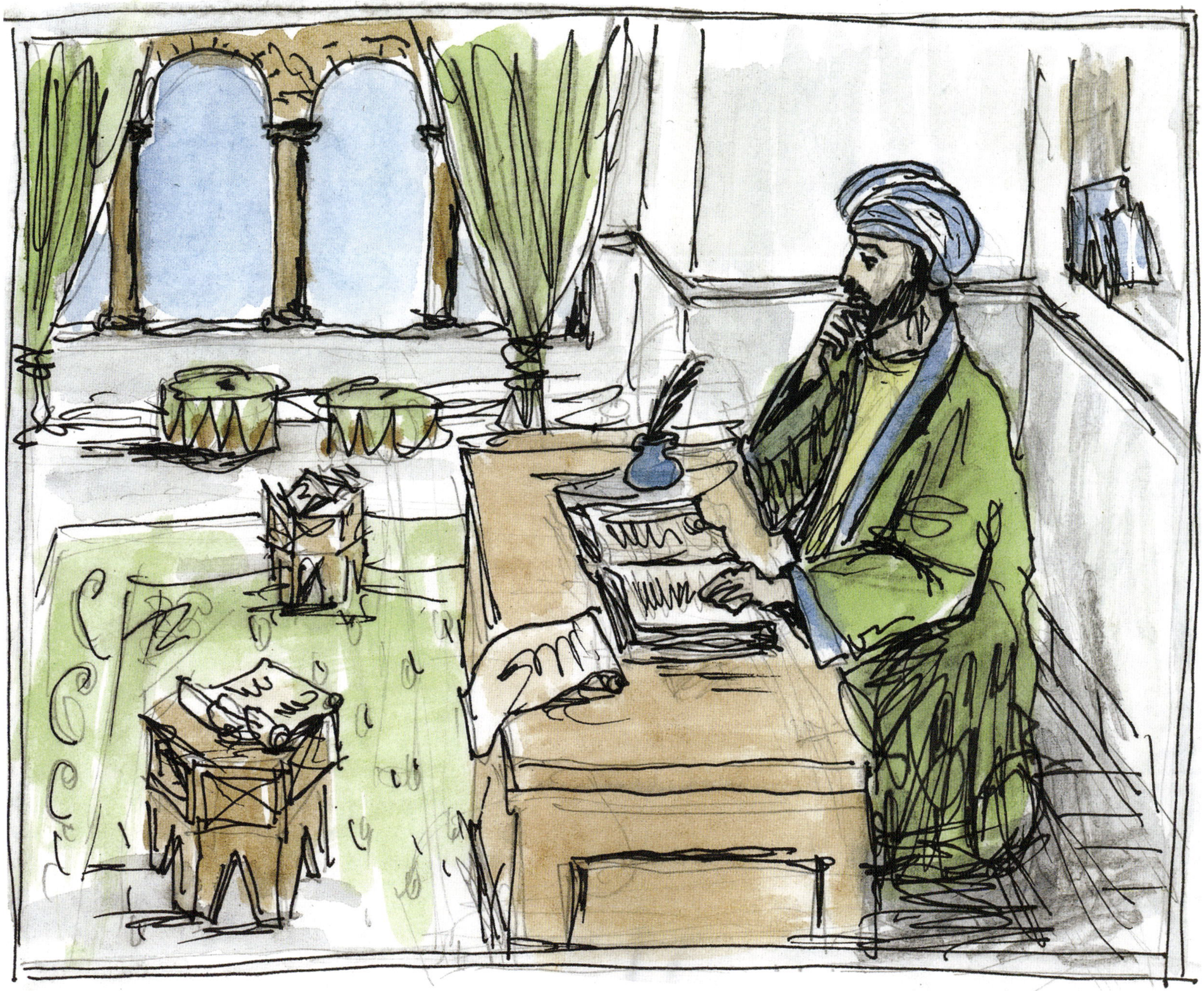

DESERT & SOWN

Nomads OUT OF AFRICA came the first human animals. They migrated into Asia and Europe, and from Asia—presumably crossing a land bridge—to America. Humans are at heart nomads. It is our very nature, looking always for better pastures. Even after we settled in cities, explorers continued to roam, sometimes going back to the deserts or, in the 19th century, into deserts of 'deepest darkest' wherevers.

Living in cities, saddled with mortgages and taxes, rules and regulations, was contrary to their nature.* When they could, the Mongols converted sown fields back to pasture. 'It is easy to conquer the world on a horse,' said Genghis Khan, 'but much more difficult to get down from the horse and rule the country.'

Nomads are the only peoples who by virtue of moving can take advantage of the lands outside the Inhabited World, or *Ecumene*, the Greek 'house,' a place you inhabit. Nomads can inhabit what is, for lack of rainfall or poor soil, the Uninhabitable World. There were never many of them. The desert can support very few, and only if those few keep moving from place to place; and they were defined by the means* of their moving, either camels or horses.

Nomads, who live to some extent outside time, conserve their language better than city people; it is the only treasure* they can carry with them in their pastoral existence. It was out of the extraordinarily rich ground* of poetry in Arabic that the Qur'an emerged, and supercharged the Arab conquest of half the Inhabited World.

Nowadays there is almost nowhere to wander anymore over miles and miles of open land, and Mongols are outmoded.* There are no more Attila the Huns, no more Ghengis Khans, no more Tamerlanes*—and today's pressure of the *Desert* on the *Sown* is the overwhelming migration from the poorer into the wealthier countries.

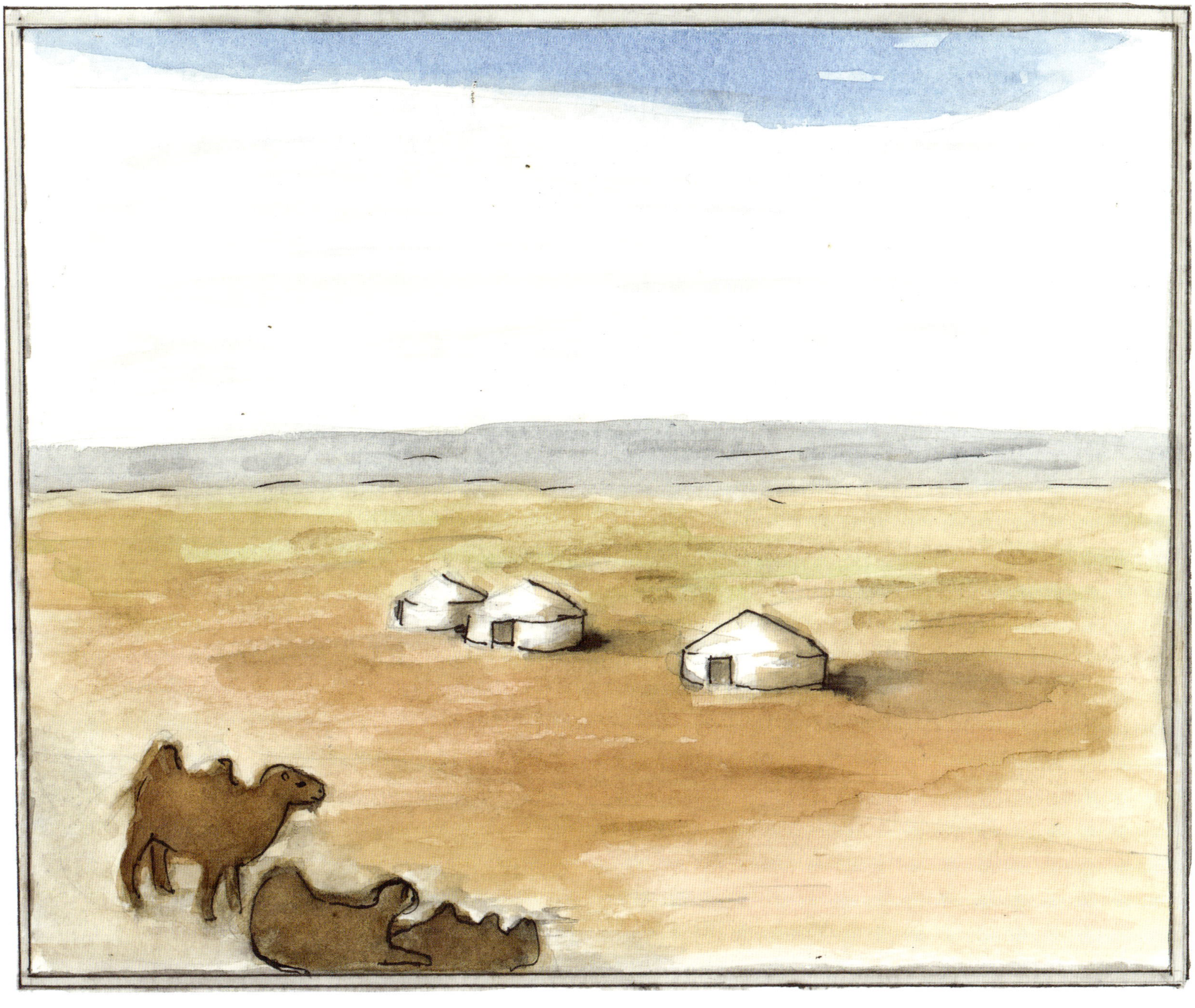

Horses, Camels, Ships

Settled people are all alike in their tendency to dig in and build walls around their houses. Nomads carry their houses with them and are different from one another in their various ways of movement. After all, this is their primary characteristic—to move or wander. In the history of mankind, there have been three principle means of moving on the surface of the earth: horses, camels, and ships. These freed humans from the limitation of one foot placed in front of the other, as well as the limitation placed on them by the trackless oceans.

This drawing represents how, at various and overlapping periods of time, these three—horse, camel, ship—powered major expansions out of Eurasia: first, the Mongols with horses; second, the Arabs with camels; and third, the Europeans who became sea nomads* and conquered the world with ships.

Seen from an imaginary point of view in outer space, the earth is like an enormous hive of insects teeming, swarming, moving this way and that over its surface. In truth, we are all nomads on the face of the earth in our passage through life.

Each nomadic movement represents an adaptation to a different climatologic zone. Each allowed humans to move into otherwise inaccessible places, which then became geopolitical fortresses: places out of which one could sortie, but into which a foe could not pursue. The deserts of Arabia are a good example, as are the steppes of Asia.

Many peoples have had access to more than one mode of transportation. What has distinguished these peoples from one another is that a horse, camel, or ship was the primary means by which they commanded their geopolitical zones. While it is true that camel and ship people* have horses, and camel and horse people have ships, the point is that even if the Arabs used horses for raiding and fighting, camels were essential to carry water into the desert for their horses. Camels were therefore the strategic key to commanding their geopolitical zone.

The farthest to the south in Africa that the camel people reached was roughly the sub-Saharan tree line—the line along which Sudan was divided in 2011.

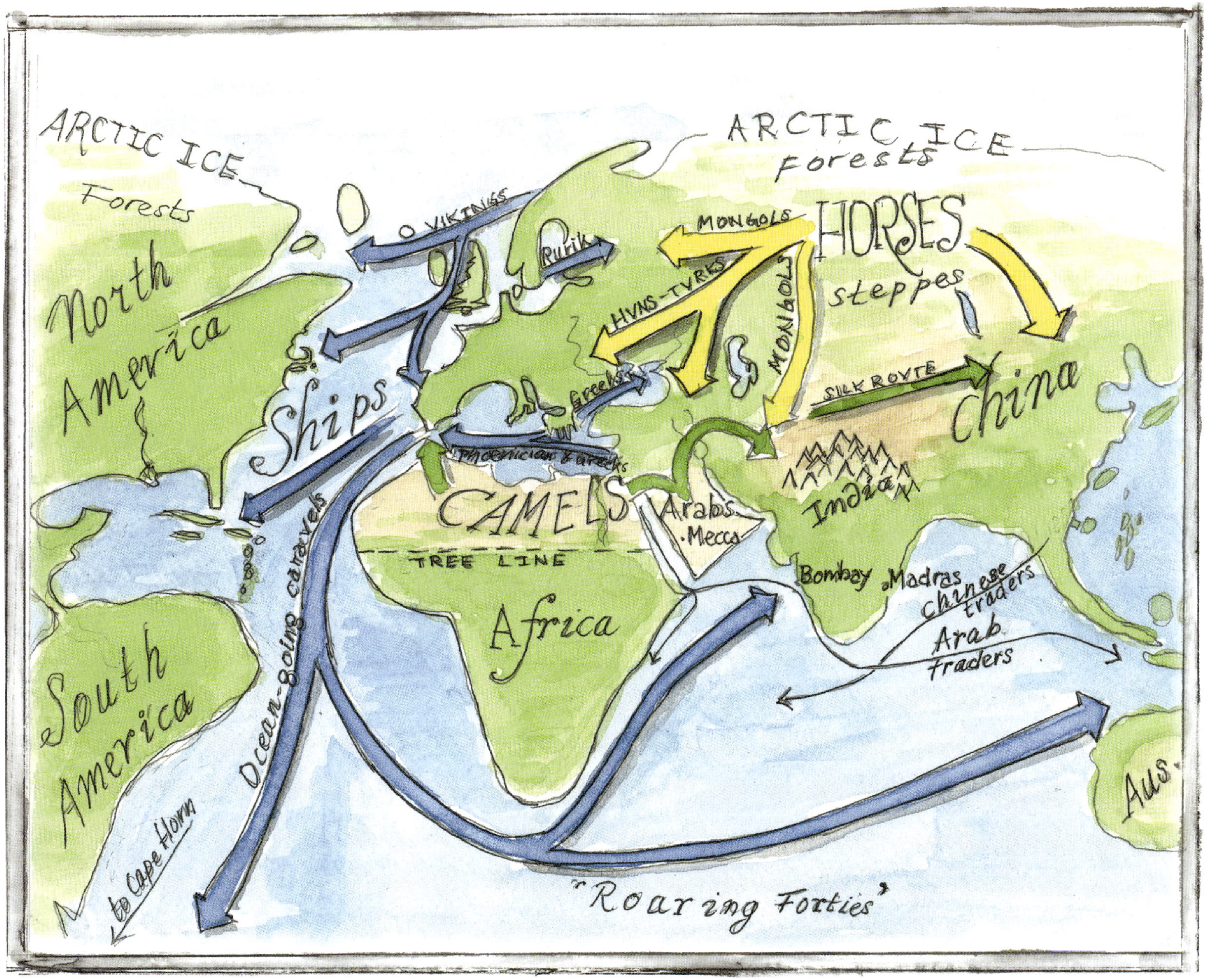
ARCTIC ICE
Forests
North America
ARCTIC ICE
Forests
VIKINGS
Rurik
MONGOLS
HORSES
steppes
HUNS-TURKS
MONGOLS
SILK ROUTE
China
Greeks
Ships
Phoenician & Greeks
CAMELS
Arabs
Mecca
India
TREE LINE
Bombay
Madras
chinese traders
Arab traders
Africa
South America
Ocean-going caravels
to Cape Horn
Aus.
"Roaring Forties"

Mongol's-Eye View

This is the way it might have looked to a Hun, or a Mongol, or a Turk—to anyone coming from the East. The steppe, a grand boulevard trending westward, flows toward the plains of Poland and Hungary and on into the fields of France. This physical characteristic of the steppeland inexorably led to the vast nomadic migrations westward and is a perfect example of how adapting to a landscape can determine human behavior. The typical pattern of migration was a peaceful movement westward, or interchange along the edge of the desert and sown. From time to time, however, a leader—a 'man on horseback'—appeared out of nowhere and united a people who then began to move en masse. As Coleridge* wrote, these leaders were 'the masters of mischief, the liberticides, and mighty hunters of mankind.'

On the steppes, nomadism was dependent upon the horse, whose origin can be traced to that narrow band south of Russia. Herding people could not travel long distances on foot away from settled areas, and the breeding of larger and larger horses,* originally very small animals, allowed them to break away and move into the steppe in search of grazing land and minerals. Horses were first beasts of burden, then people learned to ride them, and the final development in the human adaptation of the horse was the stirrup, invented around 500 BC. It made the horse into a formidable machine of war, and the horse made the steppes a geopolitical fortress.

The hordes of the horse people were not like a European army but rather a people in movement. Herding their flocks, their sustenance, with them, they increased in numbers as they moved westward. The peoples they encountered irresistibly joined the moving horde. They were stopped only when the grasslands ran into the plowed fields.

These horse-borne movements were brought to an end by the invention of gunpowder, which led to the 'gunpowder empires'* of the Ottomans, Persians, Russians, Spanish, and English, just as the last of the horse people, the Comanches, were stopped only by the Connecticut Yankee invention of the Colt revolver.

A Mongol's-Eye View of the World
Moscow
Constantinople
Black Sea
Cairo
Ain al Galat
Baghdad
Caspian S.
Sarai
Volga
Persia
DRY STEPPE
Tundra
Frozen Sea
Forests
GRAZING BETTER THIS WAY
India
Tibet
Gobi Desert
China
Beijing
Karakoram
Sacred Mountains
Pacific Ocean

Attila Playing Pool

There were many invaders from the East, but Attila penetrated farthest into Europe and cut the deepest into Western history. Imagine him as a pool player striking the racked-up balls at the beginning of the game and, with one powerful strike of the cue, scattering the tribes of Europe, called in German the *Völkenwanderrung*.*

We trace the origins of modern Europe to this scattering. Attila chased the Angles and Saxons into England. The Franks, Goths, and Roman provincials united in battle against him at Châlons in 451. From this union springs the modern French people. He destroyed Padua and Aquileia, forcing their citizens into the Venetian lagoon, which led to the eventual founding of the city of Venice. Outside of Milan in 452, Bishop Leo of Rome met him on the banks of the Mincio. For unknown reasons, Attila went no farther. Maybe Leo reminded him of how Alaric had died soon after his earlier sack of Rome in 410. Attila died in 453, and the Church won great prestige; .

The Norman conquest of England is well known; less well known is another Norman conquest—that of Russia. Rurik, who went east rather than west or south, conquered the East Slavs, founding Kievan Rus, the 'mother of all Russian cities.' Centuries later, when Rurik's descendants, the Russian princes, emerged from the domination of the Mongols, modern Russia was born under the rule of one of these princes, the grand duke of Moscovy, Ivan the Great.

Out of the struggles of opposites, of thesis and antithesis, always comes a synthesis, a new creation. The invading Huns drove the German tribes of the north into the declining Western Roman Empire of the south. Out of this struggle emerged the synthesis of the modern nations of Europe. But, despite recurrent dreams of unification, deeply embedded tribal loyalties have always kept Europe a fragmented place. For instance, the recent (1999) European monetary union, as well as the EU itself, has been challenged by this incomplete synthesis of opposites.

The East brought riches as well as raiders to the West.

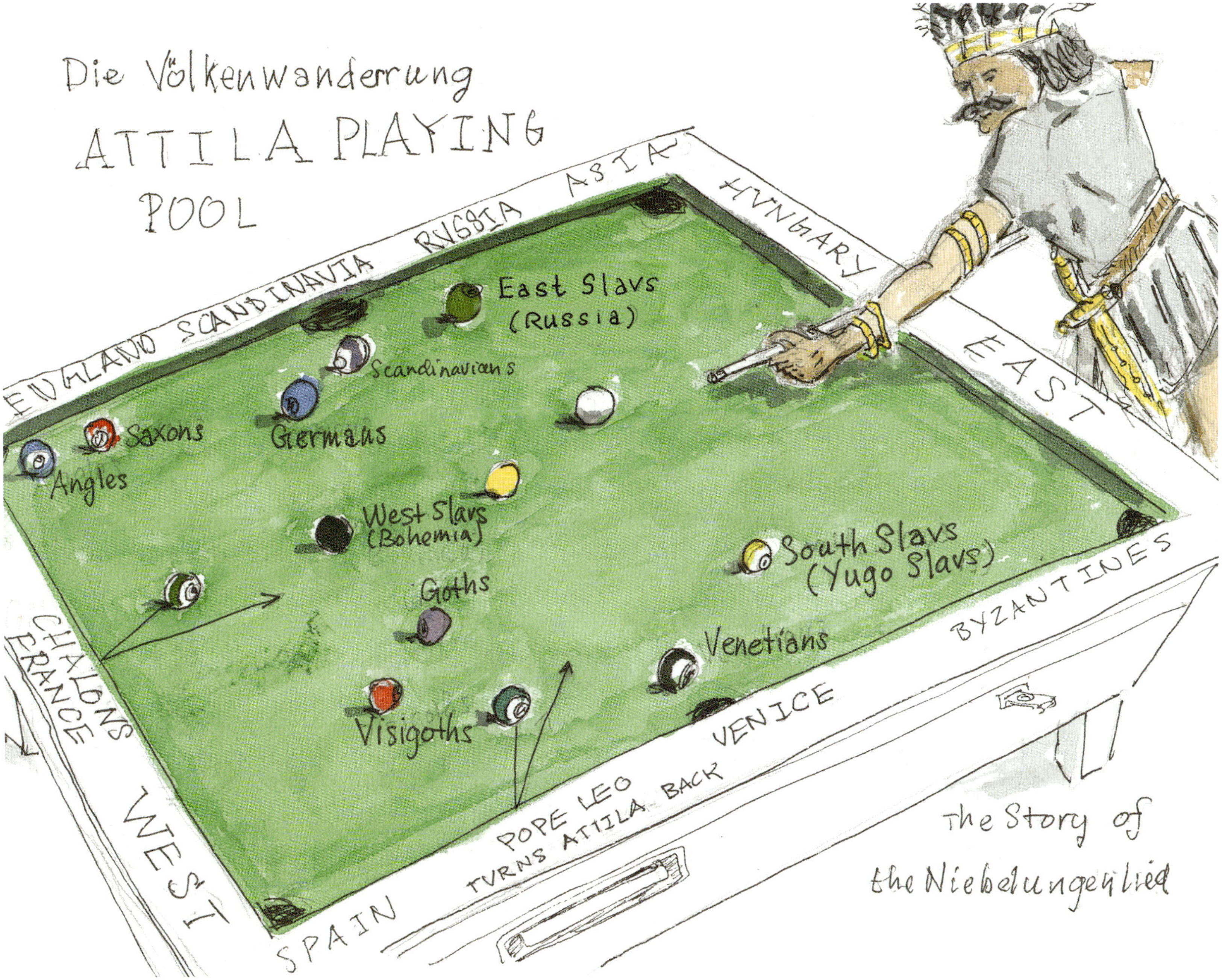
Die Völkenwanderrung
ATTILA PLAYING
POOL
ENGLAND SCANDINAVIA RUSSIA ASIA
HUNGARY
EAST
East Slavs
(Russia)
Scandinavians
Saxons
Germans
Angles
West Slavs
(Bohemia)
South Slavs
(Yugo Slavs)
Goths
CHALONS
FRANCE
Venetians
Visigoths
BYZANTINES
VENICE
POPE LEO
TURNS ATTILA BACK
WEST
SPAIN
The Story of
the Niebelungenlied

Good Stuff Comes from the East

Symbolized in the New Testament by the gifts of the Magi—Persian priests or oriental kings riding on camels—those Eastern riches were brought in enormous caravans* across the breadth of Asia. In 200-pound loads on the backs of Bactrian camels and 500-pound loads on dromedaries, these goods reached Europe through its eastern entrepôt, Venice.

The ancients were perfectly aware that all the good stuff comes from the East. As Herodotus wrote:

> It would seem to be a fact that the remotest parts of the world are the richest in minerals and produce the finest specimens of both animal and vegetable life ... the most easterly of which has gold in immense quantity. The most southerly country is Arabia; and Arabia is the only place that produces frankincense, myrrh, cassia, cinnamon.

The East gave much more to the West—silk, paper, gunpowder, as well as what today we call intellectual property: mathematics, algebra, the 'Arabic' numbers, the zero, astrology, and astronomy. All these came along the complex network of routes named, by a 19th-century German historian,* the Silk Road (*Die Seidenstrasse*).

Only with the camel—specifically the Bactrian (two humps), which can endure the extremes of cold found on the icy steppes of western Siberia and on the plains of inner Asia—was travel possible along the 5,000-mile route. The Bactrian camel, like the horse, comes from Central Asia. It is thought that the first trade on the Silk Road was in fact Chinese silk in exchange for the horses of the nomads, the horse not being native to China. The Silk Road is a geopolitical manifestation—expressed in terms of economics, culture, science, and technology—of the narrow band of deserts that cut off Africa, India, and China from the Known World but also connected them through the trade either along or across it, and then by sea on the seasonally reversing monsoon trade winds to and from India.

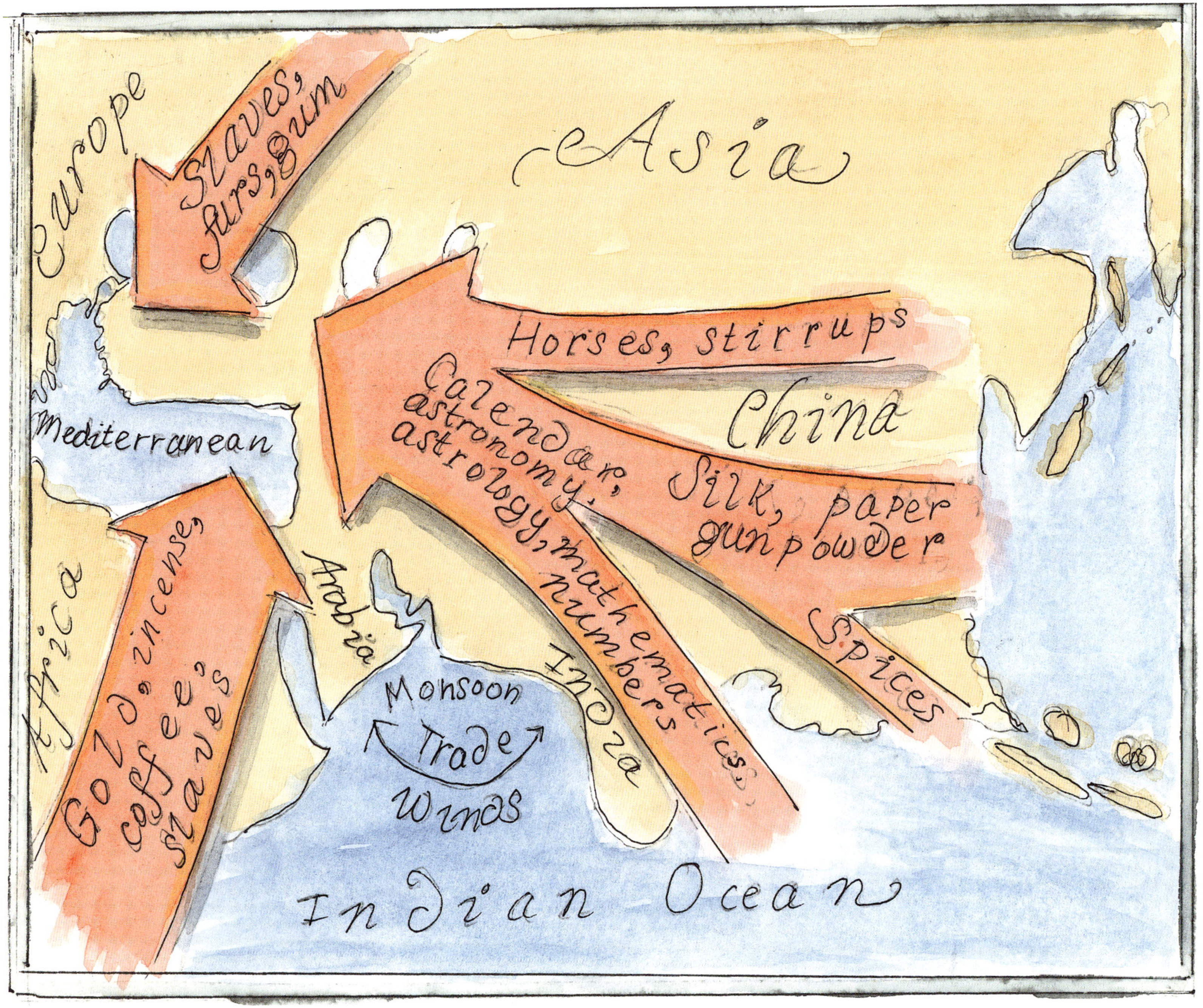

Europe
Slaves, furs, gum
Asia
Horses, stirrups
China
Calendar, astronomy, astrology, mathematics, numbers
Silk, paper gunpowder
Mediterranean
Africa
Gold, incense, coffee, slaves
Arabia
India
Spices
Monsoon Trade Winds
Indian Ocean

Silk Road

The first direct economic link between East and West was the Silk Road. Its major highway ran along the southern edge of the narrow band of the Temperate Zone; its revenues vastly enriched whatever power controlled it. From the beginning, the strategic interests of trade and empire overlapped.

The 4th-century BC conquests of Alexander the Great most likely opened the Silk Road. From the farthest east of his settlements, Alexandria Ultima in present-day Tajikistan, Greek traders are supposed to have reached China. A succession of states both protected and profited from the Silk Road. Taxes on the trade enriched the empires of Central Asia and built the cities of Tashkent, Samarkand, and Bukhara. In the 9th century, the Persian Samanids secured the Road, spreading the Persian language and culture. The Samanids fell to the rising power of the Turkish tribes, notably the Selçuks. In the continuing succession of states, the Selçuks were then overpowered by the Mongols. From the mid-13th to the mid-14th centuries, the Road became a Mongol highway connecting East and West. Marco Polo traveled along it to China, as did his Iberian Arab counterpart Ibn Battuta,* who traveled even farther. For a century under the *Pax Mongolica*, peace and prosperity flourished in Asia together.

One final gift of the East was the bacillus of the Black Plague, which was spread along the Silk Road and disrupted the trade in the middle of the 14th century. In the 16th century, the discovery of long-distance sailing routes brought the Road's primacy to an end. Diminished also were the empires that had controlled it, lastly the Ottomans.

Sea empires now both protected and profited from the new ocean trade.* In the 19th century, the Royal Navy assured the freedom of the seas and hence the wealth of the British Empire. In the 20th century, the task of protecting seaborne global trade fell to the U.S. Navy, particularly in keeping open the Iranian-dominated Strait of Hormuz, through which flows the modern 'wealth of Ormus and of Ind'*—35 percent of the world's seaborne-traded oil and 20 percent of the world's liquefied natural gas.

Die Seidenstraße
400 BC- A.D. 1400
Mare Gelatum
Tundra
Germania
Hungaria
Sarmatia
Italiæ
Steppe
Mongolia
Beijing
Gobi Desert
Scythia
Pontus
Constantinople
Caucasus
Caspium
Mare Internum
Sahara
Antioch
Aleppo
Baghdad
Alexandria
Nilus
Tyre
Damascus
Bukhara
Samarkhand
Tashkent
Dunhuang
Xi'an
Sinæ
Plateau of Tibet
Ctestiphon
Tehran
Merv
Persia
Basra
Ægyptus
Arabia Deserta
Hormuz
Gedrosia
Afghanistan
Hindu Kush
Himalaya
Lhasa
India
Borneo
Africa
Aden
Java
Æthiopia
Taprobane
Oceanus Indicus

EAST AND WEST: THE EAST

Ecumene, WE CONSTANTLY USE the term 'the West,' but what is 'the East'? To the ancients,
or west of the West there was nothing but the unknown Stream of Ocean. To the east,
Known there were only two Easts: the Greek empire and Persia.
World

The Known World was the *Ecumene*, from the Greek for 'house.'* Earlier we said that the Roman Empire was a house with a courtyard around the pool of the Mediterranean Sea, but that sea is really two seas: a western, or Latin, sea and an eastern, or Greek—later Ottoman—sea lying east of and slightly to the south of the western. The island fortress of Malta commands the passage between them. Then there is Persia, which the Romans never succeeded in conquering but was part of Alexander's Empire and thus part of the Known World. Therefore, the Ecumene really has not one, but three courtyards. Each one represents an elemental geopolitical zone, the original three characters in the drama of the Eastern Question.

In this drawing, the western courtyard represents the Western Empire, founded with Rome's conquest of Carthage. The middle courtyard represents the Eastern Empire, the successor of the Hellenistic kingdoms ruled by Alexander's generals and their descendants. Divided from the Western in AD 395, it was conquered by the Ottomans in 1453. The eastern courtyard represents Persia, high up on the natural geopolitical fortress of the Iranian plateau. Even though conquered several times, it has always tended to reassert its Persian, or Iranian, identity and continues to do so today.

The border between the Eastern and Western Roman empires was the Balkans, the Adriatic Sea, and Malta.* Iraq was the border between the Eastern Empire and Persia, and today is the border between Western interests in the Middle East and Iran.

These are the great borderlands* of the world, the killing fields of history: the Balkans, Iraq, and—to the east of Persia—Afghanistan, the end of the Known World.

SCANDANAVIE
Baltic Sea
RUSSIE
Polonie
GERMANY
Black Sea
Caspian
PAKISTAN
AFGHANISTAN
PERSIA
INDIA
FRANCE
Rhine
IRAQ
EASTERN EMPIRE
HELLESPONT
ADRIATIC-MALTA
WESTERN EMPIRE
TO INDIA
BASRA
SUEZ
GIBRALTAR
SPAIN
THE ECUMENE or "KNOWN WORLD"
Gulf
ARABIA
Red Sea
EGYPT
TUNIS
MAROC
ALGÉRIE
Nile
Mecca
Deserta

Six Geopolitical Zones

Here is the plan of the metaphorical *Ecumene* projected onto the map of the World Island showing how it is related to actual geography.

Outside the *Ecumene* of the ancient world, there are also three other geopolitical zones: the Arabian desert, the Russian steppes—Mackinder's Heartland—and the New World. Originally unknown, or *Terra Incognita*, with the expansion of geographical knowledge they were one after another revealed to the people of the original Known World. In this book, these six geopolitical zones are represented by six colors.*

Arabia was known to the Romans through trade, but was impenetrable. For them Russia and the Scandinavian north were *Ultima Thule*: beyond the beyond. And even though the Roman philosopher Seneca had prophesied that

> there will come an age,* in far-off years,
> when Ocean shall unloose the bonds of things,
> when the whole broad earth shall be revealed
> and... Thule will not be Limit of the Land....

the discovery of a land beyond Ocean (the Atlantic) would have to wait until the relatively recent age of European discovery. Eventually northern Europe and its counterparts in the New World, the U.S. and Canada, were to form a geopolitical Western zone that spanned an ocean and that during the Cold War came to be known as NATO. In the same period, this Western zone was counterpoised by the Eastern zone of the Soviet Union and its satellites that came to be known as the Warsaw Pact countries. These two zones are the northern heirs of the Eastern and Western empires.

Beyond the borders of the Known World, on the other side of the band of deserts and mountains that divides the World Island—beyond Afghanistan—are other 'world systems'* that had been connected to the *Ecumene* only by the trade of the Silk Road. In contrast to the histories of the lands to the north, which exhibited constant expansion *beyond* their natural boundaries, Africa, India, and China remained *within* their boundaries, internally witnessing the dynamic of *Order* alternating with *Fragmentation*.

NORTH AMERICAN
STEPPE
USA & CANADA
TUNDRA
pine forests
Alaska
RUSSIAN STEPPE
Moscow
Kazan
Irkutsk
WESTERN
EMPIRE
Rome
EASTERN
EMPIRE
Constant
PERSIA
Babylon
Isfahan
Alexandria
Jeru-
salem
Baghdad
Afghanistan
Gobi
Tibet
Khanbalik
CHINA
Sahara
Medina
Mecca
ARABIAN
DESERT
Aden
Delhi
INDIA
AFRICA

Persian/ Alexander's Empire/ Caliphate of Baghdad

While the Romans succeeded in once uniting the two western courtyards, the two eastern courtyards were twice united: first as Persia/Alexander's Empire and second as the Caliphate of Baghdad. A millennium separates these two empires. Their eventual fracture underlies today's geopolitical division of Sunni and Shia Islam.*

Alexander dreamed of uniting East and West. He married a princess (Roxanne) from Central Asia and ordered his generals and 10,000 of his men to likewise take Eastern brides. The mass wedding symbolically celebrated the marriage of East and West.* He adopted Persian dress and court customs. He planned to fix his capital at Babylon, from where he could rule both Persia and the Mediterranean world, but he died, and his generals—the Diadochi or 'successors'—divided his empire.

A thousand years later, the Arabs conquered Persia and, having conquered a large part of the Eastern Empire as well, essentially re-created Alexander's empire, adding large chunks of the former Roman Empire in North Africa and the Iberian Peninsula. Stretching from the Atlantic to the Indus, the Caliphate of Baghdad was far larger and lasted much longer than Alexander's empire. The great conquests of the Arab empire were made by the first three caliphs—or 'successors' of Mohammad.

The first dynasty of caliphs, the Umayyads, came to power by usurping the title from Mohammad's grandson Ali, the last of the four 'Rightly Guided' (*Rashidun*) caliphs. Here lies the dynastic division of Sunni and Shia. The Umayyads fixed their capital at Damascus. The second dynasty, the Abbasids, overthrew them and built a new capital at Baghdad in 750, not far from Babylon. Damascus had proved to be too far to the west, as Mecca was too far to the south, to rule the vast empire. Their ambition was the same as Alexander's: to rule both East and West.

With the loss of Persia, however, the caliphate was split in half, and since then, instead of being the center of an empire, Iraq has become a borderland and thus by definition a battleground.

Persian/Alexander's Empires / Caliphate of Baghdad

Map 1 — Persian/Alexander's Empire
Marseille, Barcelona, Pillars of Hercules, Rome, Carthage, Macedonia, Thracia, Byzas, Issus, Damascus, Alexandria, Jerusalem, Babylon, Susa, Persepolis, Armenia, Alexandria Eschate, Sogdiana, Bactriana, Gedrosia, Africa, Egyptus, Thebes, Arabia

Map 2 — Caliphate of Baghdad
Francia Orientalis, Leon, Andalus, Cordova, Gibel al-Tarik, Corsica, Rome, Sardinia, Sicily, Bulgaria, Serbia, Constantinople, Byzantine Empire, Caspian Sea, Khowaresm, Maghreb, Kairouan, Afrikah, Damascus, Jerusalem, Baghdad, Cairo, Irak Adshemi, Fars, Kerman, Sind, Indus, Caliphate of Baghdad

Sunni and Shia

The original dispute between Sunni and Shia was between two types of legitimacy as caliph: between the descendants of Mohammad and the descendants of his strongest generals. It was a political dispute that morphed into a religious one, and then hardened into a geopolitical reality along an ancient borderland. The history of Baghdad is a geopolitical fable. Founded as the capital of the vast Sunni Arab Caliphate, when Shia Persia split off, Baghdad eventually ended up in the middle of a battlefield.

This borderland had been the eastern frontier of the Roman Empire, which Trajan had fixed at the Tigris and Hadrian later pulled back to the Euphrates. This borderland, where the Fertile Crescent meets the Heartland, has been fortified by the U.S. with antimissile capability, but with the power vacuum created by American withdrawal, Iranian influence is advancing into Shia Iraq.

When you engage Iraq, you engage Iran. Their histories are inextricably intertwined. Coming from Iraq, the Abbasids had originally been Shia but converted to Sunnism upon becoming caliphs. When Persia broke away in the 10th century, the Abbasid caliphs lost half their empire and their rule began to weaken. Turks began migrating into the empire, and in the middle of the 11th century, the Selçuk Turk Alp Arslan became sultan at Baghdad, and the Abbasid caliph became a figurehead.* In 1258, the Mongols sacked Baghdad,* bringing the Caliphate to its end.

The Islamic world never recovered from the fall of Baghdad. Two hundred and fifty years later, in 1501, Shah Ismail converted Persia to Shiism. In 1534, the Ottoman sultan Suleiman the Magnificent, having failed to take Vienna in 1529, turned his armies eastward and conquered Baghdad. The Persian Shah Abbas reconquered it in 1632. When the Ottomans retook it in 1637, a border was established by treaty that left the Shia holy cities—Samara, Karbala, and Najaf—on the Sunni Ottoman side. This is the same border* that was disputed in the Iran-Iraq War of the 1980s. The overthrow of Saddam's minority Sunni government in 2003 once again opened the Pandora's box of civil war between Sunni and Shia.

Asia
Europe
Constantinople
Caucasus
Caspian Sea
Taurus Mtns
SUNNI
SHIA
Shia Holy Cities
Baghdad
Samara
Najaf
Karbalo
Jerusalem
Cairo
Africa
Zagros Mtns.
Persian Gulf
Red Sea
Riyadh
Medinah
Makkah

Great Mosque of Damascus

The Great Umayyad Mosque at Damascus in Syria is a palimpsest of powers rising and falling, a perfect illustration of the succession of states. It is a monument of religions, peoples, languages, arts overlaid one on top of the other: of Nabateans, Aramaeans, Romans, Byzantines, and Muslim Arabs.

It is also a monument to the struggle between Sunni and Shia, the defining moment of which was the battle of Karbala in AD 680. Here the second Umayyad caliph, Yazid, successfully defended his claim to the title by defeating Mohammad's grandson Husayn ibn-Ali. It was the first time that a son had succeeded his father as caliph and Commander of the Faithful. It represents the triumph of power over 'right.'

By right of familial inheritance, when Mohammad died in 632, the caliphate should have passed to his nephew and son-in-law Ali ibn-Abi Talib, but he was passed over three times: first by Abu Bakr, then Umar, and finally by Uthman. Ali finally became the fourth and last of the 'Rightly Guided' caliphs. He was, however, quickly overthrown by Yazid's father, Muhawiyah ibn-Umayyah, progenitor of the Umayyads, and killed near the town of Najaf, where his head is now buried. When Muhawiyah died, Ali's second son, Hussayn, tried to assert his right to be caliph, but he was killed by Yazid's forces where the town of Karbala stands today. The tragic events that ensued are mourned every year by Shias, the party of Ali. The Shia faith is based on this grievance, and the consequent desire for revenge.

Husayn's family were forced to walk from Karbala to Damascus and then made to stand for 72 hours outside the gate of the mosque before being admitted. The heads of those killed at Karbala were displayed in the court, and Husayn's son Ali was made to submit to Yazid. 'The heart is like Husayn, and separation like Yazid—it has been martyred two hundred ways in the desert of grief and affliction.'*

When the ancient structure was rebuilt by the caliph al-Walid, the head of John the Baptist was discovered and a shrine built into the new mosque. It is ironic that John, or Yahya ibn-Zachariah to Muslims, was also a tyrant's victim* and his head a trophy.

GREAT UMAYYAD MOSQUE · DAMASCUS, SYRIA · PLAN

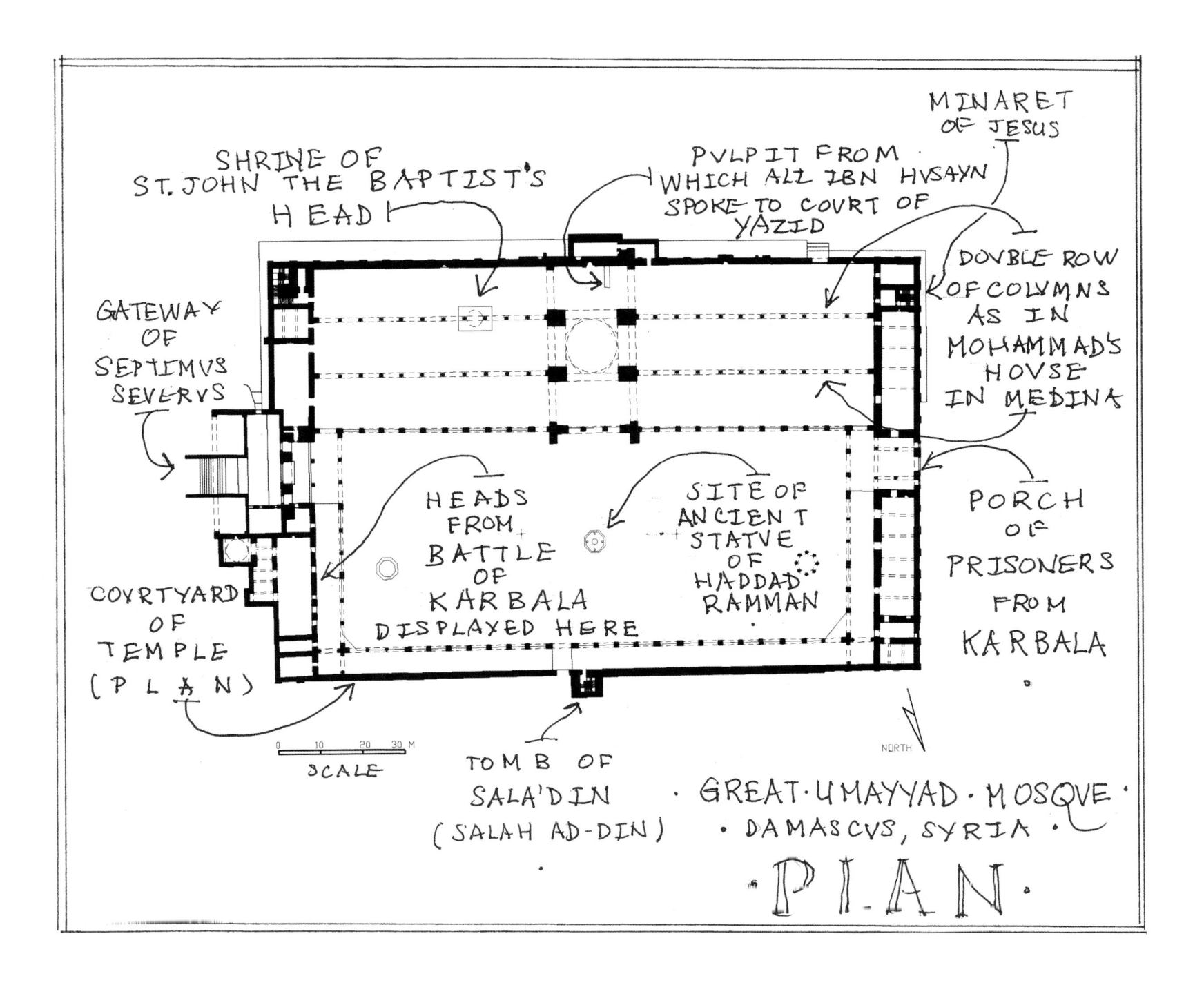

- SHRINE OF ST. JOHN THE BAPTIST'S HEAD
- PULPIT FROM WHICH ALI IBN HUSAYN SPOKE TO COURT OF YAZID
- MINARET OF JESUS
- DOUBLE ROW OF COLUMNS AS IN MOHAMMAD'S HOUSE IN MEDINA
- GATEWAY OF SEPTIMUS SEVERUS
- COURTYARD OF TEMPLE (PLAN)
- HEADS FROM BATTLE OF KARBALA DISPLAYED HERE
- SITE OF ANCIENT STATUE OF HADDAD RAMMAN
- PORCH OF PRISONERS FROM KARBALA
- TOMB OF SALA'DIN (SALAH AD-DIN)

SCALE 0 10 20 30 M

NORTH

THE TRUE EAST: TURKS, MONGOLS, RUSSIANS

Selçuks and Crusaders

THE TWO LEADING Eastern characters in the geopolitical drama of the Eastern Question in the 19th century were the Turks and the Russians. On this and the following three double-page spreads, we will discuss their origins and the struggle for control of the Heartland. We will show how the Russian Empire was the successor of the Mongol Empire; and how the Turks, the Byzantines, the Russians, and the Mongols played musical chairs in a game of succession of states.

Long before the rise of the Mongols, the Turks began entering* Arab lands as warriors in the service of the weakening Abbasid caliphate. Around the year 1000, a Turk named Selçuk led several tribes into Bukhara, where they converted to Islam. In 1039, horsemen under Selçuk's grandson Tughril crossed the Oxus River and penetrated into Iran, Iraq, and Armenia. His nephew Alp Arslan founded an empire and in 1055 was acknowledged as sultan at Baghdad. Then in 1071, the Selçuks under Alp Arslan defeated the Byzantines at Manzikert, near Lake Van in eastern Anatolia, and thereby dealt a crushing blow to the declining Byzantine Empire.* Ruling over lands conquered from the Roman Empire, the Selçuks called themselves the sultans of Rum and established their capital at Konya (Iconium).

After Manzikert, the Byzantine emperor appealed to the pope for help. In the first counter-*jihad* in the East, the Crusader knights took Jerusalem in 1099, establishing the Latin Kingdoms.* This was the West's first direct contact with the Turks. In contrast to the modern state of Israel—with which there are many parallels—for lack of immigration the West lost its tenuous grip on the eastern shore of the Mediterranean, but for a while their counter-*jihad* was successful. In 1187, Saladin, the founder of the Ayyubid dynasty in Egypt, ejected the Crusaders from Jerusalem.*

The Selçuks and the Crusaders
A.D. 1099
Ocean Sea
Ireland
Scotland
Norway
Sweden
Denmark
Prussia
Grand Duchy of Vladimir
Poland
German Empire
France
Burgundy
Hungary
Santiago de Compostella
Leon
Castile
Cordoba
Andalus
Marseille
Venice
Rome
Kingdom of Sicily
Palermo
Danube
Servia
Bulgaria
Black Sea
Constantinople
Trebizond
Nicaea
Dorylaeum
Byzantine Empire
Sultanate of Iconium
Iconium
Cilician Gates
Ephesos
Caspian Sea
Mediterranean Sea
Empire of the Almohades
Tunis
Kairouan
Tel Aviv
Gaza
Latin Kingdoms
Damascas
Jerusalem
Baghdad
Selçuk Turks
Cairo
Fatimids until 1171
Red Sea
Arabia
Medina
Mecca

Mongols

The true East is Genghisid: that is, in one way or another descended from Genghis.* This map contains a geopolitical family tree. It shows how three of Genghis's grandsons laid the foundations of the modern countries of China, Iran, and Russia; how the last conqueror from the steppes, Tamerlane, married into Genghis's family; and how a Mongol descendant, Babur, founded the Mughal dynasty of India. A third small tribe, later the Ottomans—not Genghisid themselves but followers of the Mongol horde—settled on the borders of the shrinking Byzantine Empire. These were the supreme horse people.

This map shows how the Mongols spanned the entire continent of Eurasia, stretching from the Pacific to the Mediterranean, almost reaching Africa. The map also shows where they reached their limits: at Ayn al-Galat,* where they were turned back by the Egyptian Mamluks; in Indonesia, where they were defeated by the hot, humid climate; and in Japan, where a typhoon* destroyed their fleet.

Like a vast glacier, the Mongols left a radically altered landscape when they retreated. Instead of being a barrier, the Heartland became a highway. At the time of Genghis's birth in 1162, no one had made the journey from one end of Asia to the other. At the time of his death, East and West, the core of the Heartland and the Rimlands of Europe, Asia, and North Africa, were for the first time directly connected. The first ambassadors had been exchanged; the 'artists of China and Persia vied with each other in the service of the Great Khan.'* They had no words for 'right' or 'left,' but only east and west; they were the first people to understand 'globalization,' and they created a new world order. Of all the heirs of Genghis, whether direct or not, the most important from the point of view of the West are the Ottomans and the Russians. In the 19th century, what might happen, as the former declined and the latter ascended in power, became known as the Eastern Question.

In the succession of states, after the great tidal wave of the Mongols had receded, the Russian tsars became the political successors of the khans.

Frozen Sea
TVNDRA
to Alaska
Petersburg
Moskva
Kiev
Europe
Batu Khan
Jochi
Genghis Khan
Golden Horde
Saray
Tolui
Karakorum
Constantinople
Seljuks
Attempt on Cairo
Hulegu Khan
Chagatai
Khubilai Khan
Xanadu
Attempt on Japan
Tamerlane (by marriage)
Il Khans later Safavid Persians
Baghdad
Khanbalik (Beijing)
Empire of the Great Khan
Libya
Egypt
Aynal Galat
Arabia
Bahur
Mughal Empire
Shah Jehan
1858 (last Mughal)
Sahara
Yemen
Darfur
Ethiopia
Somalia
Attempt on Indonesia
South China Sea
Pacific Ocean
Indian Ocean

Russian Façade

Imagine the modern Russian state as the successor of the Mongol Empire* with an enormous European-style façade,* designed by Italian architects,* facing west. Behind it, from the 15th to the 19th centuries, the tsars gradually conquered the vast steppes and pushed into the Heartland of Eurasia. Here's how it happened.

In the 5th century, when Attila scattered the tribes of Europe, one group, the East Slavs, settled in Russia. They were ruled over by descendants of Rurik the Norseman. In the first half of the 13th century, these princes were defeated by the Mongols who settled on the Volga at Saray (near Volgograd), a vast city of which no trace now remains.* From there they extracted tribute and homage from the princes.

At first the Russian rulers tried to throw off the galling domination, but in time they came to curry favor with the khan of the Golden Horde, vying with one another, marrying into Mongol families, and to some extent becoming Tatarized themselves. The Russian people, the Slavs, 'reproached them for* loving overmuch their masters.' One of these rulers, the prince of Moscow, succeeded so well at this game of currying favor with the khan that he eventually emerged as superior to the others.

The Black Plague and Tamerlane's sack of Saray in 1395 seriously weakened the Golden Horde. Less than one hundred years later, the grand duke of Moscow, Ivan the Great, freed himself from the Mongols at the 'Ugra standoff' in 1479. Thus, thirteen years before the discovery of America, Russia emerged as an independent nation.

The rulers of Russia, from the tsars to Putin, have thus been not only the political heirs of the old Nordic princes, the Rurikids, but also the heirs of the Mongol khans.

> The autocratic power* which has been for the last four centuries out of all comparison the most important factor in Russian history came out of the long domination of the Mongols, reinforced by the Byzantine conception of the state, the keystone of the arch of imperial autocracy.

Baltic
Rurik the Norseman
Forests
Siberia
Kamchatka
Pacific
Mongols
Kazan
Altai Mtns
Volga
Moscow
STEPPE
Turks
Saray
Slavs
Novgorod
Kiev
Tatars
Don r.
Dnepr. r.
Cossacks
Black Sea
ST PETERSBURG

Here, looking forward and backward in time, is a broad overview on a succession of states—of Turks, Mongols, Byzantines, and Russians—in a circular pattern swirling around the Heartland of Eurasia, eventually threatening the West.

Succession of States

Not only were the Russian princes the heirs of Rurik and the khans, they were also the religious and political heirs of Byzantium. Starting with Cyril and Methodius, missionaries from Constantinople brought the Christian religion to the Slavic peoples of the north. In 988, Vladimir, Grand Prince of Kiev, accepted Christianity.* Thus was established a northern home and refuge for the Eastern Orthodox Church.

Meanwhile, the Selçuk Turks swept into the Arab Caliphate and then on into Anatolia, defeating the Byzantines at Manzikert in 1071. In the 13th century, the Mongols invaded Kievan Rus, subjugating without occupying the Russian lands. In the 15th century, the Ottomans, followers of the Mongols, began to conquer the Eastern Empire both in Europe and Asia, culminating in 1453 with the Conquest. Russia was left alone as the only unconquered Christian state in the East.

Fifteen years earlier, at the Council of Florence in 1438, in a desperate attempt to get help for his threatened city from the West, the Eastern emperor had agreed to accept the supremacy of the pope over the Orthodox Church. Refusing to accept this, the Russians established an independent Patriarchate of Moscow* in 1448. When Constantinople was conquered five years later, the prince of Moscow could claim the title of Eastern Caesar, or tsar. To legitimize this claim, in 1469, Ivan the Great married Sophia Palaiologina,* the niece of the last emperor. Famously, a monk prophesied, 'Two Romes have fallen [meaning Rome and Constantinople]. A third stands [Moscow].'

From the 15th century on, the Russian tsars subdued the lands* of the former Mongol Empire, pushing east and south into Central Asia, yet always dreaming of taking Constantinople and reconquering parts of the old Eastern Empire in the Balkans. Both projects* eventually provoked the Eastern Question.

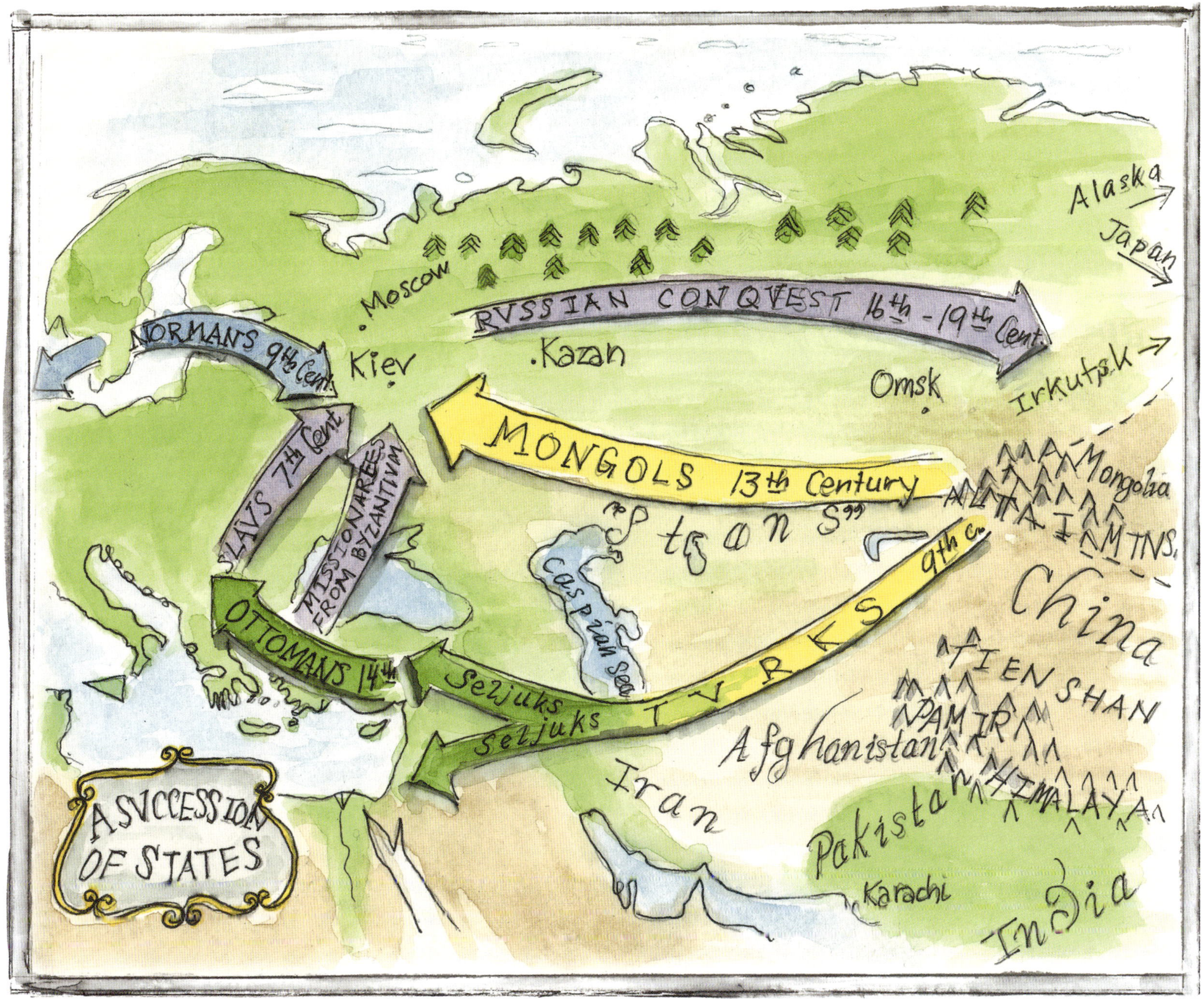
A SUCCESSION OF STATES
NORMANS 9th Cent.
SLAVS 7th Cent.
MISSIONARIES FROM BYZANTIUM
RUSSIAN CONQUEST 16th - 19th Cent.
MONGOLS 13th Century
TURKS 9th c.
OTTOMANS 14th
Seljuks
Seljuks
"Stans"
Moscow
Kiev
Kazan
Omsk
Irkutsk
Alaska
Japan
Mongolia
ALTAI MTNS.
China
TIEN SHAN
PAMIR
HIMALAYA
Afghanistan
Iran
Pakistan
Karachi
India
Caspian Sea

EAST & WEST: THE WEST

Cross and Crescent

THE MODERN EUROPEAN WEST was defined by its struggle with Islam: first the Arabs, and then the Turks. In between these two great historical *jihads* arose the Holy Roman Empire, the heart of Europe. The two *jihads* did not occur at the same time, but their farthest advance defined what Europe is and then how far its borders were pushed back,* by the *Reconquista* in the West and the Russian advance into the Ottoman Empire, the latter under the rubric of 19th-century nationalist Pan-Slavism.

The Muslims, filled with the spirit of Allah, had a mission to bring the entire world into the House of Islam, or the House of Peace, which in Arabic is Dar al' Islam—meaning the lands where the people live under a Muslim ruler for whom the Friday prayer is said in the mosques. Everything outside of this was the House of War, or Dar al' Houl—the lands of the Unbelievers—not yet conquered. The relationship between the House of Peace and the House of War is 'struggle,' or *jihad*.

After the Arabs lost their original impetus with two failed attempts to take Constantinople, the Turks picked up the *jihad*. In 1071, they defeated the Byzantines at Manzikert. In 1095, the pope preached a sermon that led to the First Crusade.

> Can anyone tolerate* that we do not even share equally with
> the Moslems the inhabited earth? They have made Asia, which
> is a third of the world, their homeland. They have forcibly
> held Africa for over 200 years. There remains Europe, the
> third continent. How small a portion of it is inhabited by us
> Christians!

Neither the Ottoman Empire nor the Golden Horde existed at this time, though the Duchy of Moscovy did. I show them to emphasize these future characters in the drama of the Eastern Question. Persia has always been there.

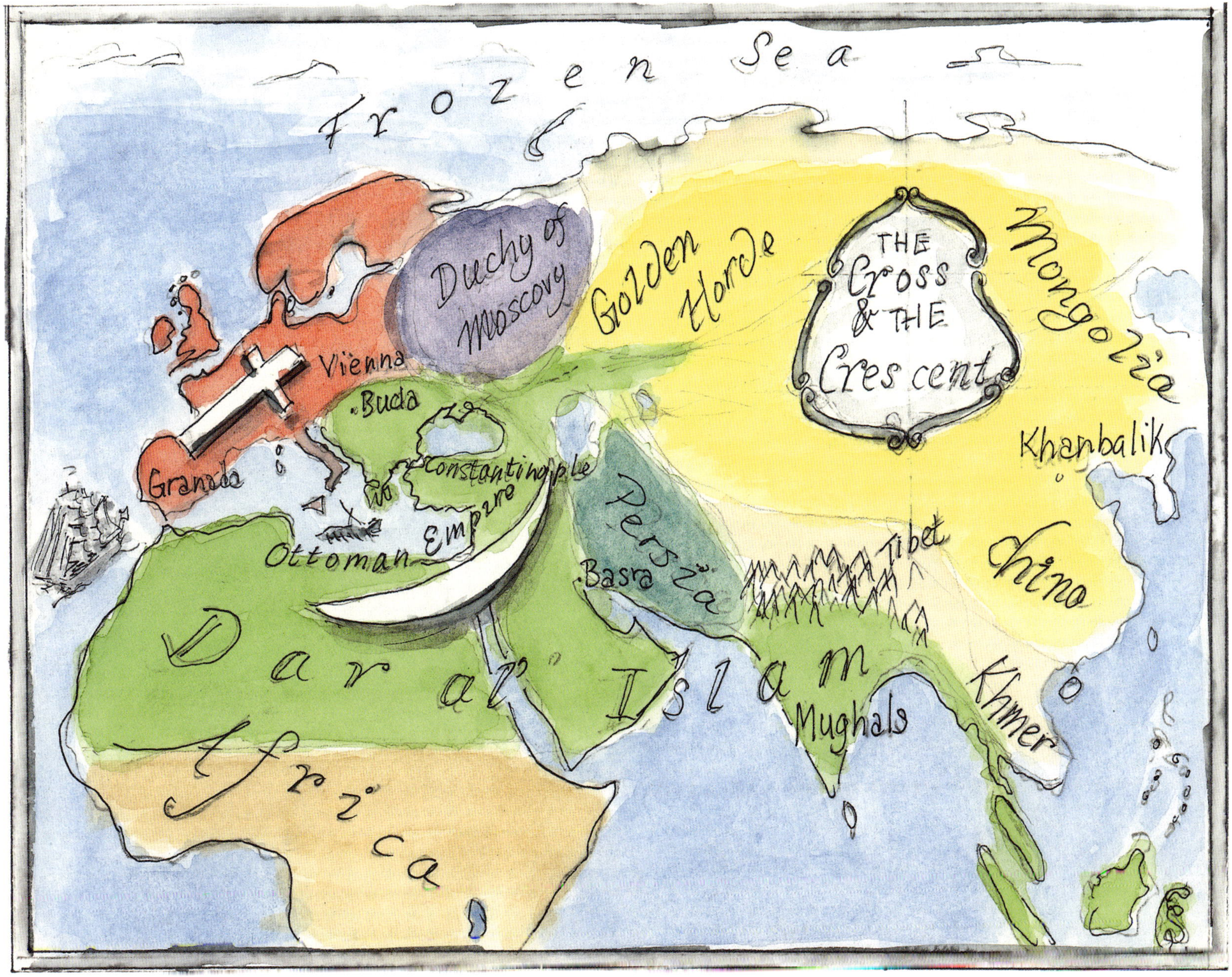
Frozen Sea
Duchy of Moscovy
Golden Horde
THE Cross & THE Crescent
Mongolia
Vienna
Buda
Granada
Constantinople
Ottoman Empire
Khanbalik
Persia
Basra
Tibet
China
Dar al Islam
Mughals
Khmer
Africa

Two Great Jihads**

The Arab plan had originally been to encircle the diminished Christian West and to crush it in a classic pincer movement: from Spain in the West and from the Byzantine Empire in the East. But the Byzantines, the last remnant of the old Roman Empire, resisted the onslaught. The Arab and Turkish conquests were astonishing and are comparable only to those of the Mongols in the 13th and those of the Europeans from the 16th to the 20th century. All three created successively vaster new world orders.

As if driven by the desert winds, the Muslims, led by Mohammad's successors, or caliphs, in 633 burst out of Arabia. Within three years* they had taken Damascus; within six, Jerusalem, then all of Syria; within a decade, Egypt and Armenia; within two decades, the Persian empire; and within three, Afghanistan and most of the Punjab. In 711, after having rapidly run the length the entire coast of North Africa, they crossed into Spain at Gibraltar. In the battle of Guadalete near Jerez de la Frontera, they conquered the Visigothic kingdoms of the Iberian peninsula, and then crossed the Pyrenees into France and reached the Loire, where their progress was finally checked in 732, exactly a century after Mohammad's death. They had conquered more than half of the former Roman territory, including the oldest Christian cities of Antioch, Alexandria, and Jerusalem. However, the Arab dream of a pincer movement evaporated with the failure to conquer Constantinople, which was reserved for the Turks.

> **Arab *jihad*** (632–1050) Arabs take the lands of the former Roman Empire from the Pyrenees Mountains and Marseille in the West to Syria as far as the Taurus Mountains in the East. The Byzantine Empire serves as a buffer state on the border of Western Christendom. The Mongol sack of Baghdad in 1258 marks the final end of the Arab Empire.
>
> **Turkish *jihad*** (1050–1683) The Ottoman Turks take Constantinople and all of the Eastern Empire and become its successor state. In this phase, the Catholic Hapsburg Empire of Spain, Austria, and Hungary defends the marches of Western Europe from the Turks.

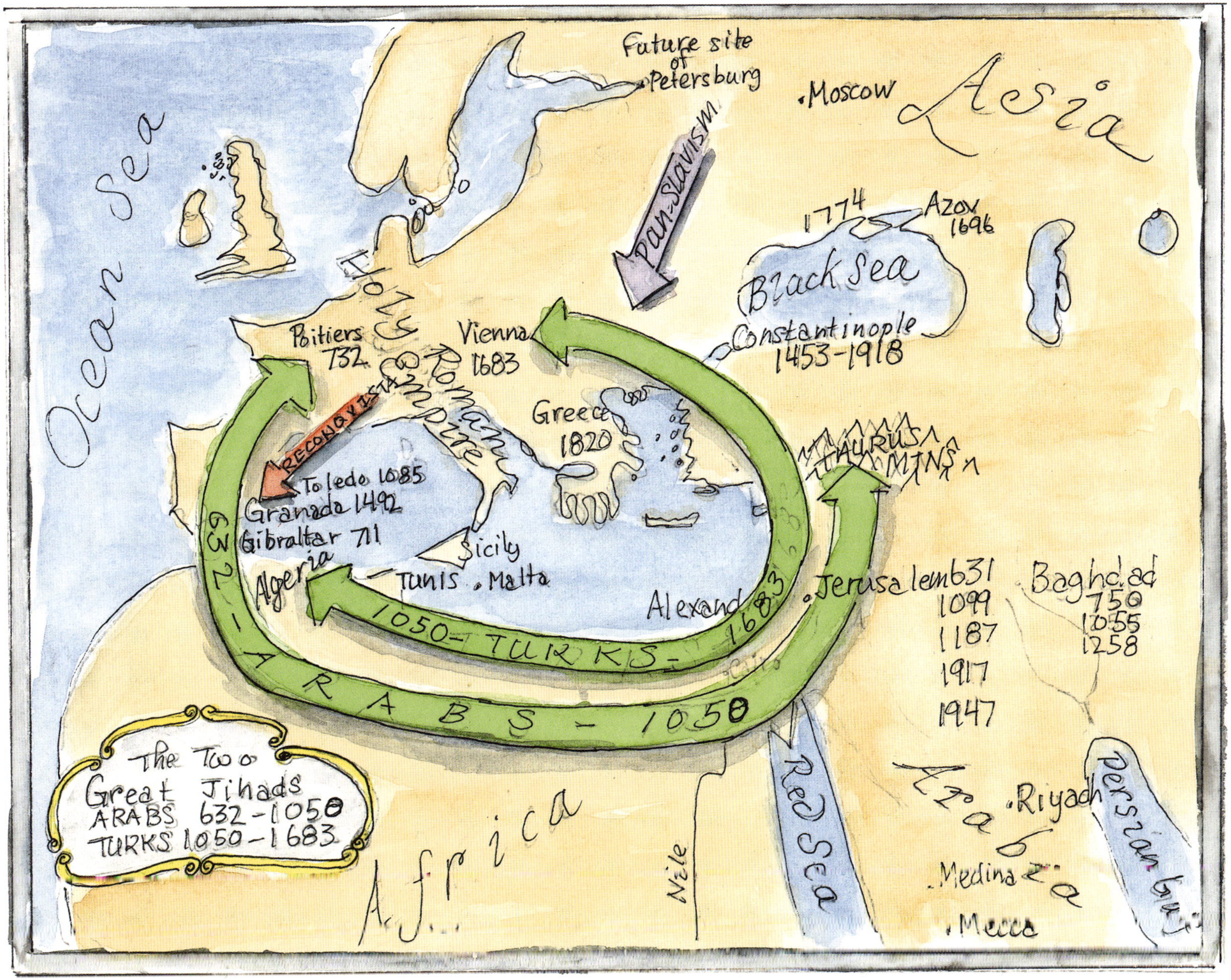
Future site of Petersburg
Moscow
Asia
Ocean Sea
Pan-Slavism
1774
Azov 1696
Black Sea
Holy Roman Empire
Poitiers 732
Vienna 1683
Constantinople 1453-1918
Reconquista
Greece 1820
Taurus Mtns
Toledo 1085
Granada 1492
Gibraltar 711
Sicily
Algeria
Tunis
Malta
Alexand
Jerusalem 631 1099 1187 1917 1947
Baghdad 750 1055 1258
1050 - TURKS - 1683
632 - ARABS - 1050
The Two Great Jihads
ARABS 632-1050
TURKS 1050-1683
Africa
Nile
Red Sea
Arabia
Riyadh
Persian Gulf
Medina
Mecca

Holy Roman Empire

The tremendous onslaught of the Arab *jihad* brought the Western Roman Empire to its end and led to the birth of its faint shadow, the Holy Roman Empire. The Arab war fleets cut the trade routes across the Mediterranean, transforming this former 'middle-earth' sea into a moat dividing Dar al' Islam and Christendom. The unity of the Roman world was broken, and another age had begun. The southern shore of Europe now lay across from enemy territory,* and the political center of Europe, no longer at Rome, nor even at Ravenna, now lay in the heart of the European peninsula along the Rhine River. With Charlemagne, a new consolidating power arose north of the Alps. Without the rise of Islam, 'Charlemagne would have been inconceivable.'*

To Muslims, Europeans were the *Ferenghi*, that is, the Franks, Charlemagne's Germanic tribe. At his death, his kingdom split in half* east and west: the origin of the modern countries of Germany and France. Germany became the Holy Roman Empire, the First Reich, an empire in name only. At the Reformation, it split north and south along a linguistic and climatic divide.* Having already seized the title of emperor for himself, Napoleon abolished the Holy Roman Empire in 1806. Having defeated Napoleon III in 1871, Bismarck founded the Second Reich and took back the title of emperor for the Germans. In the 20th century, the borders of Charlemagne's kingdom re-emerged more or less as the borders of the original European Union.*

In 962, however, Europe was not called Europe; it was Christendom. It only became defined as such in contradistinction to Dar al' Islam. From the 7th to the 17th centuries, Islam 'harassed Christendom with its vigorous aggressions,'* taking more than half of the former Roman Christian empire. In the 11th century, the spirit of a counter-*jihad* infused Europeans to such a degree that war appeared to be the most holy and praiseworthy response. Like Islam for the Arabs, the Christian faith became a rallying cry. From all over Christendom, people made pilgrimages to Compostela in Spain, dedicated to the patron saint of the *Reconquista*, Christ's brother Saint James, who had been transformed into *Matamoros*, or 'the Moor-killer.'*

Holy Roman Empire AD 962

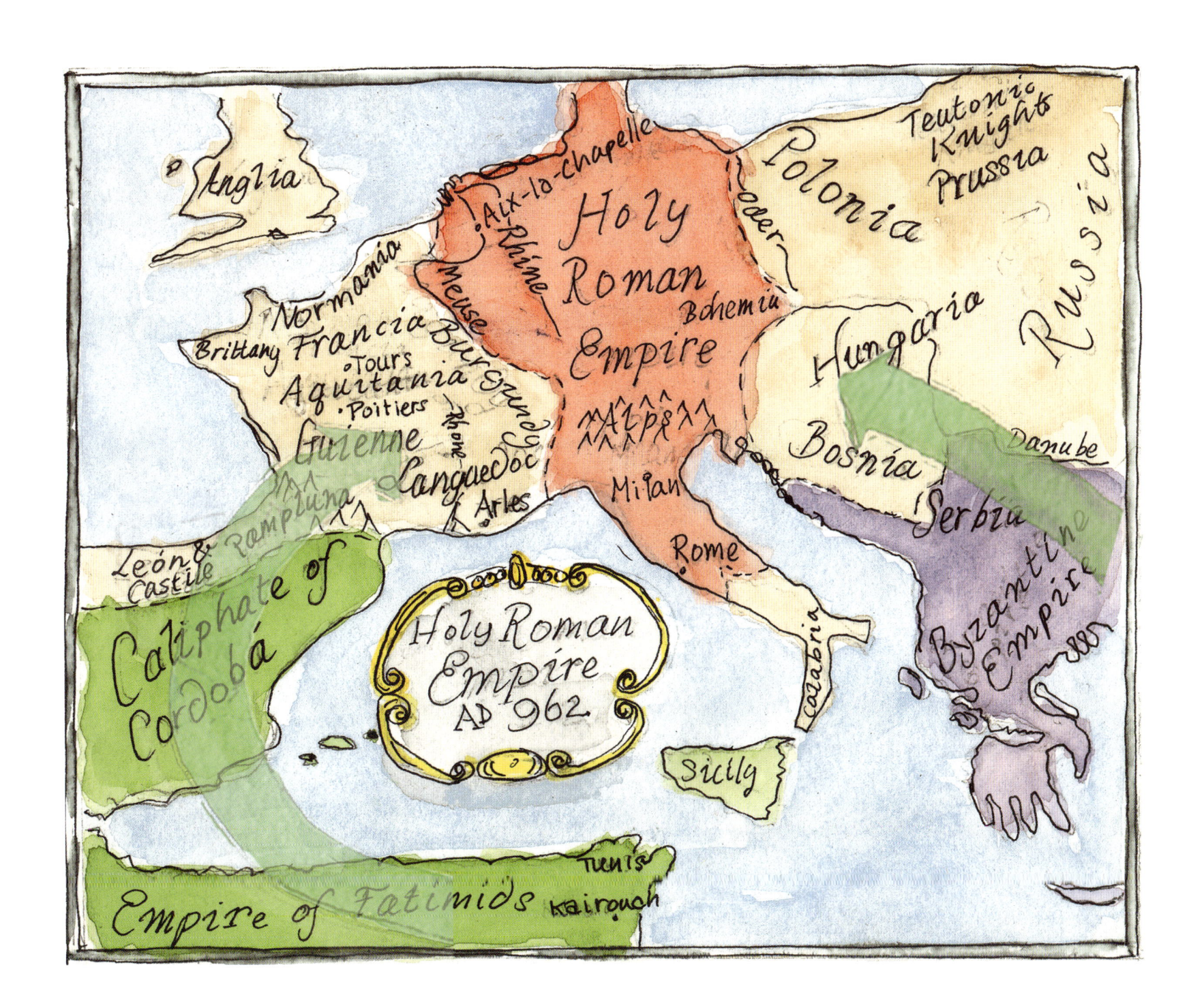

Peninsularity of Europe

Even though highly divided internally, Christendom managed to survive the onslaught of a unified Islam, and all the incursions of Mongols, Huns, Arabs, Turks, and Bolsheviks—from the west and from the east—due to one simple geographic fact: it is an extremely long peninsula, an 'almost island,' with a highly indented coast. It is a moated fortress stretching from Cape St. Vincent in Spain eastward... to where?

Here in this map I have drawn the peninsula with the East at the top, as in a medieval map, to emphasize this peninsularity. As Gibbon wrote of the Arab advance:

> A victorious line of march* had been prolonged above a thousand miles, from the Rock of Gibraltar to the banks of the Loire; the repetition of an equal space [another thousand miles] would have carried the Saracens to the confines of Poland and the highlands of Scotland.

But the Arabs had encountered the classic military problem of an overextended supply line and the Loire was their limit. During the Second World War, the Allies had great difficulty moving—even against a dispirited enemy—from Africa to Sicily and then up the boot of Italy, the supposed 'soft underbelly' of the Fortress of Europe. Hitler's Third Reich was the only power to rule almost the entire peninsula.*

While Europe's maritime limits are clear, the border to the east is not. If we are to define it as a peninsula, the line would lie at the narrow neck where this peninsula joins the continent of Asia, between the head of the Gulf of Finland and the head of the Sea of Azov, leaving Moscow to the east and Kiev to the west. Even though most atlases extend a 'European' Russia as far as the Urals, the Michelin road map of Europe goes only as far as Moscow, leaving most of Russia in Asia.*

Just as peninsular Europe is a geopolitical fortress, so is vast Russia—for the same reason. They are equally inviolable because of the danger of overextended supply lines. The ever-shifting border between these fortresses is also the border between the Sea Power of the West and the Land Power of the East.

MONGOLS
HVNS
TVRKS
Petersburg
Moscau
Azov
Gulf of Finland
Kiev
Ukraine
Constantinople
Kingdom of Sweden
Lithuania
Poland
Prussia
DENMARK
Hungary
Romania
Bulgaria
Serbia
Bosnia
Berlin
Vienna
Ilyria
Greece
VIKINGS
London
Italy
Rome
Sicily
Chalons
Poitiers
Mare Mediterraneum
Kairouan
Ifrikiyah
ARABS
Jerusalem
Spain
Magreb
Gibel al' Tarik
Mare Oceanum
E
N
S
W
Islas Canarias
The Peninsularity of Europe

Eastern Borders of Europe

Borders, or marches, are wide zones within which the lines drawn on maps are always shifting. The steppes of Asia reach through the plains of Poland and Hungary right into the wheat fields of France practically without a break except for rivers. The lines have been placed where armies in the field laid down their guns, and diplomats at treaty tables picked up their pens. Sometimes they agree to place the line on an *uti posseditis*,* or 'as possessed' basis, sometimes they agree to adjust it with concessions granted or insisted on, depending who has the upper hand. There have been at least four lines drawn here. They are being redrawn as we speak.

Prince Metternich, the architect of post-Napoleonic Europe, claimed that the East began outside the city wall of Vienna, to which the Ottomans twice laid siege. Founded on the Danube as a Roman border outpost against the Ostrogoths (East Goths), Vienna remained an outpost against the Ottomans when Austria—or Austreich, the Eastern Realm—was the farthest bastion of the West.

> A man seems to take* leave of our world [when he leaves Vienna], and before he comes to Buda seems to enter upon a new stage of the world, quite different from that of Western countries… enters upons habits, manners, and a course of life which with no great variety but under some conformity extends unto China and the utmost parts of Asia.

Along the narrow corridor between Vienna and Istanbul, the Turkish wars were waged back and forth across the football field of the Balkans,* as the armies of the sultan advanced and then retreated in a series of battles from the 14th until the 17th centuries, battles with names like Kosovo and Mohács, where the Hungarian nobles in their heavy armor were wiped out by the swift-moving Janissaries. After this, the Austrian Hapsburgs inherited the thrones of Hungary and Bohemia, and became the defenders of the eastern marches of Christendom.

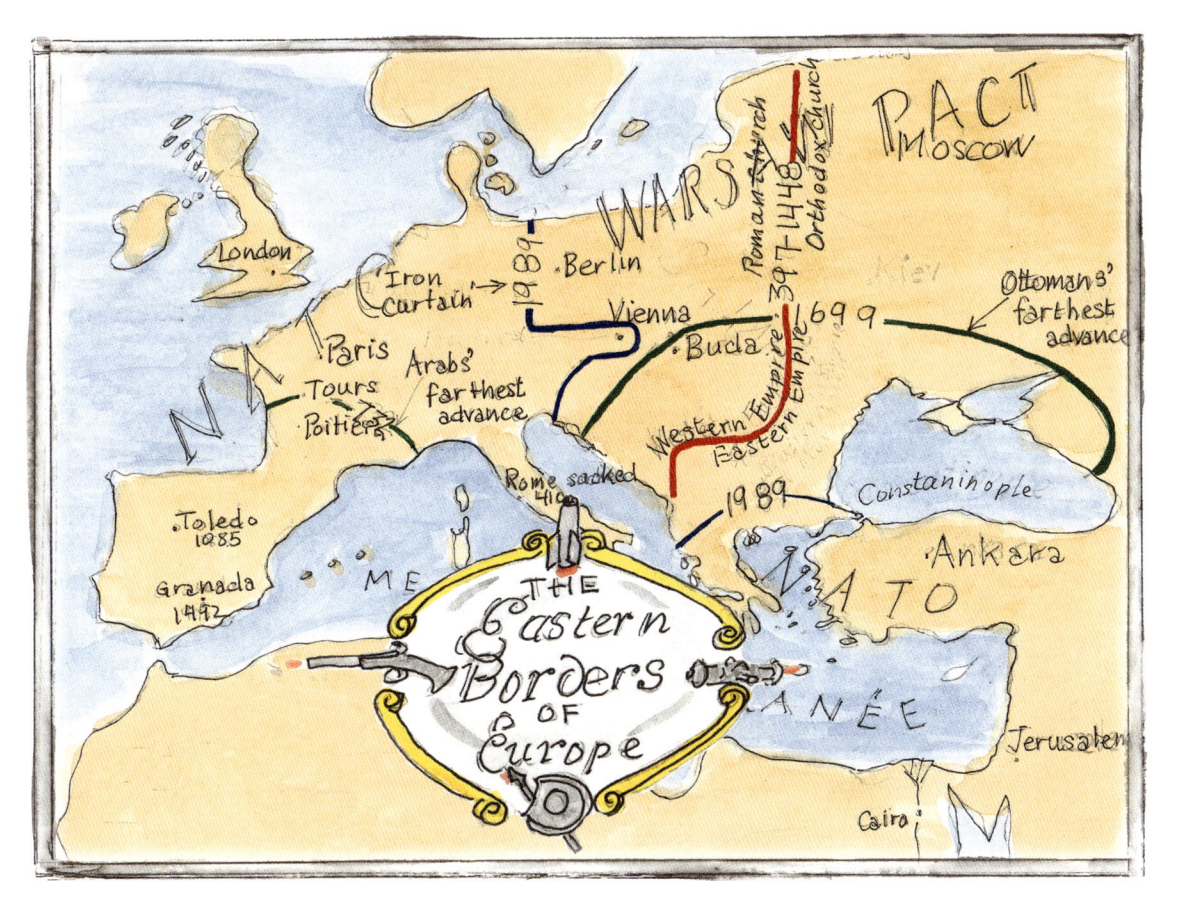

397 The old division between the Western and Eastern Roman empires, with the death of Emperor Theodosius

1448 The later border between the Roman Church and the Russian Orthodox Church, with the establishment of the Patriarchate of Moscow

1699 The line of farthest advance of the Ottoman Empire into Europe, before the Treaty of Carlowitz

1989 The farthest reach of Eastern power* into Western Europe, the 'Iron Curtain' of the Cold War, before the fall of the Berlin Wall

THE WEST: A MIGHTY FORTRESS

Ein Feste Burg* IMAGINE THE WEST as a fortress built on a 16th-century model for defense against the Ottoman Empire. This fort has two outer walls. The outermost, the *Counterscarp*, had been the Byzantine Empire until it was breached in 1453 with the Conquest of Constantinople. The city had survived two Arab assaults, in 674 and 718, more crucial to the survival of the West than Charles Martel's lauded victory at Poitiers in 732. If Constantinople had fallen then, the West would most likely not have survived the Arab *jihad*. The hitherto impregnable walls of the city were finally breached in 1453 by a huge gun manufactured by a renegade Hungarian* named Urban. By this time the inner *Bastion* of southern Catholic Hapsburg Europe was now strong enough to hold out against the onslaught, even though Vienna was twice besieged.

The innermost redoubt of the fortress, the *Cavalier*, of northern Protestant Europe never had to fight this Long War,* but a few mercenaries, like John Smith, volunteered. He earned the title of captain in the Turkish wars, before sailing for Virginia. But for the most part, northern Protestant Europe and its heir in the New World, the United States, could turn its back on this struggle.

This was the last phase of that Long War in which Christendom fought against the onslaught of Islam from 632 to 1683. By the end of the 16th century, a relatively stable border had developed along a 1,200-mile-long arc like a scimitar with its tip at Croatia and its hilt at Crimea, close to the western edge of the Heartland. (See previous page.) For its service to the West, Pope Leo X gave Croatia the title of the Counterscarp of Christianity (*Antemurale Christianitatis*), and the job of manning the garrison fell to the Austrian Hapsburgs. Luckily for them, their foes the Ottomans had their own foes the heretical Shia Persians to contend with at their rear.

Ein Feste Berg
THE FORTRESS OF EVROPE
1453 – 1683
"Cavalier"
Northern Eur.
Protestants
"Bastion"
Southern Europe
Catholic
Hapsburgs
"Counterscarp"
Eastern
Orthodox
Byzantines
conquered by
Ottoman Turks.
The Great Gun of Urban
"The outer ramparts were breached, but the inner ones held."
The Grand Turk's tent pitched before Vienna
Transylvania
Wallachia
Vienna
Budapest
Constantinople 1453

Two-Fronted Wars

Who were these Hapsburgs? Despite being the oldest dynasty in Europe, and Holy Roman Emperors, from beginning to end, they were drab. 'Drabness was their secret. Drabness and patience. Manipulative, industrious, strangely modest, inexorable, decent, stodgy, and staunch.'*

Originally from Switzerland, they became dukes of Austria in 1273, twenty-six years before Osman declared his independence from the Selçuk sultan. By a series of brilliant marriages*—and deaths, leaving in several cases only one heir—the Hapsburgs became the rulers of the first modern European world colonial empire. In 1520, Charles V, the only grandson of Ferdinand and Isabella, inherited Spain and the lands Spain claimed in the New World. From his paternal grandfather, Emperor Maximilian, he inherited Austria, Burgundy, and the Low Countries. With the defeat of the French at Pavia,* he gained control of northern Italy. With the death at Mohács of Louis of Hungary, he became defender of the eastern marches of Christendom. At the time of the Reformation, as a devout Catholic he became defender of the Roman Church.*

The Hapsburgs held off the irresistible onslaught of the Turks. They relieved the siege of Malta in 1565. They gave the Turks their first defeat, in the great sea battle off Lepanto* in 1571, the hero of which was Charles's natural son Don Juan of Austria.* Here the novelist Cervantes was wounded, earning the sobriquet *el manco de Lepanto.**

History has shown that fighting two-fronted wars is perilous. The Hapsburgs could never devote their full strength to fighting the Ottomans for fear of the northern European Protestants at their rear; likewise, the Ottomans could never devote their full strength to fighting the Hapsburgs for fear of the Safavid Shias of Persia at their rear. Wrote Ghislain de Busbecq, Charles's ambassador to Constantinople:

> Persia alone* interposes in our favor, for the enemy, as he hastens
> to attack, must keep his eye on the menace to his rear... Persia
> alone is delaying our fate; it cannot save us. When the Turks have
> settled with Persia, they will fly at our throats, supported by the
> might of the whole East; how prepared we are I dare not say.

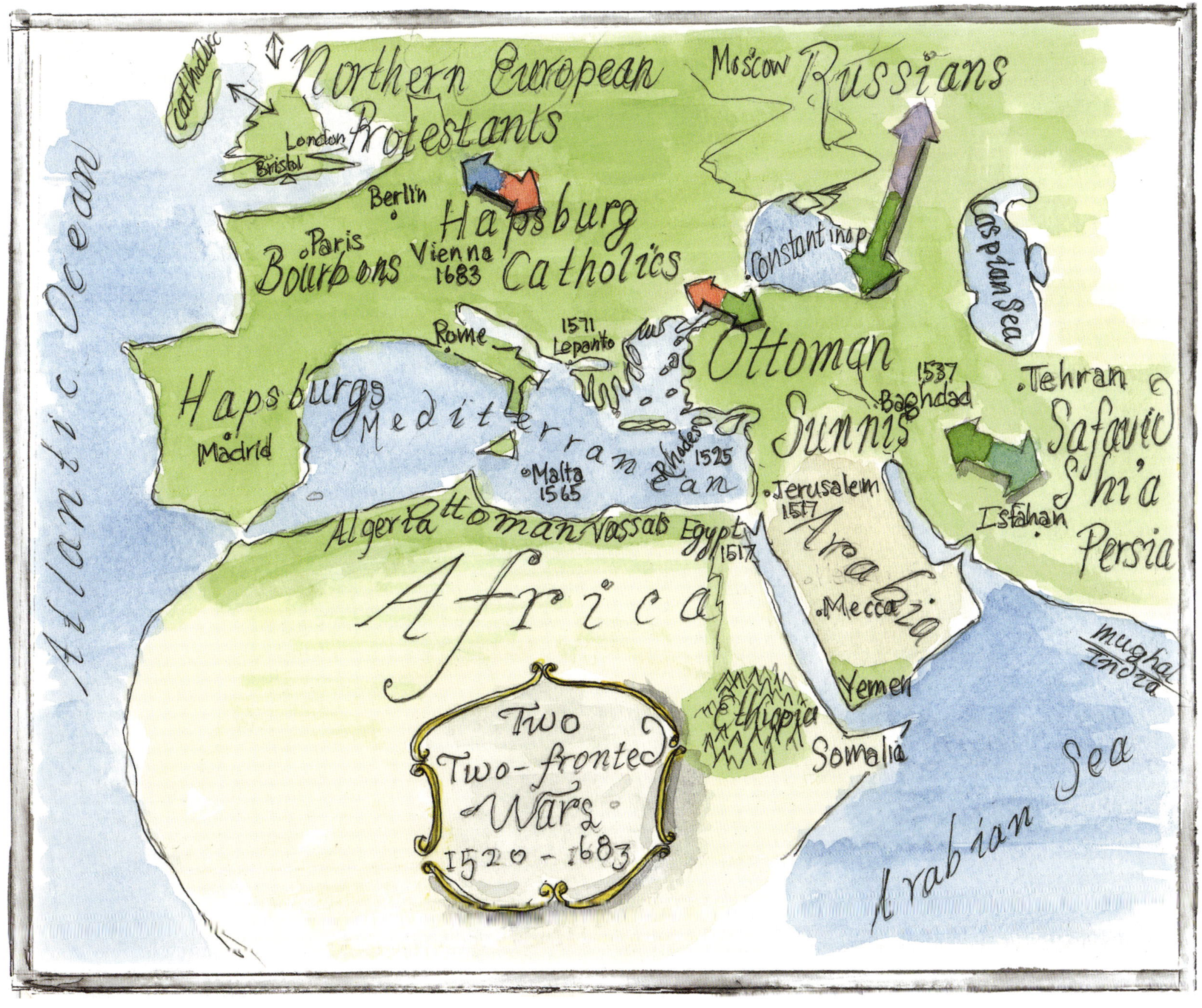

Northern European Protestants
Catholic
London
Bristol
Berlin
Moscow
Russians
Hapsburg Catholics
Paris
Bourbons
Vienna 1683
Constantinop
Caspian Sea
Rome
1571 Lepanto
Ottoman
Hapsburgs
Madrid
Mediterranean
Malta 1565
Rhodes 1525
1537 Baghdad
Tehran
Sunnis
Safavid Shi'a Persia
Isfahan
Jerusalem 1517
Algeria
Ottoman Vassals
Egypt 1517
Arabia
Mecca
Africa
Atlantic Ocean
Yemen
Ethiopia
Somalia
Mughal India
Arabian Sea
Two Two-fronted Wars 1520 - 1683

Hapsburg Military Frontier

Here is the border between East and West in the Balkans, where the Ottomans held territory for half a millennium, and the struggle between these two 'fell and incensed points of mighty opposites' surged back and forth in those formidable mountains, the Dinaric Alps. At the end of the Long War between Islam and Christendom, it became the 'Hapsburg Military Frontier.' It was the inner bastion of the mighty fortress of the West that held after the Byzantine counterscarp was breached.

The small Ottoman state became an empire in the 14th century by rapidly advancing into these weak borderlands. Even today many Turks trace their families back to the Balkans. Here were recruited as a tax (*devshirme*) Christian boys to be trained as Janissaries, the Ottoman warriors who struck fear into the heart of the West. The frontier is the western tip of the scimitar that marks the line of the farthest advance of the Ottoman Empire into Europe. The checkerboard of the frontier flies today as the flag of scimitar-shaped Croatia.

The struggle with the Ottomans in the Dinaric Alps above the Dalmatian coast of Croatia is the background to *The Mountain Wreath* of Prince Petar II Petrovic-Njegoš of Montenegro. In 1846, he set down the oral folk epic of the Balkans, which celebrates the heroic death of the Serbian Prince Lazar, who assassinated the victorious sultan after the battle of Kosovo in 1389. Half a millennium later, on the exact anniversary* of the battle, the Serbian nationalist Gavrilo Princip—who knew this poem by heart—assassinated the Austrian archduke at Sarajevo in Bosnia.

In the new age of 19th-century nationalism, the Serbians and Bosnians had no desire to be ruled by the Austrian Hapsburgs after they had finally shaken off the rule of the Ottomans. In 1919, the Treaty of Versailles united these disparate elements as the country of Yugoslavia, the bloody fragmentation of which in the 1990s was an extension of the fragmentation of the Roman Empire in miserable miniature—pitting Catholic, Orthodox, and Muslim against one another.

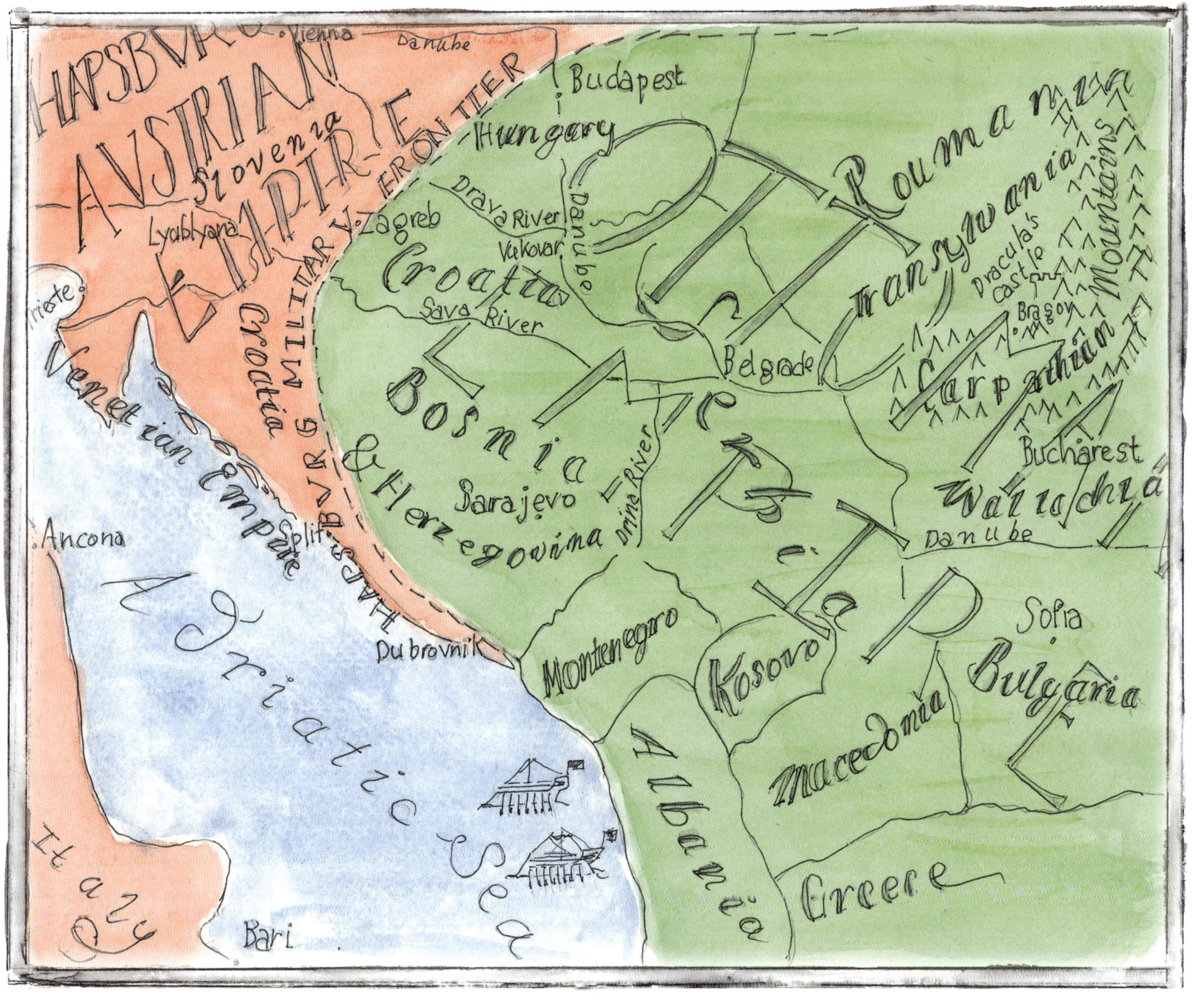

HAPSBURG
AUSTRIAN EMPIRE
Vienna
Danube
Budapest
Hungary
Slovenia
Lyablyana
Trieste
Venetian Empire
Croatia
MILITARY FRONTIER
Zagreb
Drava River
Vukovar
Danube
Croatia
Sava River
Belgrade
Bosnia & Herzegovina
Sarajevo
Drina River
Split
Ancona
Adriatic Sea
Dubrovnik
Montenegro
Kosovo
Albania
Macedonia
Greece
Italy
Bari
Roumania
Transylvania
Dracula's castle
Brasov
Carpathian Mountains
Bucharest
Wallachia
Danube
Sofia
Bulgaria
OTTOMAN EMPIRE

EMPIRE: ORDER & FRAGMENTATION

The World Egg Broken

WHAT IS MEANT by the words 'the fall of the Roman Empire'? Only the birth of the modern world. Ever since its 'fall,' the world that empire encompassed has been fracturing into smaller and smaller pieces that we call nations. Two large empires were re-created from its remains: the Caliphate of Baghdad and then the Ottoman Empire. The fracturing of these two subsequent empires, as well as of the Western Empire, is still being felt. Imagine the fallen Roman Empire as a giant broken egg.

There are many words to describe this tendency toward fragmentation or division—frangible, friable, fissiparous, fractious—but in the realm of politics they all mean struggle, strife, war. If we consider the story of the fragmentation, or division, of the empire as a play in the genre of *commedia della storia* mentioned at the beginning of this book, it would be a geopolitical comedy in five acts.

ACT 1 The division between the Eastern and Western empires

ACT 2 The rise of Arab Islam on one side of the Mediterranean opposed to the rise of a European power on the other side

ACT 3 The rise of the Turks and the end of the Greek-speaking Eastern Roman Empire

ACT 4 The rise of the West and Russia; and the decline, fall, and partition of the Ottoman Empire

ACT 5 The New War: America's Eastern Question

Imagine the characters as large and gorgeously dressed Sicilian puppets,* their lines spoken by the puppeteers who are pulling the strings, vaunting their feats in the dramatic triangle of the West, Dar al' Islam, and Russia.

The World Egg Broken

The Roman Empire had many a wall,
 and mighty was its great domain;
 nevertheless it had a great fall—
 and neither duke nor emperor,
 no, neither caliph nor Grand Turk,
no, neither Hitler nor *le roi Charlemeyne*
 could e'er put it back together again.

Act One: Empire Divided, AD 395

Theodosius I divided the empire between my two sons, Arcadius and Honorius, East and West. I had to. The empire was simply too big to rule from a single capital, which by this time in the West was Ravenna.

AD 395

Honorius RED I got the bad end of the deal. My part, the Latin/Western, was going downhill rapidly. Four centuries earlier, our ancestors had united the Eastern and Western halves under one rule. But, as Mr. Gibbon points out, we never succeeded in imposing our language on them. The Romans built roads and were practical people, while the Greeks sat around arguing about theology. In the end, it didn't help that my brother, encouraged by evil advisers, deflected the Ostro-Goths unto us in the West.

Arcadius PURPLE I got the Eastern half of the empire, as my father stated, but as for 'deflecting' the barbarians, that's just smear tactics. We had much more culture to protect than those illiterate cross-gartered barbarians that had come to rule the Western Empire… bunch of Germans, if you ask me. Yes, Alaric the Ostro-Goth did get them pretty quickly after the division of the empire; *we* kept the culture of the world alive for another thousand years.

405

Honorius RED Yes, brother, but in the end they got you, too, you and your fancy prancing Byzantines, but by then Emperor Constantine's great city had shrunk to a village inside the walls with a bunch of ruined palaces, and—to paraphrase the Persian poet Saadi—with the spiders weaving its curtains and the owl doing guard duty on its ramparts.

1453

Arcadius PURPLE Yes, brother, but—to adapt Robert Frost—good geopolitical fences make good geopolitical neighbors. The border between us was the Adriatic Sea and that mess of rivers in the Balkans that no one can figure out. It's a good border, though… so good they used it again during the Cold War… and then again in the Balkan wars of the 1990s.

1991

Honorius RED Speaking of borders, look at the one between your territory and mine in North Africa that cuts today's Libya in half. The war between the eastern part, Cyrenaica—where the rebellion started in 2011—and Gaddafi's western part was a distant echo of this division.

2011

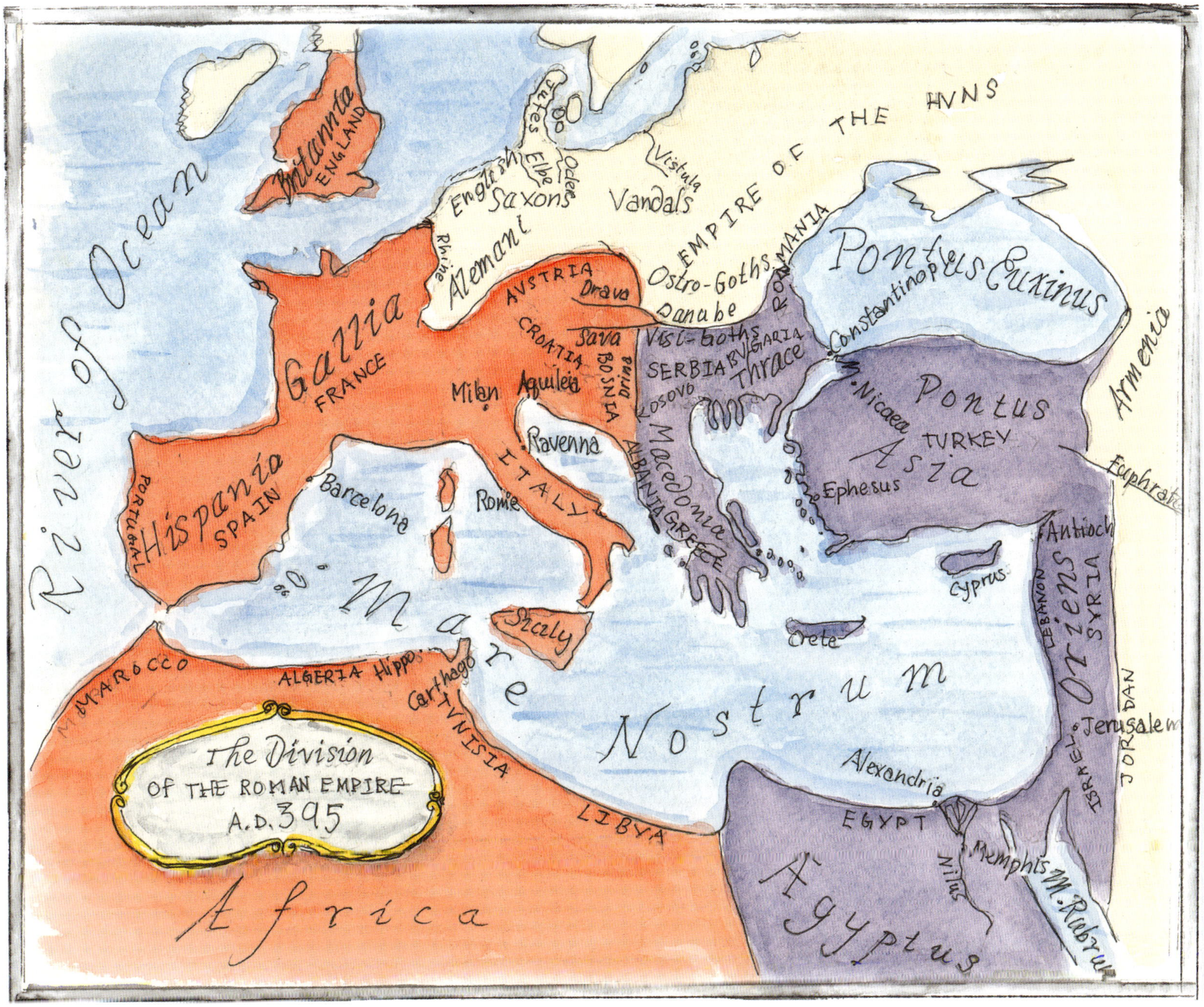

The Division
OF THE ROMAN EMPIRE
A.D. 395
River of Ocean
Britannia
ENGLAND
English
Saxons
Jutes
Elbe
Oder
Vistula
Vandals
EMPIRE OF THE HVNS
Alemani
Rhine
Gallia
FRANCE
AVSTRIA
Drava
Danube
Ostro-Goths
ROMANIA
Pontus Euxinus
Constantinople
Armenia
CROATIA
Sava
BOSNIA
Drina
Visi-Goths
BVLGARIA
Thrace
SERBIA
KOSOVO
Milan
Aquileia
Ravenna
Hispania
SPAIN
PORTUGAL
Barcelona
Rome
ITALY
ALBANIA
Macedonia
GREECE
Nicaea
Pontus
TURKEY
Asia
Ephesus
Euphrates
Antioch
Cyprus
LEBANON
Oriens
SYRIA
Mare
Sicily
Crete
Nostrum
MAROCCO
ALGERIA
Hippo
Carthago
TVNISIA
LIBYA
Alexandria
EGYPT
Memphis
Nilus
Jerusalem
ISRAEL
JORDAN
Africa
Ægyptus

Act Two: Empire Divided, 1292

Abu Bakr GREEN (First Caliph) 'Mohammad is dead, but God lives,' I said when he died. I led the first conquests of the Muslims when we burst out of the 'vasty wilds / of wide Arabia.'* We were the caliphs, Mohammad's successors as Commanders of the Faithful.   AD 632

Within three years, we took Damascus; within six, Jerusalem and all of Syria; within three decades, Egypt, Armenia, the Persian Empire, Afghanistan, Gibraltar—which is named after our general Tarik—then Spain. Defeating the Visigoths, we crossed the Pyrenees into France, where our advance pretty much petered out in 732, exactly a century after we had started out of the desert. We overextended our supply lines. This conquest is one of the most extraordinary events in the history of the world. Only those of the Mongols and the Europeans come close.   711

Charlemagne RED It didn't just 'peter out.' My grandfather Charles Martel (the Hammer) stopped them dead in their tracks between Tours and Poitiers. I founded the European Union, more or less. My kingdom had roughly the same boundaries as those of the EU in 1993. That's the reason *The Economist* magazine named its column on EU affairs after me.   800

Harun Al-Rashid GREEN I didn't found Baghdad, but I enriched its libraries and scientific institutions. I was the caliph of the Arabian Nights.   800

Byzantine Emperor PURPLE (*after Manzikert*) If you guys in the West don't help us, we are done for!   1071

Pope Urban II RED (*preaching the First Crusade*) Can anyone bear it that the infidels occupy half of the world? Twenty years ago, my predecessor may have split the church in two by excommunicating the Eastern Church, but now we should launch a crusade.   1095

Batu Khan YELLOW (*Genghis's grandson, leader of the Golden Horde, to the Russian princes*) You pay me tribute, or we pay you a second visit.   1240

Selçuk Sultan GREEN (*to the last Crusaders*) GO HOME! You guys invaded when we Muslims were weak, and there was a power vacuum. But now you must go. Your little colonial experiment failed; go try it somewhere else. Maybe on the other side of the Ocean Sea? Shouldn't be very far…   1292

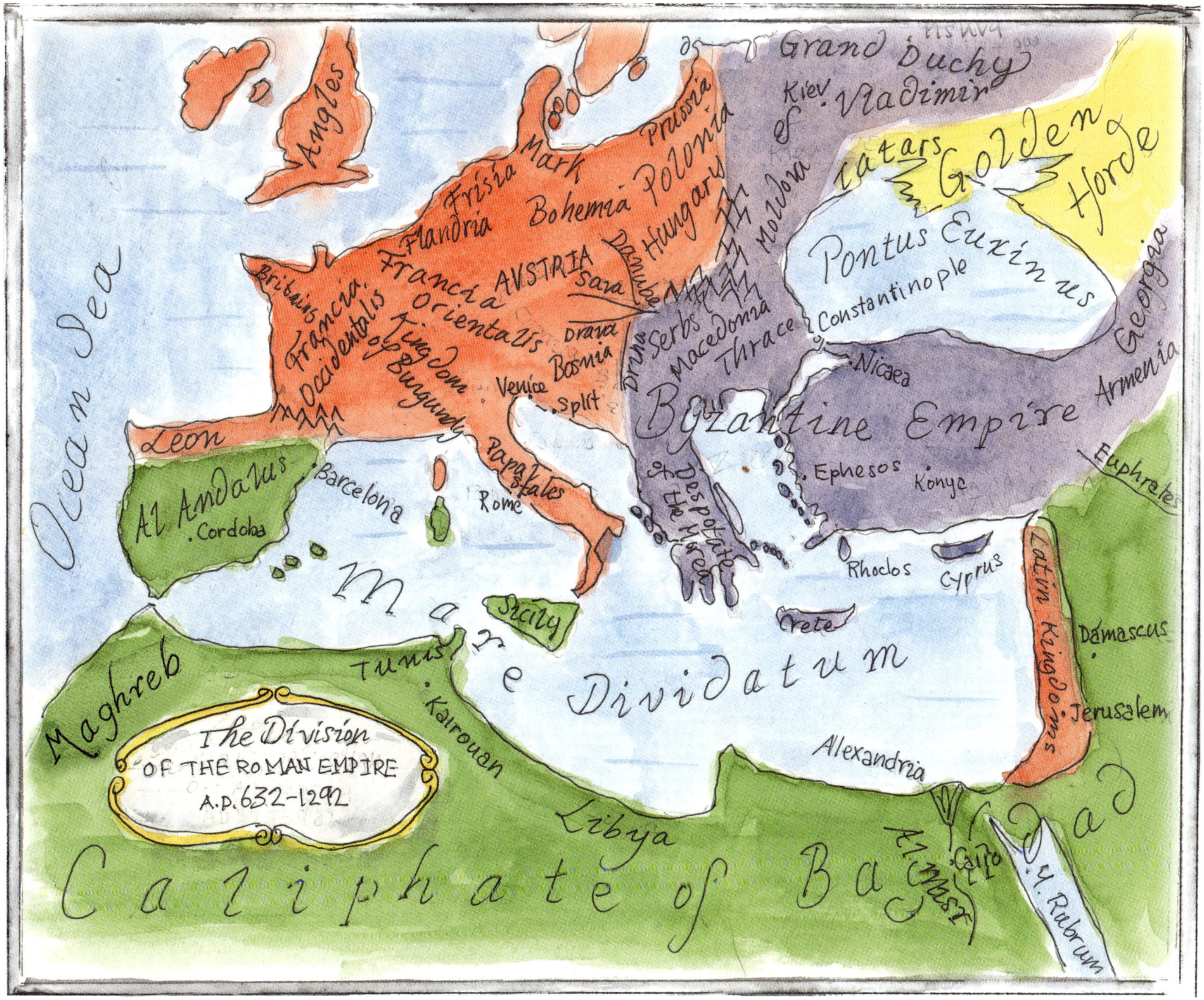
The Division
OF THE ROMAN EMPIRE
A.D. 632-1292
Ocean Sea
Angles
Frisia
Mark
Prussia
Polonia
Bohemia
Flandria
Hungary
Danube
Francia Occidentalis
Francia Orientalis
AVSTRIA
Sava
Drava
Kingdom of Burgundy
Britains
Venice
Split
Bosnia
Drina
Serbs
Macedonia
Thrace
Grand Duchy of Vladimir
Kiev
Moldova
Tatars
Golden Horde
Pontus Euxinus
Constantinople
Georgia
Armenia
Nicaea
Byzantine Empire
Ephesos
Konya
Euphrates
Despotate of the Morea
Leon
Al Andalus
Cordoba
Barcelona
Rome
Papal States
Sicily
Rhodos
Cyprus
Crete
Mare Dividatum
Latin Kingdoms
Damascus
Jerusalem
Tunis
Kairouan
Maghreb
Alexandria
Libya
Cairo
Al Masr
Caliphate of Bagdad
M. Rabrum

Act Three: Empire Divided, 1699

St. Patrick   RED   I brought the Roman Church to Ireland.   AD 430

Mohammad   GREEN   In Mecca was I born. Look what my Muslims did!   570

St. Augustine   BLUE   No... I'm not that Augustine: not the first saint by that name but the later one. I brought Christianity to the Angles and Saxons in Britain.   579

St. Boniface   BLUE ... and I brought it from there to the Germans.   743

Cyril and Methodius   PURPLE   We brought the Eastern Orthodox Church to the lands of the Slavs, establishing a northern refuge for Eastern Orthodoxy before the empire had been entirely lost to the Turks.   862

Premier of Kiev   PURPLE   I established Eastern Christianity in what was to become Russia, and gave it that northern refuge.   998

Otto von Hapsburg   RED   I became duke of Austria, and by a series of brilliant marriages my descendants became rulers of the Western world, both the Old and the Newly Discovered one. As kings of Hungary and Bohemia, they defended the marches of Christendom against the Turks of the East and the heretic Protestants in the north. The last direct descendant of my line—who died in 2011—sat in the Parliament of the European Union.   1273

Osman, Son of Ertoğrul Gazi   GREEN   (*to Selçuk Sultan*) Lord of the Byzantine marches am I now. You people caved in to the Mongols... the same way that the Russians did... and paid tribute. We will carry the *jihad* farther than anyone else into the lands of the infidels. The Arabs were stopped by the Taurus Mountains; nothing stops us.   1299

Mehmet II   GREEN   *Fatih* was I, the Conqueror of Constantinople, the Red Apple of Islamic dreams. I fulfilled the prophecy of the Qur'an and brought the Roman Empire to its final end.   1453

Sultan Selim the Grim   GREEN   I conquered Syria, Palestine, and Egypt. I ruled over the holy cities of Mecca and Medina and made Jerusalem Islamic again. I brought peace to the Middle East; perhaps Turkey will do so again.   1517

Martin Luther   BLUE   I led the Germanic-language people of the north out of the Roman Church, that ghost of the Roman Empire.*   1517

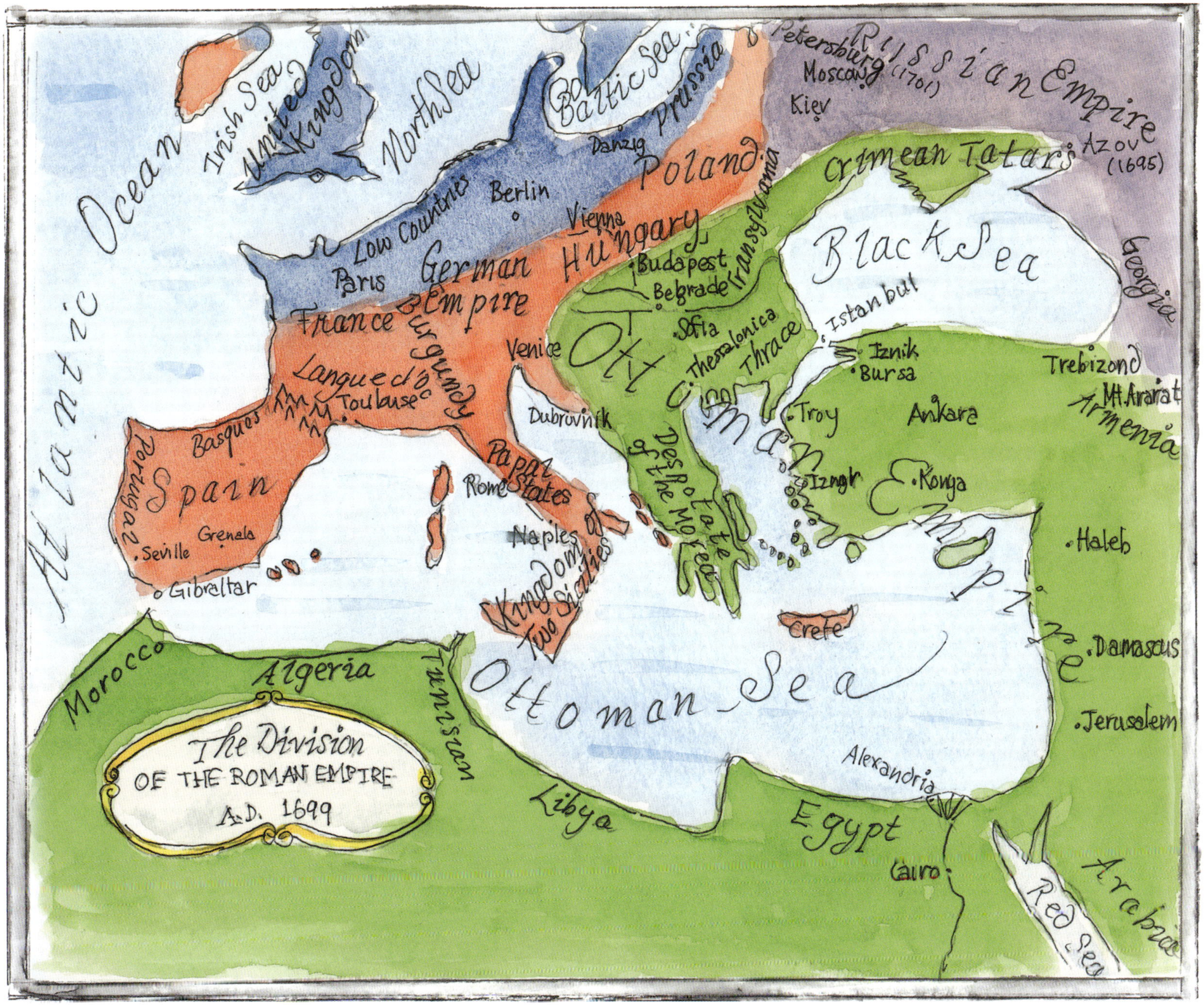
The Division
OF THE ROMAN EMPIRE
A.D. 1699
Atlantic Ocean
Irish Sea
United Kingdom
North Sea
Baltic Sea
Prussia
St Petersburg (1701)
Russian Empire
Moscow
Kiev
Azov (1695)
Danzig
Poland
Crimean Tatars
Low Countries
Berlin
Vienna
Hungary
Transylvania
Black Sea
Georgia
Paris
German Empire
Budapest
Belgrade
France
Burgundy
Istanbul
Sofia
Thessalonica
Thrace
Iznik
Bursa
Trebizond
Venice
Ottoman Empire
Languedoc
Toulouse
Dubrovnik
Troy
Ankara
Mt. Ararat
Armenia
Basques
Portugal
Spain
Papal States
Despotate of the Morea
Izmir
Konya
Rome
Naples
Kingdom of Two Sicilies
Grenada
Seville
Haleb
Gibraltar
Crete
Damascus
Morocco
Algeria
Tunisia
Ottoman Sea
Jerusalem
Alexandria
Libya
Egypt
Cairo
Red Sea
Arabia

Intermission: Analysis of the Plot

With the rise of Russia in the East and of northern Europe in the West, the Former Roman Empire was now divided into four quarters—four of the geopolitical characters in our play. The four quarters are southern Europe, northern Europe, Russia, and the Ottoman Empire.

A little more than half a century after the conversion of Russia, the two churches—Eastern Orthodox and Latin Catholic—split in 1054. Officially, the issue was doctrinal, but this division really reflected the political division of the empire, following closely the old border through the Balkans. Projected north, around Transylvania, the new border left Poland and Hungary to the west and Russia to the east. The 'Pale of Settlement,' where Jews were forced by the tsar to live in the 19th century, lies on this border.

Then, 500 years after this Schism—and 50 years after the Conquest of Constantinople—a fourth part split off at the Protestant Reformation, essentially along another linguistic divide. The Teutonic-speaking peoples, the Germanic tribes of the north, who lived along the border of the Roman Empire, became increasingly uncomfortable under the rule of the empire's ghost, the Roman Church. As a sense of national or tribal identity arose, they began to resist the claims of a catholic or universal church.

The Protestant north suffered a series of fracturings into a multitude of sects, dividing more or less along national lines: German and Scandinavian Lutherans, Swiss Calvinists, Scots Presbyterians, English Anglicans, Bohemian Hussites… In our modern secular world, these divisions have largely been submerged, blurred over as with the loss of memory, but they were bitterly and bloodily contended in the 16th and 17th centuries.

We can imagine this division of the Former Roman Empire in terms of a medieval world map, or *Orbis Terrarum* (circle of the earth), a reference to a line from Isaiah

(40:22): 'It is he that sitteth upon the circle of the earth.' These schematic maps are often divided by the four rivers of paradise, with Jerusalem at the center, the East at the top.

Imagine a modern, secular, and political *Orbis*, showing the four-part division of the world. Starting in the lower right quadrant, we have the Former Eastern Empire—now Dar al' Islam (the House of Islam), the most powerful state of which was the Ottoman Empire. It lies to the east of Europe and is divided from it by the Mediterranean Sea and the Balkans. In the lower left quadrant, we have Counter-Reform Catholic southern Europe.

In the upper left quadrant, to the north of the Alps, we have the rising power of northern Europe—the lands of the Reform, the Enlightenment, and the modern corporation. To the east is Orthodox Russia, later the Soviet Union. Between them, during the Cold War, was the Iron Curtain. And coming full circle, to the south of Russia, across the Black Sea, was the Ottoman Empire.

With the decline of the southern quadrants in the 17th century, the struggle between East and West moved north—between the northern quadrants.

In the middle of the 17th century, the West began its rise to world power, sailing west and south, while at the same time Russia began to look south toward Constantinople and east to the steppe lands of Asia, the former Mongol Empire.

There now came to be two lords in the East: one rising, the other declining.

Act Four: The Red Apple*

A Monk *(to Tsar Ivan III)* Two Romes have fallen [meaning Rome and Constantinople]. A third stands [meaning Moscow]. — 1501

Tsar Peter the Great I briefly opened a window onto the Black Sea and the south. These actions frightened the British, who thought that I would threaten their colony in India and the route to it. Their fears were premature, but under Catherine we did get the Crimea. — 1696

Sultan I will not condescend to any peace discussions except on the condition of your giving me back the Crimea and the renunciation of your lordship over the Tatars. — 1789

Catherine the Great Eastern Empress and Tsarina am I now, so don't ask for any lands back. We plan to put the cross back on Hagia Sofia. — 1790

Sultan Sultan am I of the Ottomans, Allah's Deputy on Earth, Lord of the Lords of This World, Possessor of Men's Necks, King of Believers and Unbelievers, King of Kings, Emperor of the East and West, Emperor of the Chakans of Great Authority, Prince and Lord of the Most Happy Constellation, Mighty Caesar, Seal of Victory, Refuge of All the People of the Whole World, the Shadow of the Almighty Dispensing Quiet in the Earth… and I will not let you get our Red Apple!

Tsar Nicholas Maybe, maybe not… but you are sick, and if you'll pardon me speaking directly, you're dying. All of us young people are just wondering what's going to happen with your estate. *(Aside, in stage whisper)* It would be a great misfortune if one of these days the old man should slip away from us before the necessary arrangements are made. — 1853

Sultan We have ruled over the Slavs of the Balkans for four centuries, and they were happy to be relieved of the intolerant tyranny of your Christian churches.

Tsar You enslaved them. You made slaves of all the Slavs.* But not anymore. We will free them and restore Christianity… and what's more, we'll take Jerusalem from your heathen hands.

Atatürk Do your worst! But you will never get the Straits. — 1915

Two Lords of the East

Act Five: Zagros Mountains

In September 2012, it was reported* that the U.S. was racing to complete a broad arc of antimissile defenses* against the clear and present danger Iran represents to the West. What the U.S. has been fortifying—having destroyed the buffer state of Iraq—was once the eastern border of the Roman house, the edge of the Western world.*

This is the border where Crassus, the ancient Roman real estate mogul and would-be general, was defeated by the Parthians, the ancestors of the modern Iranians, putting a limit to eastward Roman expansion. The Parthians are said to have used his head as a prop in a Greek tragedy, Euripdes' *Bacchae*.*

Here across the valley is where the Byzantines battled the Sassanian Persian Empire. Here, too, is where the Sunni Ottomans battled the Shia Persians, with possession of Baghdad going back and forth between them. Here is where British troops from India fought the Ottoman Turks in the First World War, protecting the oil refinery on Abadan Island at the head of the Persian Gulf, their oil fields in Iran, and the route to India itself. Here is where the United States still has boots on the ground, defending its oil interests and fighting perceived threats to world order after 9/11. Here, across the valley of Mesopotamia and the Persian Gulf, rise the Zagros Mountains, the ramparts of the southwestern bastion of the Iranian plateau.

Why do we fight battles in the East over and over again in the same place? That question would not puzzle a 19th-century British statesman. If a Lord Palmerston* were to come back to life today, even though he might be saddened by the decline of the empire, he would likely be fascinated by the turn of events—and amused that it is now the Americans who are stuck with the Eastern Question.

We will get back to these questions at the end of the book, where regional actors and their reactions to Western intrusions and interests in the Middle East will get their due, but meanwhile let's look at our story as a fable, to see what these characters are in the abstract, distilled down to geopolitical essences.

ZAGROS MTNS.
Veni, vidi...., NON vinci!
Friggin' Shias!!
Sheeet, man!
Quite.....
PERSIA
Persian Gulf
SPQR
USA
Baghdad
Babylon
KUWAIT
TRUCIAL STATES
Alexander returning from India
Dubai
CRASSVS
You boys back for more fun?
IRAQ
Riyahd
ARABIA

A Geopolitical Fable

Once upon a time, led by a great prophet, a Camel People tried to conquer the entire world, bringing it into what they called the House of Peace—and almost succeeded. They had established a trade route through the band of deserts and mountains that split the World Island in half north and south, but which was a highway east and west. They founded the original Islamic Empire. As there are limits to all things, there were limits to these conquests. The remnants of the fragmented Western Empire put a stop to the Camel People's expansion in Iberia and Gaul. For a time, so did the remnant of the Eastern Empire, still unified but declining for centuries.

In time, the Camel People were overtaken by the Horse People, invaders from the vast steppes of Central Asia, and the founders of the Great Medieval Islamic Slave Empire (GMISE), which was the heir and successor of both the Old Christian and Islamic empires. The invention of guns had made this empire powerful and allowed it to put an end to further invasions of Horse People out of the steppes of Asia. The GMISE conquered the remnant of the Old Christian Empire and thus came to occupy one of the most strategic places in the world, a Great City with a great harbor commanding the strait that controlled the trade into the Black Sea, thence to Central Asia, and also to the Great Land Empire, landlocked in the Heartland, which desired a warm-water outlet via that great city.

The conquest by the GMISE of the Great City of Byzantium had an unintended consequence: the Christian Greek scholars who held the key to the secrets of science fled to the West. Empowered by this science, the Sea Empires arose and— with stout weatherly ships developed from those of the Viking Norsemen for sailing the cold seas of the rough North Atlantic—made an end run around the control of trade. Being able to penetrate into the heretofore impenetrable, dark, and forbidding oceans, the Sea Empires conquered the world, planting colonies for their excess populations. With their science they forged the magic Ring of Power and Industry.

At the same time the Great Land Empire was conquering the geopolitical fortress

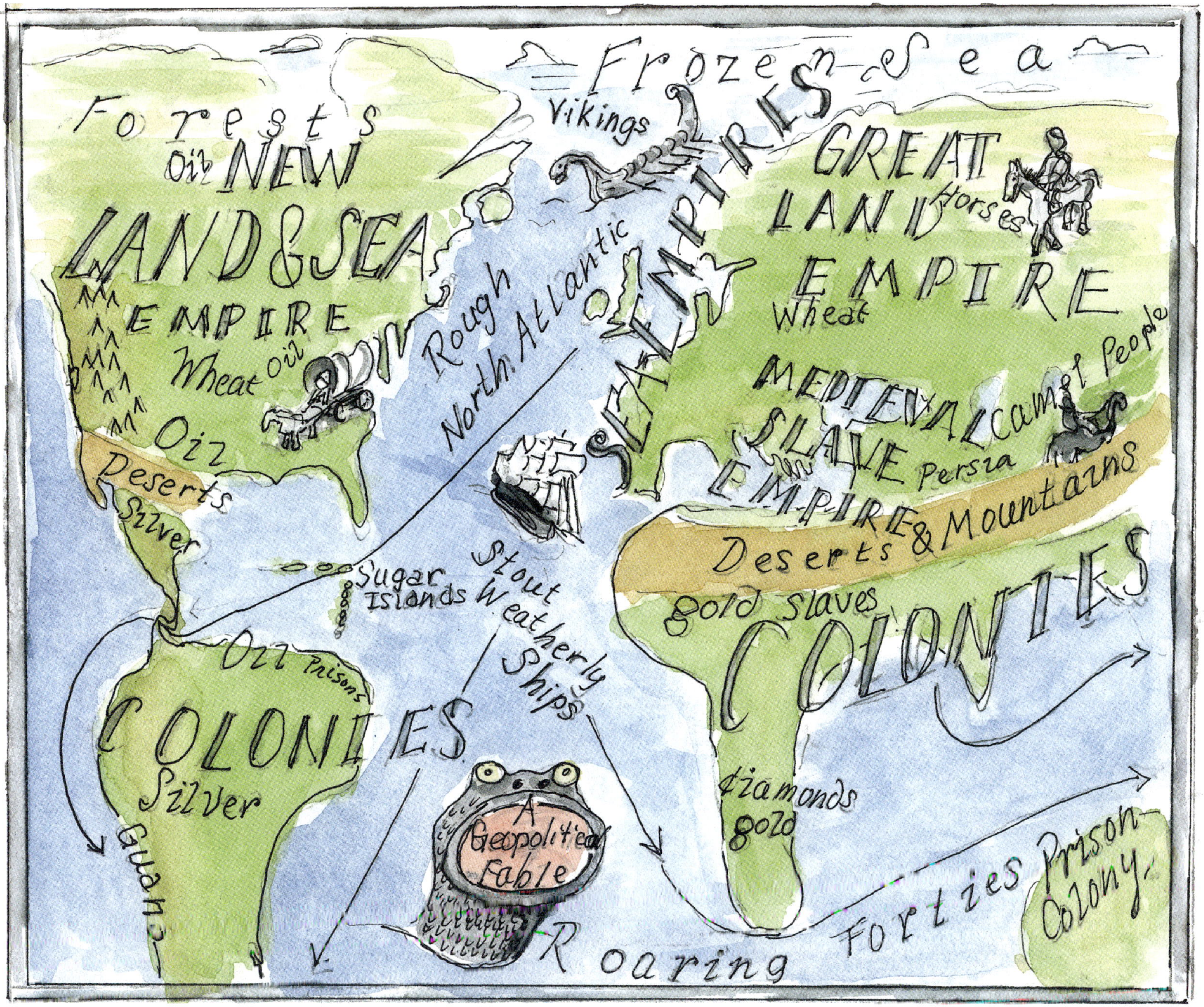

Frozen Sea
Forests
Oil
NEW LAND & SEA EMPIRE
Wheat
Oil
Oil
Deserts
Silver
Vikings
SEA EMPIRES
GREAT LAND EMPIRE
Horses
Wheat
MEDIEVAL SLAVE EMPIRE
camel People
Persia
Deserts & Mountains
Rough North Atlantic
Sugar Islands
Stout Weatherly Ships
gold slaves
COLONIES
Oil
Prisons
COLONIES
Silver
Guano
diamonds
gold
A Geopolitical Fable
Roaring Forties
Prison Colony

A Geopolitical Fable (cont.)

of the steppes of Asia. Then—both for the Great Land Empire of the East and the Great Sea Empires of the West—there were no more worlds to conquer except one: the declining GMISE. Who would get it became the Eastern Question. The Great Sea Empires, of which there were now only two—but really one, based on the British Isles—were determined that the Great Land Empire of the tsars would not, by conquering the remains of the GMISE, threaten either the new canal route to the Great Colony in the Monsoon Rimlands of southeastern Asia or that colony itself, through the mountain passes that separated it from the Heartland where the Great Land Empire was rapidly expanding south. The struggle between them here became known as the Great Game.

When these empires finally came to blows in world war, it turned into a murderous war in the trenches, thanks to the development of highly efficient killing machines. After that first war, the GMISE was defeated and broken up into its constituent parts, all of which fell to fighting one another.

Meanwhile, a New Land & Sea Empire had arisen in a former colony on the other side of the rough North Atlantic, endowed with tremendous mineral resources and especially oil, the most strategic commodity of them all. It was oil that fueled the Great Machine of Technology and Industry. Oil was also discovered in the Great Land Empire and, by virtue of that oil, the New Land & Sea Empire and the Great Land Empire emerged out of the cataclysm of a second world war as victors. The old Great Sea Empires declined in power and had to give up all their colonies. These former colonies came to be known as the Third World, in which was fought—by proxy with secret agents overthrowing unfriendly governments—a second Great Game, called the Cold War.

The Great Land Empire developed an entirely new system for the organization of society, and in the end the struggle between East and West became a struggle between two competing systems. The Great Land Empire and the New Land & Sea

Empire both tried to extend their systems into the Third World. Depending on one's point of view, these empires were called either the First World or the Second World. But the system of the Great Land Empire was unable to provide the economic success that the system of the New Land & Sea Empire could, and so it collapsed. This left the New Land & Sea Empire in possession of the field, achieving the dream of every conqueror or crank: World Conquest. The collapse of the former Great Land Empire left a power vacuum in the East and, since Nature abhors a vacuum, a new force flowed into that empty space.

Mujahedin—*gazi* or *jihadi*—traditional fighters for Islam, had helped the New Land & Sea Power defeat the former Great Land Empire in the world's ancient battleground of the mountain passes of Afghanistan. Now, having defeated one power, these *mujahedin* thought, Why not another? So they turned the sights of their hand-carried rocket launchers on the New Land & Sea Empire. This led to a third Great Game, yet another war in Afghanistan, and then another in Iraq, the borderland of the GMISE with Iran sitting up in another geopolitical fortress, the Iranian Plateau, behind the Zagros Mountains, looking down with menace and threats toward Israel, the New Land & Sea Empire's easternmost outpost.

II. The Eastern Empire

[He is] a young man of twenty-six years of age, who aspires to equal the glory of Alexander the Great, and every day has histories of Rome and other nations read to him...

—VENETIAN REPORT ON MEHMET II, 1453

THE LEGACY OF THE EASTERN EMPIRE

A Virtual Tour of the Former Ottoman Empire

THE LEGACY of the old Greek-speaking Eastern Empire is the West's most precious cultural possession, and in this section we will show what that means, and how this Christian Greek empire was transformed into the Islamic Ottoman Empire.

Since the Eastern Empire no longer exists as an intact geopolitical entity—and therefore is hard to grasp—let us take a quick tour of its last manifestation as the Ottoman Empire, if only in our imaginations. There are several options on this tour. We could go either by sea from Venice, or from Vienna by land through the Balkans, stopping to visit some battlefields in this borderland between East and West, between Islam and Christendom. Either way, we get to Istanbul.

We could then tour the Black Sea—formerly an Ottoman lake—another ancient border between the Heartland and Western Rimlands going back to the time of Jason and the Argonauts.

We could drive across Anatolia, visiting Troy, just across from the Ottomans' first foothold in Europe, Gallipoli. Then to Bursa, their first capital—where they first settled and ceased being nomads—and then drive on to Konya, passing through the battlefields of the 20th-century Turkish War of Independence. In Konya, we could visit the poet Rumi's tomb. From Konya we might go through the Cilician Gate in the Taurus Mountains and then visit the battlefield of Issus, where Alexander the Great defeated the Persian King Darius III. Then cross into Syria and visit the Great Mosque of Damascus. We could then visit Lebanon, Israel, Jordan, Iraq, Saudi Arabia, Egypt, Libya, Tunisia, and Algeria, the farthest extent of the Ottoman Empire in North Africa. A final option would be to circle the whole thing by private jet, flying along the rim of what might be called the petri dish of the world.

A Virtual Tour
Visit the Scenic Ottoman Empire
Berlin
Germany
Vienna
Russia
France
Venice
Trieste
Istria
Split
Dubrovnik
Sarajevo
Bucharest
Mohács
Belgrade
Transylvania
Kosovo
Crimean Tatars
Azov
Sofia
Edirne
Sebastopol
Black Sea
Istanbul
Trabzon
Batumi
Georgia
Armenia
Mt. Ararat
Caspian
Spain
Gibraltar
Algiers
Algeria
Tunis
Zama
Maroc
Atlas Mts
Malta
Libya
Cyrenaica
Ottoman Sea
Crete
Rhodes
Alexandria
Cyprus
Butrint
Lepanto
Marathon
Salamis
Troy
Bursa
Ephesus
Bodrum
Samsun
Konya
Tarsus
Issus
Aleppo
Mosul
Kirkuk
Tehran
Iran
Samarra
Baghdad
Damascus
Beirut
Sidon &Tyre
Jerusalem
Karbala
Najaf
Basrah
Kuwait
Adaban Island
Strait of Hormuz
Riyadh
Medina
Mecca
Saudi Arabia
Qatar
Emirates
Dubai
Oman
Cairo
Egypt
Red Sea
Sahara
Nile R.
Omdurman
Khartoum
Sana
Yemen
Aden
Indian Ocean
Mali
Niger
Chad
Sudan
Darfur
Ethiopia
Somalia

The Petri Dish

A petri dish is a glass plate used by biologists to grow cultures. The *Ecumene* was a petri dish in which grew the culture of the Western world, watered by the climate of the Mediterranean Sea and the rivers of Egypt and Iraq. With the arrival of the mysterious 'Peoples of the Sea' sometime toward the end of the second millennium BC, communication between the Mediterranean and Mesopotamian world was cut. In the words of Fernand Braudel:

> This schism,* which was never healed, contained in embryo the future great cultural divide between East and West.

Alexander tried to heal that schism. He founded the Eastern Empire by creating the Greek-speaking world around the eastern basin of the Mediterranean Sea even though under his successors his empire fragmented, and was eventually conquered by the Arabs and the Turks. He was king of semibarbaric Macedonia, but his family was Greek. He was steeped in Greek culture. His tutor had been Aristotle. He settled his soldiers in Greek-speaking cities that he named for himself all over his empire.

Putting aside changes of religion, culture, and language, this empire was to survive for 2,256 years, from Alexander to Atatürk, a stretch that makes it—together with China and Persia—a member of the very select club of 2,000-year-old empires.

This 'Eastern Empire' I define as a distinct, discrete geopolitical entity within which, over the course of two millennia, one state succeeded another. These four Successor States, expanding to their natural limits and taking a long time to decline, demonstrate that this Eastern Empire is in fact a geopolitical entity.

Let's do a chronology of these Successor States. By a happy accident of numerology, such a chronology moves by the number three.

333 BC The battle of Issus: Alexander defeats the Persian King Darius III. Later, his empire is broken up into the ***Hellenistic Kingdoms.***

33 Battle of Actium: The Eastern Empire becomes the **Eastern Roman Empire**

AD 33 Traditional date for the death of Jesus. Christianity flourishes in the culture of the Hellenistic world

333 Constantinople founded as the capital of the Eastern Empire, which—after the end of the Western (475)—we refer to as the **Byzantine Empire**

632 Death of Mohammad: the beginning of the historic process by which Islam eventually conquers the entire Eastern Empire

1453 Conquest of Constantinople, by which the **Ottoman Empire** becomes the final, and fourth, successor in this chain of empires

1923 Treaty of Lausanne: the effective end of the Ottoman Empire. In founding the modern Republic of Turkey in Anatolia, Mustafa Kemal Atatürk salvages a remnant of the Eastern Empire, which—even if fragmented into the modern nations of the Middle East—remains a geopolitical entity

An enormous part of the cultural inheritance of the West comes from the Eastern Empire—its religion, its artistic and literary culture, its science—all carried, like the trade goods of the Silk Road, along with the nomadic migrations of peoples from East to West. In the petri dish of the Mediterranean world, all these influences flourished.

Battle of Issus

Here is the very moment of the creation of the Eastern Empire—its birth agony—drawn from the mosaic floor of a house in Pompeii, now in the Archaeological Museum of Naples. It represents the moment during the battle of Issus in 333 BC when the Persian 'King of Kings' (*Shahenshah*) turned and fled the field. He abandoned his luxurious tent, the sumptuousness of which tempted Alexander to pursue his campaign farther and farther to

> ...where the East* with richest hand
> showers on her kings barbaric pearl and gold.

It is said that the Persian Wars that Herodotus recounts in his histories were the beginning of the struggle of East and West. The Persians had mounted what might be called in modern terms a 'counterinsurgency' operation—a preemptive strike—against the Greeks in punishment for their support of the rebellious Lydians. From the Greek point of view, the Persian Wars were a struggle against tyranny and oppression. And in the event, as often happens with such operations designed to intimidate by 'shock and awe,' the Persian attack backfired.

The real beginning, in a global sense, of the struggle of East and West was the counterstrike that Alexander mounted in revenge. Without this event—this battle with the state that was to become modern Iran—history would be something entirely different. Alexander has been called the 'artisan of the world.'* By spreading Greek culture in the future eastern half of the Roman Empire, he laid the foundation of the 'Greco-' part of Western culture. Anytime you scratch Roman culture, you find Greek just under the skin. This Roman mosaic, for instance, is a copy of a Greek painting.

He was certainly the great hero of antiquity. His enduring importance is underscored by the many 'Alexander legends' of the Middle Ages, in one of which his sister became a mermaid* who would surface near a becalmed ship and demand of the sailors, 'Does my brother Alexander yet live?' The only acceptable answer was 'Yes, he lives and reigns.' Otherwise, she killed them. In a sense, he still does live and reign.

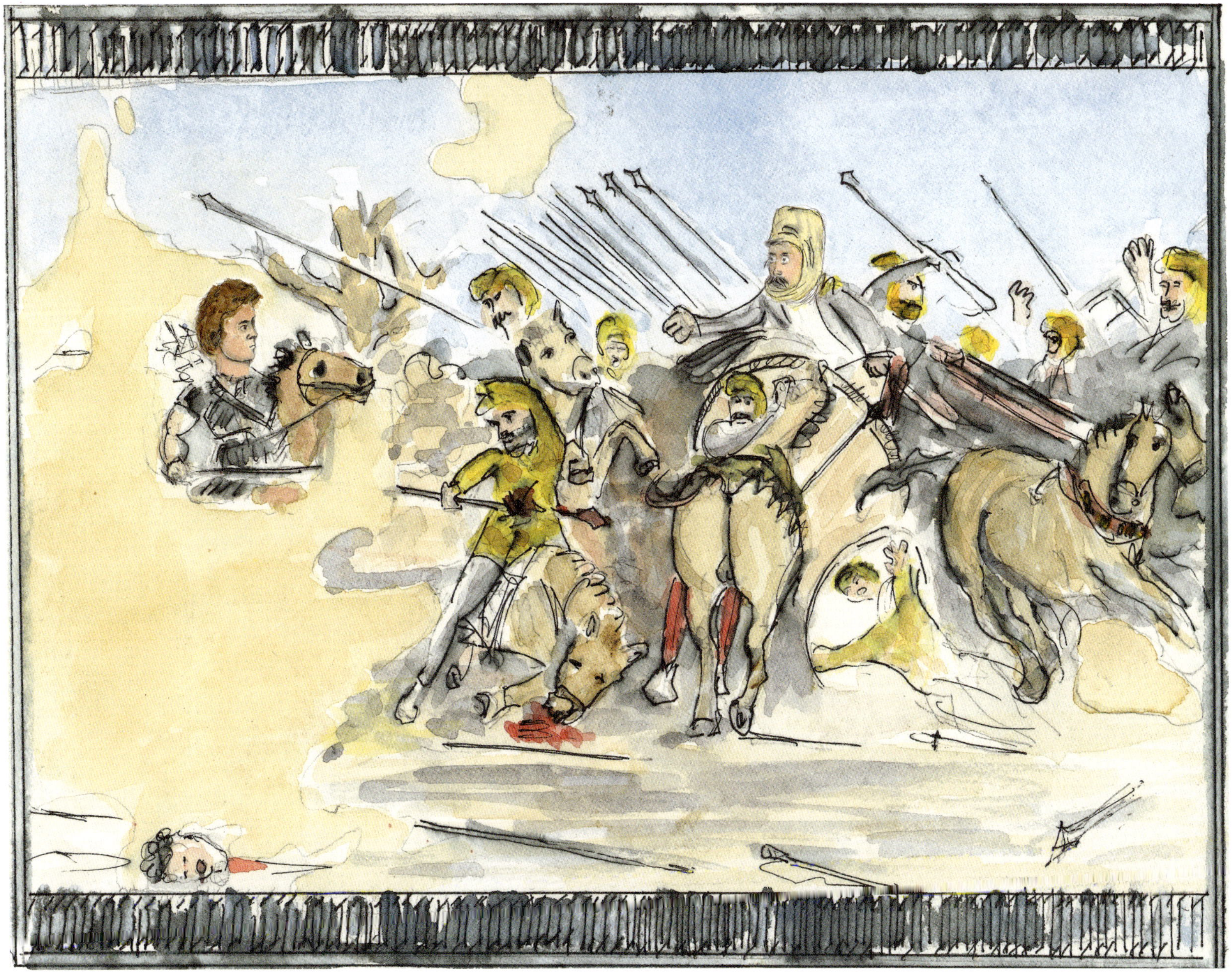

Voyages of Saul of Tarsus

Mohammad's journey from Mecca to Medina in 632 is the beginning of the Muslim calendar, the first year of the Islamic era. Its anniversary is celebrated every year by tens of thousands of pilgrims who make the Hegira, but who celebrates* the equally epochal voyage of Saul (or Paul) of Tarsus from Troy to Philippi—that is, from Asia to Europe, from East to West?

A Roman citizen, a Jew, and a Greek-speaker, he was perfectly suited to be the means by which Christianity was brought to the Gentiles. These Gentiles were 'the people of the nations,' or *gentium* in Latin—specifically the multiethnic, multireligious people of the Hellenistic world of the Eastern Roman Empire. Without the missionary voyages of the apostle Paul, Christianity would most likely not have survived the Roman destruction of Jerusalem in AD 70, and Jesus would be known only* as a Jewish rebel who was executed by crucifixion. Paul wrote Christianity's earliest texts—his Epistles, in the vernacular Greek of traders*—to encourage and sometimes chastise the small Christian Gentile communities principally in Ephesus, Phillipi, Thessalonica, Corinth, and Rome, some of which he had helped to establish.

The voyage, recorded in Acts 16:11–12—'Therefore loosing from Troas, we came with a straight course to Samothrace, and the next day to Neapolis; And from thence to Philippi…'—is the symbolic act of the bringing of the new religion to the West.

Alexander's conquests had created the cultural medium in which Christianity—the future religion of the West—would be born, flourish, and spread. The West is indebted to the East for its religion and culture, which grew in the petri dish of this Hellenistic world. The Romans adopted the Greek gods and gave them Roman names. In art and literature, the best they could do, as Horace says, was to copy the Greeks. True, the Western legal system comes from the Romans, as well as concrete, the arch, the dome, and half the English language, but it was the Greeks who were the originators of *their* culture.

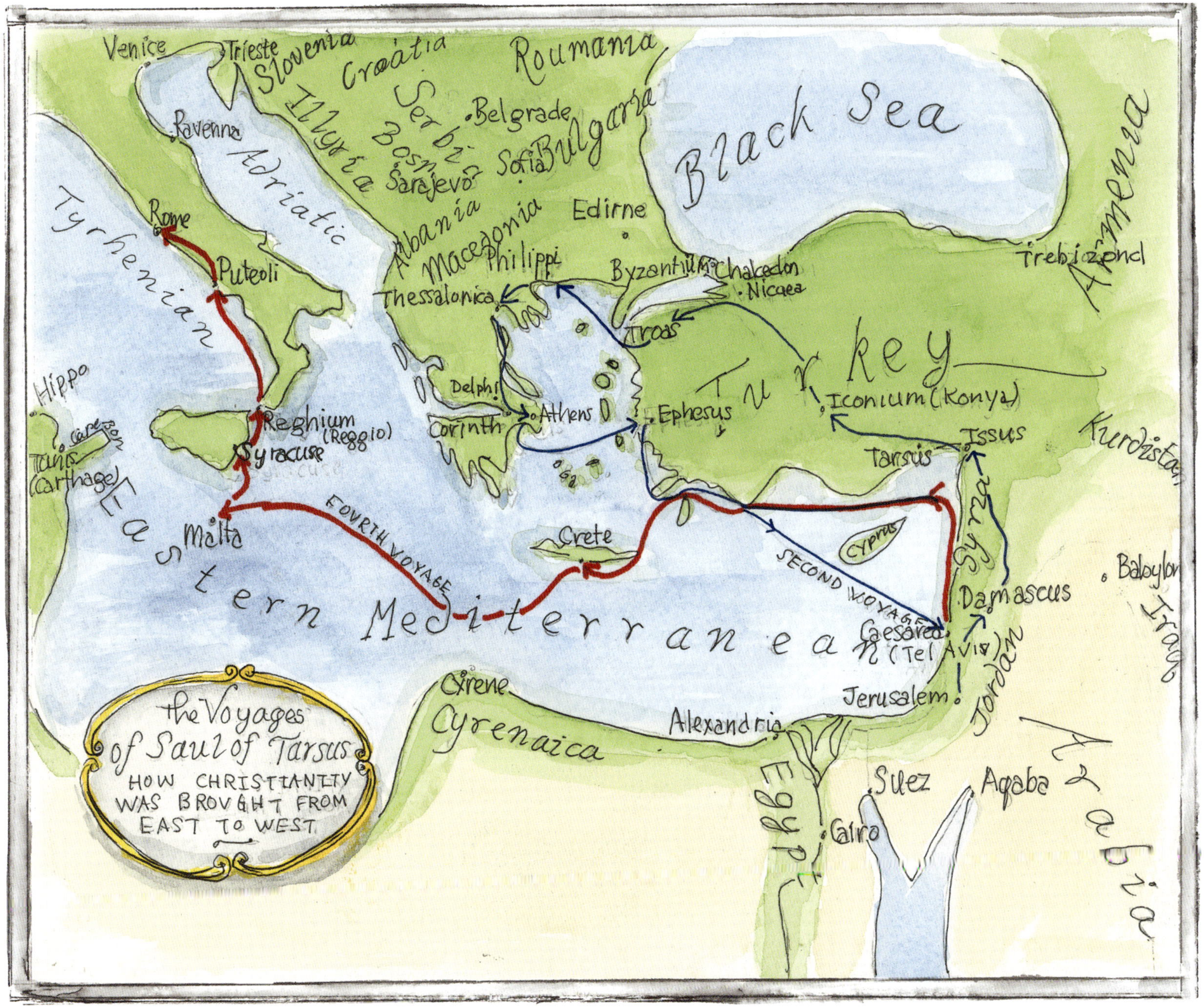
the Voyages of Saul of Tarsus
HOW CHRISTIANITY WAS BROUGHT FROM EAST TO WEST
Venice
Trieste
Slovenia
Croatia
Roumania
Serbia
Bosnia
Belgrade
Sofia
Bulgaria
Sarajevo
Illyria
Ravenna
Adriatic
Black Sea
Armenia
Tyrhenian
Rome
Puteoli
Albania
Macedonia
Edirne
Philippi
Byzantium
Chalcedon
Nicaea
Trebizond
Thessalonica
Troas
Turkey
Hippo
Delphi
Athens
Ephesus
Iconium (Konya)
Corinth
Reghium (Reggio)
Syracuse
Tarsus
Issus
Kurdistan
Cape Bon
Tunis (Carthage)
FOURTH VOYAGE
Malta
Crete
SECOND VOYAGE
Cyprus
Syria
Babylon
Damascus
Eastern Mediterranean
Caesarea (Tel Aviv)
Iraq
Cyrene
Jerusalem
Jordan
Cyrenaica
Alexandria
Arabia
Egypt
Suez
Aqaba
Cairo

Epic as History

Paul's voyage from Troy followed in the wake of the epic voyages of Odysseus and Aeneas: from Troy to Spain in the case of Odysseus, and from Troy to Rome in the case of Aeneas. Troy was the point of departure for both literature and religion.

In an epic, the proportion of historical fact to fiction is small, but an epic does possess a truth beyond truth, a super- or hypertruth. As the historian Steven Runciman observed, 'Homer as well as Herodotus was a father of history.' The first of the Greek epics, the *Iliad* tells the origin of the battle of East and West, as does Herodotus in the very first sentence of his book,* and Virgil in the *Aeneid*, who sings of 'how fate compelled the worlds of Europe and Asia to clash in war.'

The second Homeric epic, the *Odyssey*, prefigures the Greek exploration and colonization of what the Romans called *Magna Graecia*, or Greater Greece, in southern Italy and Sicily. Here the Greeks founded the city of Naples, or *Neapolis* (New City). They themselves were only following in the wake of the Phoenicians, who left no epics but founded the cites of Carthage, Barcelona, and Marseille—from *marsa*, or 'port' in Phoenician.

Jason's voyage in the *Argo* with his 'Argonauts,' or *Argo*-sailors, prefigures the Greek exploration in the other direction: eastward past Troy, the city that guarded the Straits and became wealthy controlling them. By stealing the Golden Fleece, Jason symbolically broke into the trade on the Black Sea, prefiguring the commercial relationship between Byzantium and Russia in furs, beeswax, and slaves (Slavs). Greek colonists from the city of Megara founded Byzas, the future Constantinople.

An epic tells what a people want to believe about themselves: who they think they are as defined against other peoples, whom they are not, but with whom they struggle. In the *Iliad* the European Greeks struggled against the Asian Trojans, whom they are not. The Turks today see themselves as heirs to the Trojans, certainly *not* as heirs to the Greeks. There is talk of building a monumental statue of Hector, the Trojan hero, at Gallipoli* across from Troy.

EPIC as HISTORY

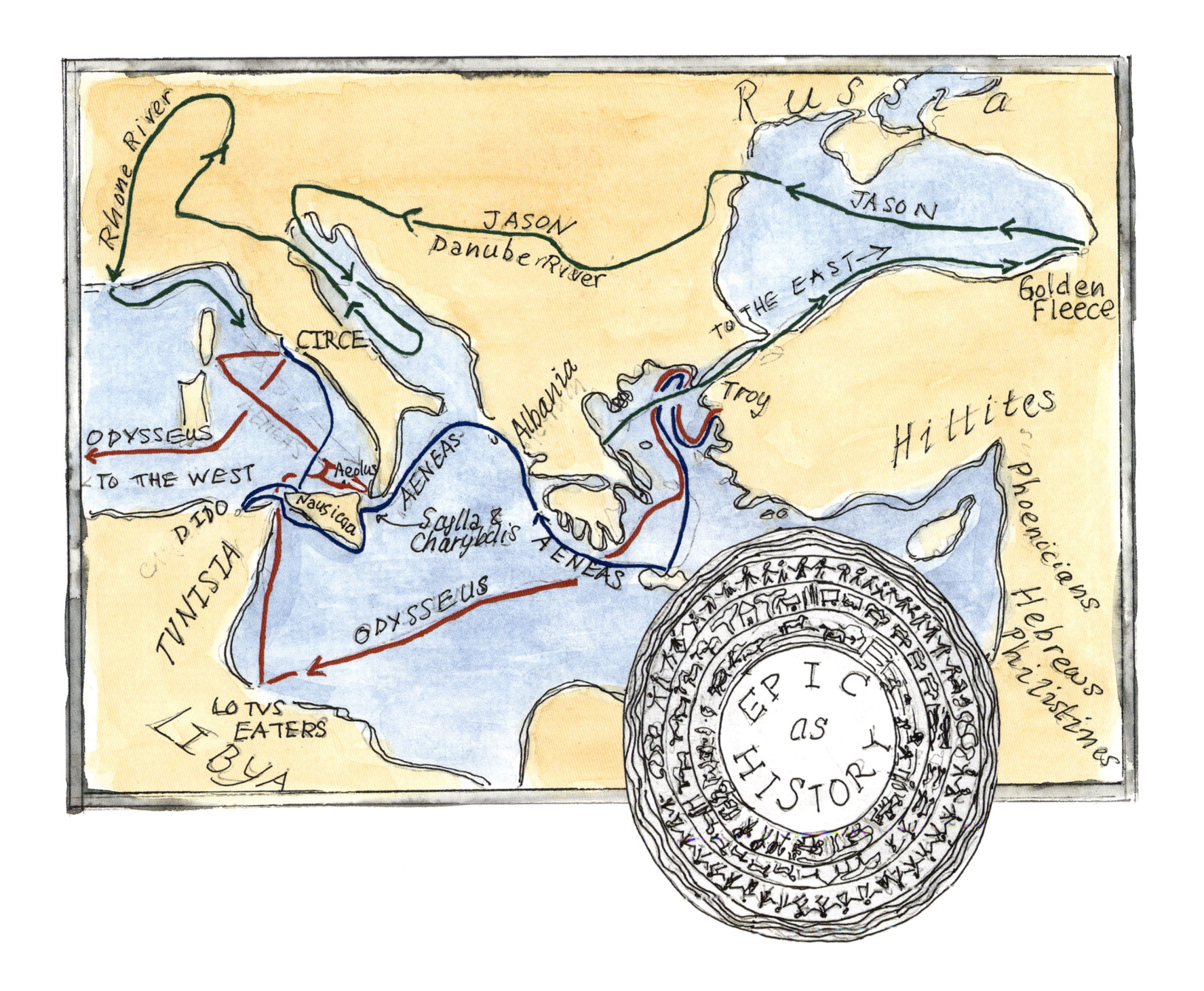

Greek Letters Encircle the Mediterranean

An understanding of the geopolitical role played by Greek letters is key to an understanding of history. Ancient Greek literature, including its scientific works, escaped the destruction of the Byzantine Empire and became the medium by which learning was preserved and transmitted to the modern world. It was the recovery of the knowledge of Greek by the West at the time of the Renaissance that gave it the scientific and technological prowess that ultimately allowed for the worldwide expansion of the West. The language of science with its various disciplines, its '-ologies,' '-nomies,' '-graphies,' and '-metries,' is Greek.

Alexander's conquests spread the Greek language and culture in the petri dish of the Eastern Mediterranean, but it was via the Arabs in the Middle Ages that these texts were first preserved and then spread west. Beginning in the 9th century in Baghdad, the Greek scientific texts were translated by Nestorian Christians into Arabic by order of the caliph al-Ma'mūn. These texts formed the basis of Arabic science and were brought to Muslim Spain in the 10th century. At the time of the *Reconquista* in the 11th and 12th centuries, they were translated by Jewish scholars into Latin and thus Aquinas gained his knowledge of Aristotle.* The ability to read Greek had by then almost entirely died out* in the West, but in the 15th century, scholars fleeing Constantinople with their manuscripts sought refuge in Italy and taught the early humanists to read the language. In the Renaissance, Latinized Arab translations were supplanted by the Greek originals.

These texts represent the precious remnant of the ancient world. As the Arab historian Ibn Khaldūn, who had been born in Spain, wrote in the 13th century:

> Where are the sciences of the Chaldeans, the Syrians, and the Babylonians? Where are the sciences of the Copts, their predecessors? The sciences of only one nation, the Greeks, have come down to us, because they were translated through al-Ma'mūn's efforts. He was successful because he had many translators at his disposal and spent much money.... Of the sciences of others, nothing has come down to our attention.

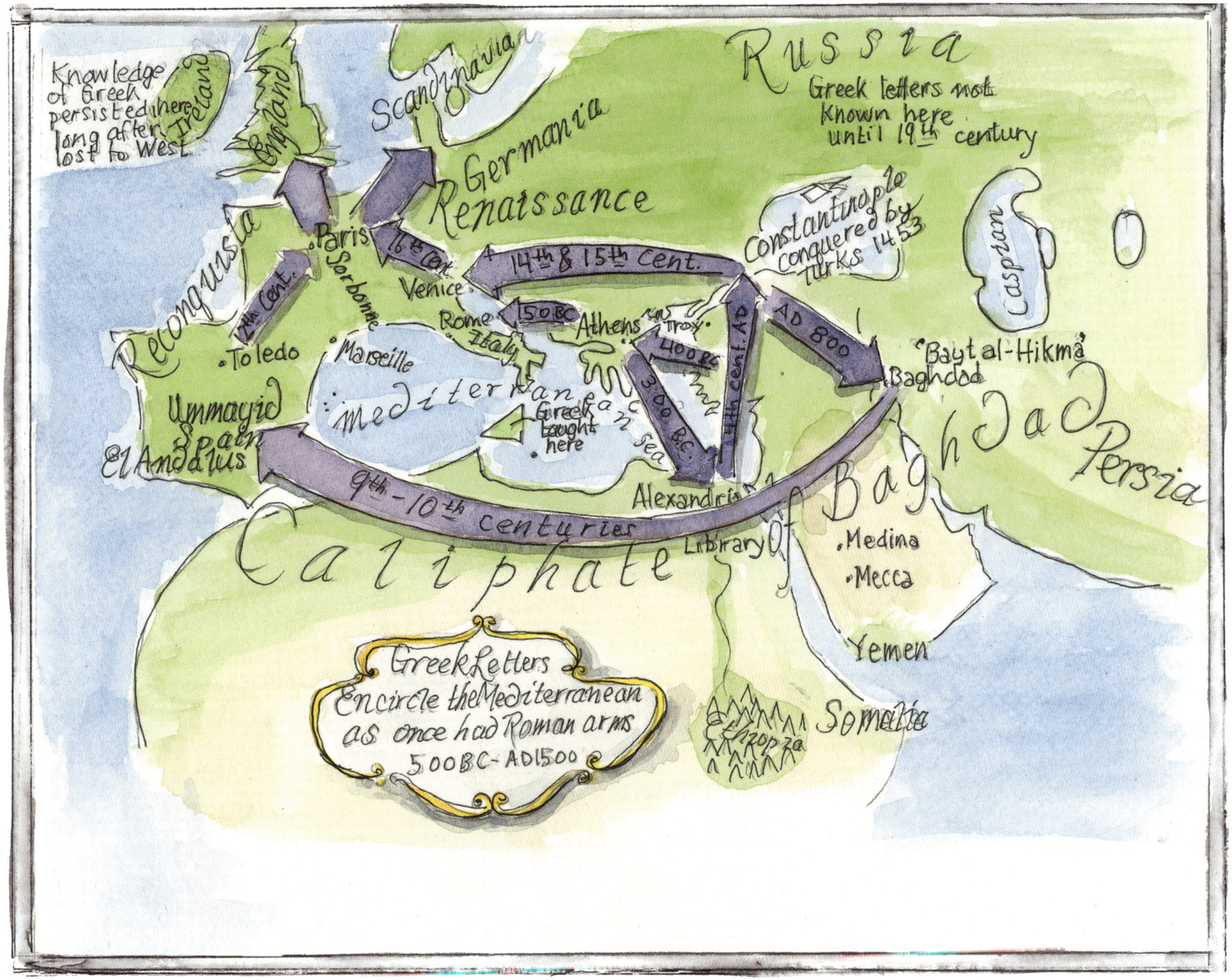

Knowledge of Greek persisted here long after lost to West
Ireland
England
Scandinavian
Russia
Greek letters not known here until 19th century
Germania
Renaissance
Reconquista
Paris
Sorbonne
16th cent.
14th & 15th cent.
Constantinople conquered by Turks 1453
Caspian
7th cent.
Venice
150 BC
Rome
Italy
Athens
Troy
400 BC
4th cent. AD
AD 800
"Bayt al-Hikma"
Baghdad
Toledo
Marseille
Ummayid Spain
El Andalus
Mediterranean Sea
Greek taught here
300 BC
Alexandria
Persia
9th-10th centuries
Caliphate of Baghdad
Library
Medina
Mecca
Yemen
Somalia
Ethiopia
Greek Letters Encircle the Mediterranean as once had Roman arms
500 BC - AD 1500

Unremitting movements, driven by politics expressed as religion, swirled around the geography of the Mediterranean in a dynamic similar to that of the Roman conquest and the spread of Greek learning.

Religion as Politics

Religion is another way that people define themselves politically. I started this drawing to show how the spread of Christianity* into northern Europe and Russia—Greek Orthodoxy in the East and Latin Roman Catholicism in the West—followed the ancient political division of the Roman Empire projected northward. Then it occurred to me that religion is politics expressed in diasporas, conquests, conversions, and expulsions of peoples from one place to another. 'Islam is politics,'* said the Iranian Ayatollah Khomeini.

The invasions of the Arabs and then the Turks into the Mediterranean world are classic examples of the dynamic of *Desert & Sown*, but there were other movements within the sown driven by politics. There was the First Diaspora of Jews released by King Cyrus of Persia from captivity in Babylon, and their subsequent dispersion in the Hellenistic world. After the destruction of the Second Temple by the Romans in AD 70, there was a Second Diaspora in which Jews began to move into northern Europe and Spain. The Arab conquests divided the Mediterranean and pushed the center of Christianity north into Europe. It was in this period that missionaries evangelized the pagan tribes of northern Europe.*

There was a Third Diaspora of Jewish people: those who, with the Moors, were expelled by Ferdinand and Isabella after the fall of Grenada in 1492. A descendant of one of these families, Baruch Espinoza, or Spinoza, lived in Amsterdam. By day he supported himself grinding lenses; by night he peered into the future with the lens of his mind. He was one of the first philosophers to posit the ideas upon which the modern Western society of the Enlightenment is founded. His ideas are embodied in the Preamble of the Declaration of Independence.*

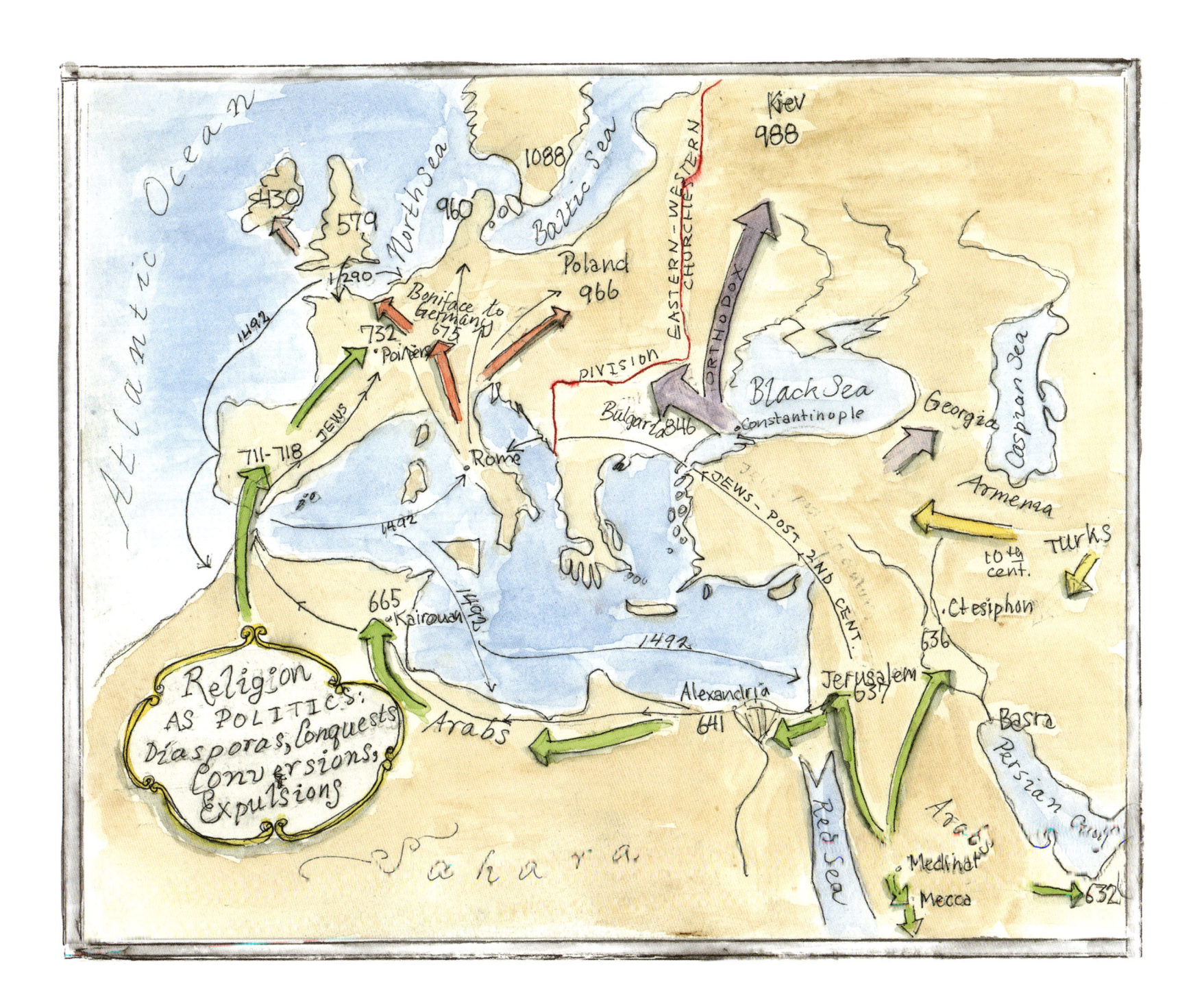

Religion as Politics: Diasporas, Conquests, Conversions, Expulsions

Jerusalem the Golden

In the struggle of East and West, Jerusalem will always be central. Geographically, it stands on the brink of the two, on the ridge that divides the sea world of the Mediterranean from the Mesopotamian land of the rivers to the east.

In the Canaanite language, the word 'Hebrew' means raider. The Hebrews were nomads coming out of the desert and settling into the sown, the land of the Philistines, for whom today's Palestinians are named. Here is a chronology of Zion's violent history. The struggle continues, the battle cry as ever, *Gerusalemme liberata!**

1000 BC	Presumed date of the building of Solomon's temple on the Temple Mount
597	Jerusalem conquered by Babylonians; Jews taken into captivity
588	Second deportation of Jews
538	Cyrus frees Jews; ends Babylonian Captivity
520	Foundations of the Second Temple laid; later finished by King Herod
63	Roman general Pompey conquers Jerusalem; desecrates Temple
AD 70	Suppression of Jewish revolt; destruction of Second Temple
135	Hadrian rebuilds the city as *Aelia Capitalina*; beginning of Second Diaspora
335	Emperor Constantine builds the Church of the Holy Sepulchre
638	Conquered by Arab Caliph Umar
698	Dome of the Rock built on Temple Mount by Umayyad Caliph Al-Walid
1099	Taken by French Crusader knights under Godfrey of Bouillon
1187	Battle of Horns of Hattin (Galilee); Jerusalem retaken by Saladin
1517	Taken by Ottomans, who subsequently build existing walls
1917	Taken by British General Allenby* (December 9)
1947	UN General Assembly votes to create the state of Israel

114

TO BAGHDAD
Golan Heights
Dome of the Rock
Calvary
WEST BANK
SACRIFICE OF ISAAC - MOHAMMAD'S NIGHT FLIGHT
VIA DOLOROSA
church of the Holy Sepulchre
CONSTANTINE'S MOTHER, HELENA, DISCOVERS THE TRUE CROSS HERE
THE TEMPLE BUILT BY SOLOMON, DESTROYED BY BABYLONIANS REBUILT BY HEROD, DESTROYED BY ROMANS; ONE WALL REMAINS OF THE VAST PLATFORM ON WHICH IT ONCE STOOD, ONE REMNANT.
ZION CITY OF OUR GOD
CONSTANTINOPLE
MECCA
ROME
Ottoman Walls
Mosque Tomb of Patriarchs
Gaza Strip

Intersection of Three Major Language Groups

If we in the West have no clear concept of what the Eastern Empire was, it is because it was completely overtaken first by the Arabs and then by the Turks. These conquests were one of the greatest seismic shifts in world history—the complete overlay of one culture by another—of a Romanized, Greek-speaking, Judeo-Christian culture by an Arabic- and Turkic-speaking Islamic one. As a matter of comparison, Chinese culture was never obliterated—merely altered—by the nomads from the Heartland who from time to time conquered China.

The obliteration of the Greek culture* of the Eastern Mediterranean by the Muslims cut the link between the Indo-European-speaking people of Europe on one hand, and India and Persia on the other. You can see on the map that the yellow and green of Turkish and Arabic completely sever the turquoise of Indo-European.

These Arabic and Turkish language zones are living monuments to the conquest of the sown by the nomad warriors based in the deserts of Arabia and the Heartland. Arabic, the language of the Qur'an, unites all Muslims worldwide and is the spoken language from Morocco to Saudi Arabia. The Turkic languages unite a people who live between the Balkan Peninsula and the Altai Mountains in Central Asia. What today are called the 'stans' are really part of a vast nation based in the Heartland. The Ottomans were the farthest westward expansion of the Turkic people. The flag of the modern republic of Turkey is red, in ancient Turkish signifying 'west.'

When the Ottoman Empire was in its last days, the nationalist Young Turks—who seized power in 1909—dreamed of uniting all these peoples. The ancient Christian country of Armenia lies in the middle of this projected Turkic nation, as does the northern part of Shia Persia. Ironically, the leader of the Young Turks, Enver Pasha, after the War, was installed by the Soviets as the ruler of Bukhara.

Besides Arabic and Turkic, a third ancient language unites an enormous cultural zone stretching from Istanbul in the West to Tashkent in the East: Persian.

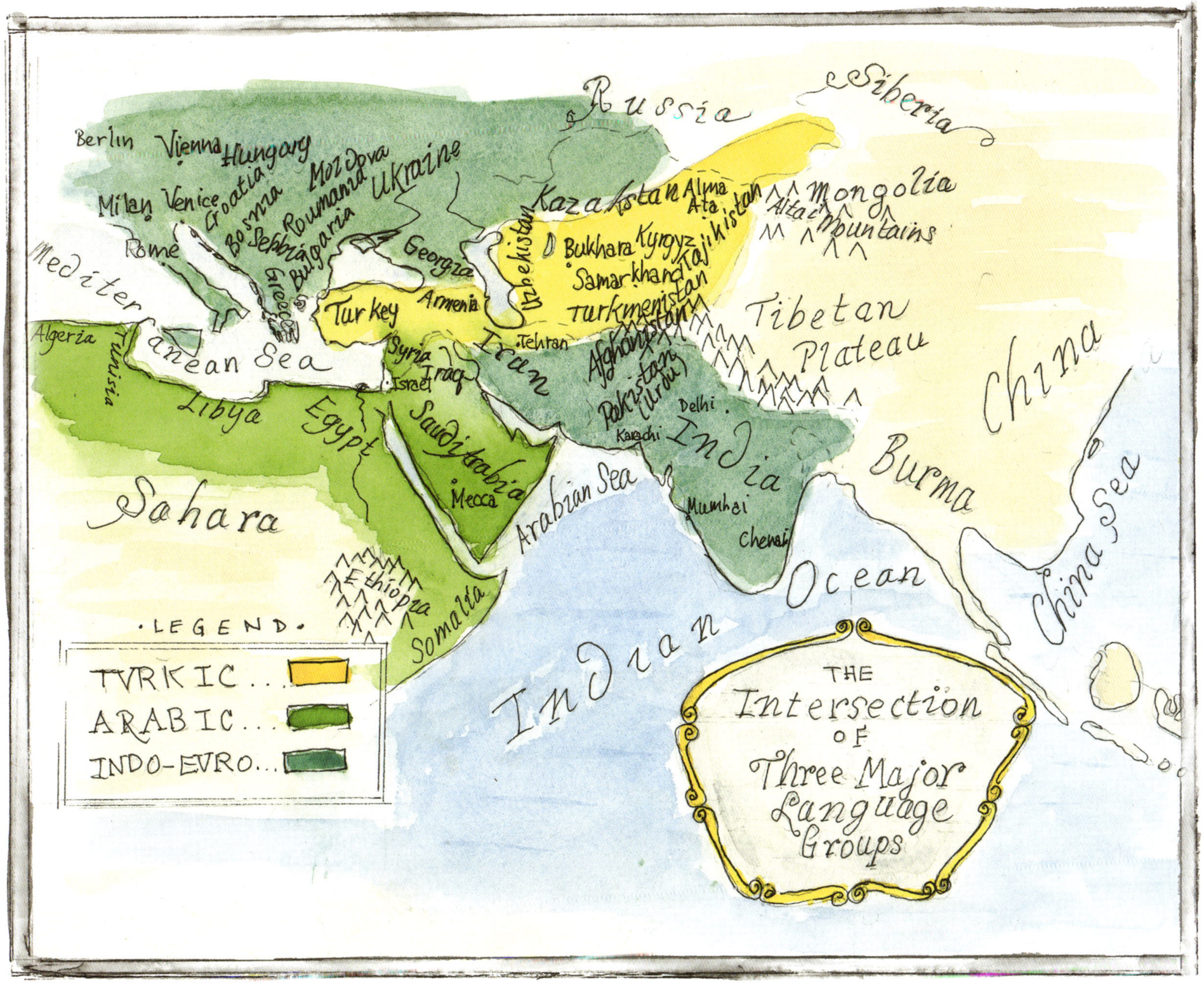

THE Intersection OF Three Major Language Groups
LEGEND
TURKIC
ARABIC
INDO-EURO
Russia
Siberia
Berlin
Vienna
Hungary
Moldova
Ukraine
Milan
Venice
Croatia
Bosnia
Roumania
Serbia
Bulgaria
Rome
Greece
Georgia
Armenia
Turkey
Mediterranean Sea
Kazakstan
Alma Ata
Kyrgyz
Tajikistan
Mongolia
Altai Mountains
Uzbekistan
Bukhara
Samarkhand
Turkmenistan
Tibetan Plateau
China
Algeria
Tunisia
Syria
Iraq
Iran
Tehran
Israel
Afghanistan
Pakistan
(Urdu)
Delhi
Karachi
India
Libya
Egypt
Saudi Arabia
Mecca
Arabian Sea
Mumbai
Chenai
Burma
China Sea
Sahara
Ethiopia
Somalia
Indian Ocean

Persian Letters

To write so much about Greek and nothing about Persian letters would be to give a distinctly imbalanced view—a very un-Greek thing to do. The West may have Greek letters, but the East has Persian. While the ancient language of the western Mediterranean was Latin, and that of the eastern Greek, in the geopolitical fortress of the Iranian plateau it was and is Persian. Just as Spanish, French, and Italian literature would be unimaginable without Latin, and Western science and theology unimaginable without Greek, so in the East both Turkish and Urdu literature would be unimaginable without Persian.

The history of Persia is a series of destructive conquests by outside forces from the desert and subsequent revivals from within under new dynasties. Persian poetry was born in one of these revivals, when the Samanids reversed the Arab conquests. The first Persian lyrics were written at the Samanid court of Bukhara in the 10th century. The 50,000 verses of the Persian epic the *Shahnamah* (Book of Kings) were written by the poet Firdausi (d. 1020) at the court of Mahmoud of Ghazna (r. 999–1030)* in eastern Afghanistan.

Ostensibly the story of the pre-Islamic kings, the *Shahnamah* can also be read as a meditation on the legitimacy of power. It celebrates a return to Persian identity symbolized by the Sassanian dynasty, an identity that had been previously reasserted with the ejection of the Seleucid Greeks, heirs of one of Alexander's generals. In this epic, we read what the Persians want to believe about themselves and how they define themselves with respect to other peoples. One of the last major Persian poets, Muhammad Iqbal (d. 1938), is also associated with the political assertion of identity. He was the founder of the Pakistan Movement, which led to the creation of that country at the Partition of 1947.

Persian literature is an empire in itself. It challenges borders and incorporates languages. It has been in the mouths of many people, from shahs and sultans in Iran and Turkey to peasants and merchants in Pakistan and India.

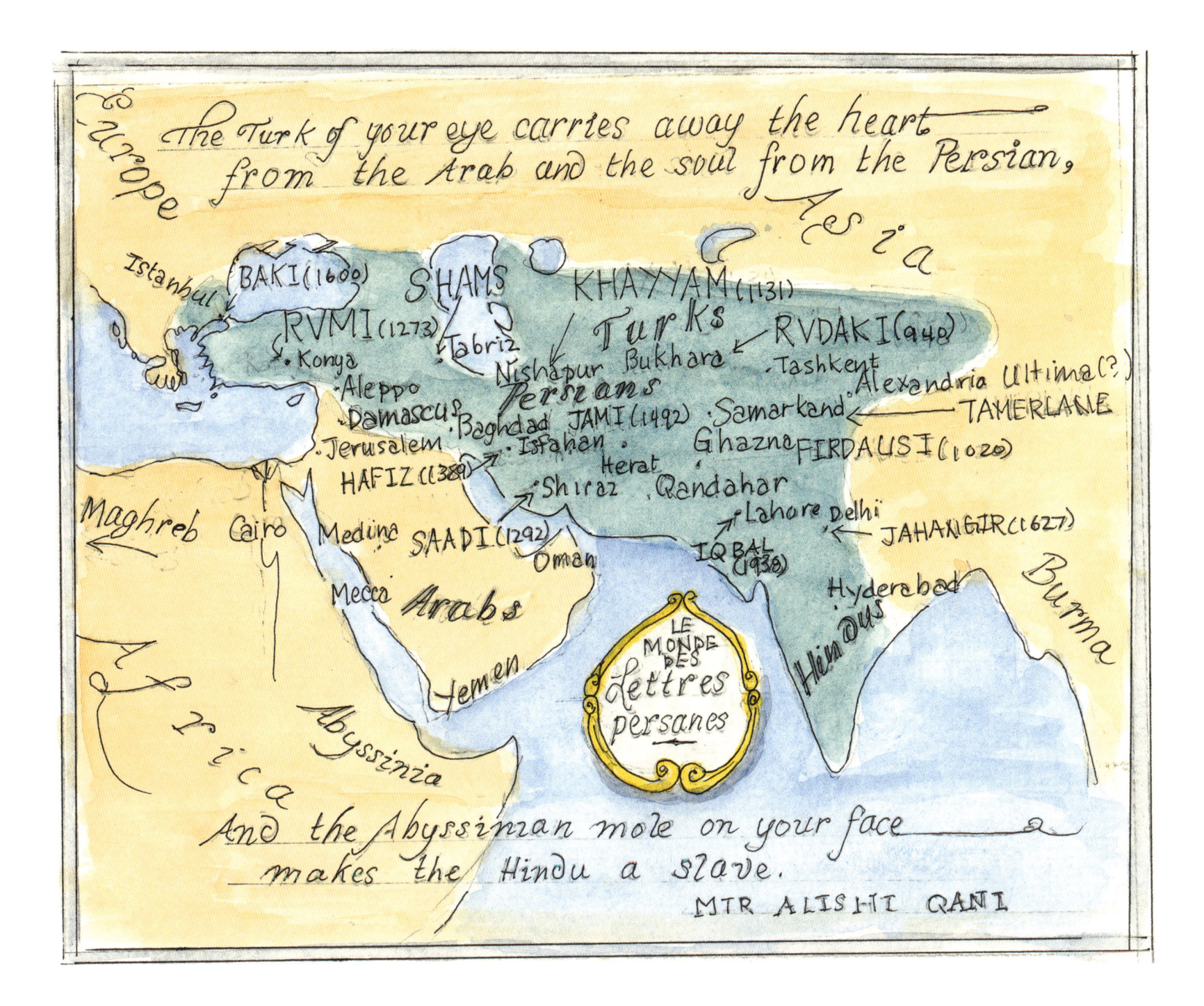

*The Turk of your eye carries away the heart from the Arab and the soul from the Persian,
And the Abyssinian mole on your face makes the Hindu a slave.*

— MIR ALISHI QANI

Rumi's Tomb

To the greatest of Persian poets, Hafiz and Rumi, all religions were more or less one, arising out of the ground of universal human experience—both of the Seen and of the Unseen worlds. Their doctrine was one of love and toleration; their appeal knows no borders. Rumi might be the most popular poet in America; one of his poems, or an extract, is often read after yoga classes.

Rumi was born in Afghanistan, but his family fled political unrest and the impending Mongol assault. They took shelter in the territory of the Selçuk sultan, where Rumi studied sharia law and became an Islamic jurist, issuing fatwas, giving sermons in the mosques, and teaching in the madrassas.

Known in Turkey as Mevlana, Rumi is buried in Konya, the old capital of the Sultanate of Rum, where he lived and taught. With its beautiful Selçuk conical dome, his tomb draws pilgrims from all over the world. His poetry is now popular in Iran.

For such a warlike people, the Ottomans had curious saints: the Whirling Dervishes of the Mevlevi Order, famous for the Sufi dance known as the Sama ceremony. The order was founded by Rumi's son Sultan Walad and his followers. Mosques all over the former Ottoman Empire—along with soup kitchens and other charitable institutions—have lodges for traveling dervishes and madrassas for them to teach in.

The word 'dervish' means doorway, and their dance is a doorway into the divine world; they whirl out of the world of Time and into the world of

Timelessness. The story is that Rumi was walking along the street of the goldsmiths in Konya. Hearing the rhythm of their beating gold to airy thinness, he began to dance, an ecstatic dance of surrender, a letting go of the Self, a spiritual remembrance of the Presence at the center of the universe.

The observatory of the Karatay madrassa was built just before Rumi began to write his couplets, the *Mathnawi*. Its dome seems emblematic not only of Rumi's work, but also of the spiritual nature of the East. Around the base of the dome is a band of highly stylized Kufic calligraphy. The design leads upward to the tile-covered dome set in a star pattern of enormous complexity. The eye tries vainly to follow the pattern until it reaches the oculus at the center, open to the sky: the many leading to the one.

At night the stars are reflected in a small pool of water directly below. Looking down into the water, the dome appears to be a bowl full of stars.

> Awake! for morning in the bowl of night
> Has flung the stone that puts the stars to flight
> And lo! the hunter of the East has caught
> The Sultan's turret in a noose of light.
>
> —'FITZKHAYYAM'*

Architecture, East and West

Architecture has left the most evident remains of past cultures. What do we do when we travel but visit famous buildings? As a historical record it is the most easily read. We can clearly see the difference between the Eastern and Western empires in the churches, or mosques, that they built.

The Christian basilica derives from Roman civic, secular buildings. In the European north, the Gothic style predominates, where it replicates the experience of living in the woods under the arching limbs of massive trees. Early Arab mosques are also a forest of columns creating powerful orthogonal vistas, but with one difference. The *mihrab* of a mosque is not its main architectural focus, as the apse is in a basilica.

The Byzantines developed the simple dome of the Romans, like that of the Pantheon, into the vast vertical space of Hagia Sophia,* so full of awe—in which 'the sunbeams, all we know of heaven, / Cross and recross in their descent…'* Suspended a hundred and fifty feet above the floor, the majestic dome's supports invisibly flow down* through semidomed apses and exedras. The plan is a circle inscribed in a square, emblematic of the divine world. One of the two architects of Hagia Sophia, a geometer (or 'earth measurer') named Isidore of Meletus, was the last director of the pagan university of Athens, closed by Emperor Justinian. A millennium later, the Ottoman architect Sinan brought this model to its ultimate apotheosis.

How different they are, East and West! The straightforward, narrow, terrestrial, clear, dogmatic view of the West—the one true story—contrasted with the Eastern model: round, domed, billowing, without visible support, 'a circle whose circumference is everywhere.'* How beautiful are the imperial mosques of Sinan, crowning the ridge of Istanbul's skyline! It was in Edirne,* however, that he created the supreme work of Ottoman architecture.

> There might be no other* space that expresses so brilliantly the idea
> of Islam, that God sees through everything, and everybody is equal
> in the eyes of God: one feels as if wrapped in the universe itself.

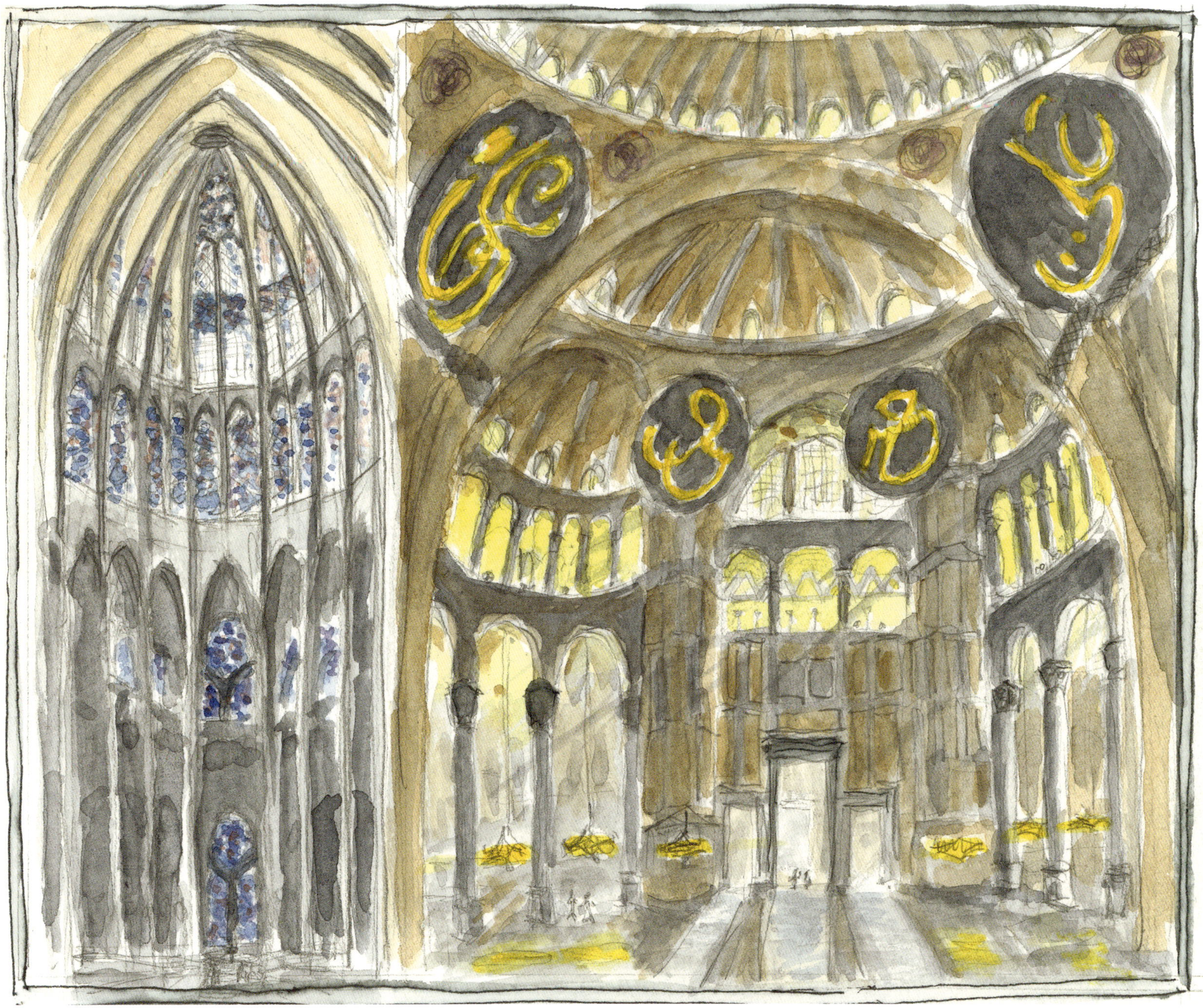

Time and Space in Church and Mosque

The difference between mosque and church is the difference between Time and Space. The Western church 'reflects Time in the form of Space,'* while the mosque reflects Space in the form of a circle whose center is the Ka'aba in Mecca. The orientation of the church is preferably easterly, toward a cyclical astronomical event—the rising of the sun—and therefore related to Time. The orientation of a mosque depends on its terrestrial relationship to Mecca and therefore to Space.

In Christianity, the movable feast of Easter is celebrated on the first Sunday after the first full moon after the vernal equinox, when the sun crosses the equator in the spring. The movements of the sun, moon, and planets across the background of the constellations of the zodiac are how humans measure time in years, months, days, and hours. Easter* was originally a pagan holiday celebrating the rites of spring, the rebirth of Nature, the return of the sun to the Northern Hemisphere at the vernal equinox. The very name of Easter means East, as does the word 'orientation,' or *oriens*, rising—in Christianity the symbol of the Risen Christ.

When Muslims converted a basilican church into a mosque, they were mostly able to change the easterly longitudinal orientation to a southerly transversal one, with the south wall becoming the *qibla*, the direction of Mecca marked by the *mihrab*, or prayer niche. The model of all 'peristyle' mosques—that is, those built with rows of columns instead of covered over by a dome as in the Ottoman manner inspired by Hagia Sophia—was Mohammad's house in Medina.

> This house* was nothing more than two rows of palm trunks on one side of a courtyard, the side facing Mecca. The palm trunks supported a roof of branches for shade. The floor was hard-packed earth, in a mosque the sacred element upon which the Muslim prostrates himself in prayer, touching his forehead to the ground. A sitting position on the ground is the normal place of rest and contemplation. The interior of a mosque is meant to be seen from this position, making each and every spot a center unto itself.

N
OCCIDENS
ORIENS
W
E
SETTING
RISING
S

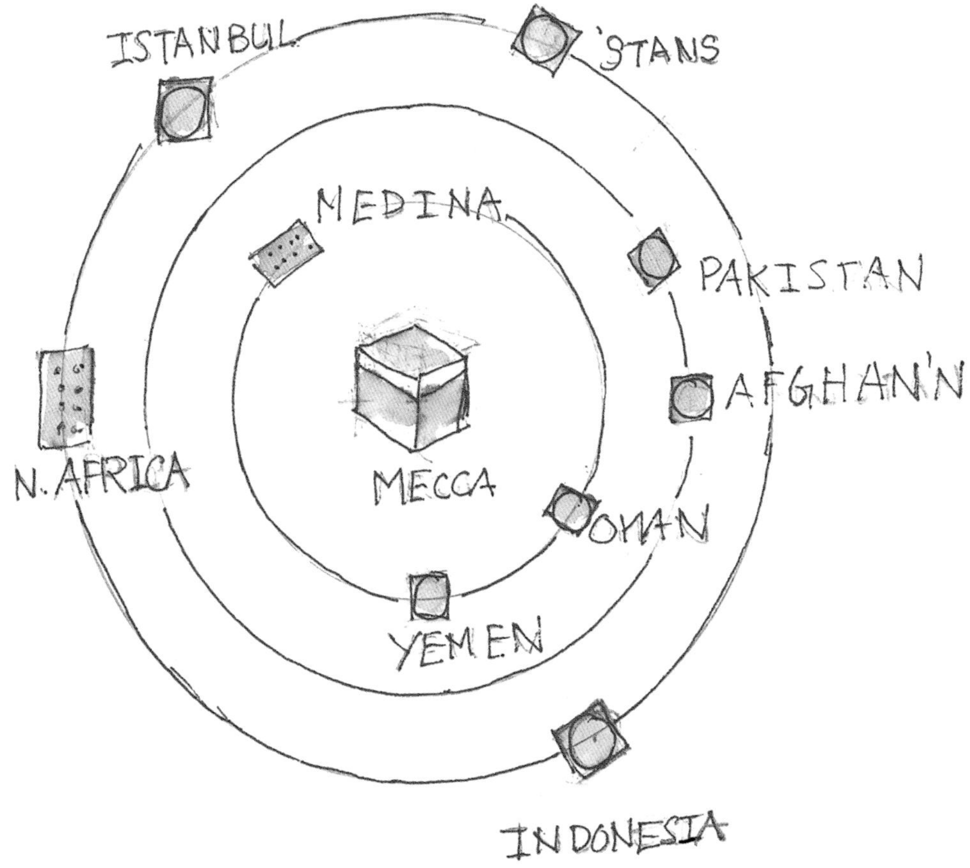
ISTANBUL
'STANS
MEDINA
PAKISTAN
AFGHAN'N
N. AFRICA
MECCA
OMAN
YEMEN
INDONESIA

THE OTTOMAN EMPIRE

The Ottoman Rhinoceros

FOR A LONG TIME—for Europe, for the West—the East was the Ottoman Empire. Imagine a huge African rhinoceros sticking its horns into the Balkans, its forefeet treading on the islands of Crete and Rhodes, its back feet on Egypt and Arabia. From Libya, Tunisia, and Algeria, the Empire's North African provinces, pirates* harried the southern coast of Europe for white slaves while brandishing the 'damasked blade of jihad.'* It was a medieval Islamic state that lasted from 1299 until 1922.

A 16th-century historian of the Turks wrote, 'They are the present Terrour of the World.' The breakup of the Ottoman Empire in the 20th century precipitated a modern form of terror that in the 21st is being exported from its former provinces.

War was the Ottoman Empire's *raison d'être*; and *jihad* was its *raison d'état*, the moral and practical imperative of its policy. Its methods were conquest and the collection of taxes. Conquest gave the *gazi*, warriors for Islam, a holy mission; collecting taxes and tribute kept the Treasury filled and the soldiers paid. The sultan used the excess of income over expense for the administration of the state, and his personal needs.

This is a very old model. As Ibn Khaldūn writes, 'Royal authority exists through the army, the army through money, money through taxes, taxes through justice, and justice through the improvement of officials and from the ruler's personal supervision....'*

The bureaucrats—from tax collectors to the grand vizier—came as part of the revenue. They were slaves mostly taken as boys from Christian families in the Balkans, a tax in kind due every five years. It was an excellent business model, but with the discovery of America and the importation of bullion into Europe—which brought the great inflation of the 16th century—the economic climate changed, and costs began to outrun revenue. The model, nevertheless, worked for centuries.

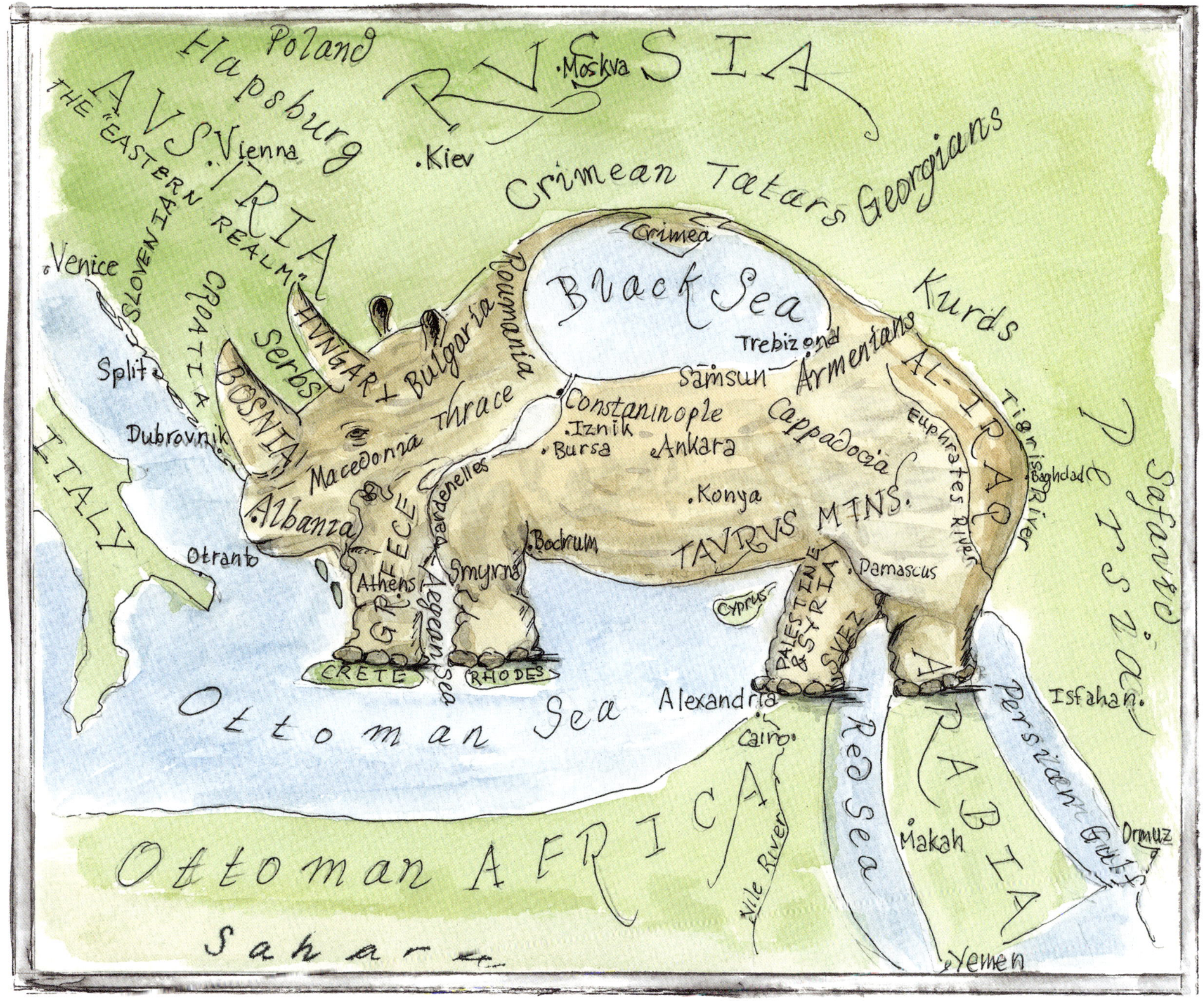

Poland
Hapsburg
AUSTRIA
THE "EASTERN REALM"
.Vienna
RUSSIA
.Moskva
.Kiev
Crimean Tatars
Georgians
Crimea
Black Sea
Kurds
.Venice
SLOVENIA
CROATIA
Split
Dubrovnik
Serbs
HUNGARY
BOSNIA
Bulgaria
Roumania
Trebizond
Samsun
Armenians
AL-IRAQ
Thrace
Constaninople
.Iznik
.Bursa
Ankara
Cappadocia
Euphrates River
Tigris River
Baghdad
Persia
Safavid
ITALY
Macedonia
Dardenelles
.Konya
TAURUS MTNS.
Albania
GREECE
Bodrum
Otranto
Athens
Aegean Sea
Smyrna
Damascus
PALESTINE & SYRIA
SUEZ
Cyprus
CRETE
RHODES
Ottoman Sea
Alexandria
Cairo
Persian Gulf
Isfahan
Red Sea
ARABIA
Makah
Ormuz
Ottoman AFRICA
Nile River
Sahara
Yemen

Topkapi Palace

For a long time, the Ottoman Empire was a sleek and efficient machine, with low overhead. Look at the size of the palace in Istanbul. It was the White House, the Pentagon, the U.S. Treasury, the IRS, Customs Office, and Department of Justice, all in one small collection of buildings. There were three departments of state: 'the sword' (the army), 'finance' (tax collection), and 'the pen' (scribes to keep the complex records).

There was no Congress, just a cabinet, the Divan, composed of slave bureaucrats who were the sultan's chief officers of state. He listened from behind a grille, the Dangerous Window, to their proceedings. When he sat in judgment at the entrance to the Inner Palace, his executioner stood behind him, ready to carry out the sentence. Nearby is a fountain* where that other officer of state washed his hands and sword.

When Mehmet the Conqueror built the Topkapi Palace (*Yeni Saray*), he constructed not just a building, but 'the very heart of Ottoman society.' The entire empire existed to service it. He placed the palace on the site of the Byzantine acropolis, overlooking the Bosphorus and Asia. Over the gate Mehmet set his title:

> Sultan of the Two Continents and Emperor of the Two Seas,
> Shadow of God Dispensing Peace in this World, Mighty Caesar,
> Favorite of God on the Two Horizons [i.e., East and West].

Mehmet was perfectly aware of history and his role in it. Described by the Venetian ambassador, he was

> a young man* of twenty-six years of age, who aspires to equal the glory of Alexander the Great, and every day has histories of Rome and other nations read to him.... He is inexorably set upon the destruction of the Christians. He says that Caesar and Hannibal were of no account compared to himself, and that Alexander entered Asia with a smaller force than his. Now, he says, times have changed... that he will march from the East to the West, as West once marched against the East.

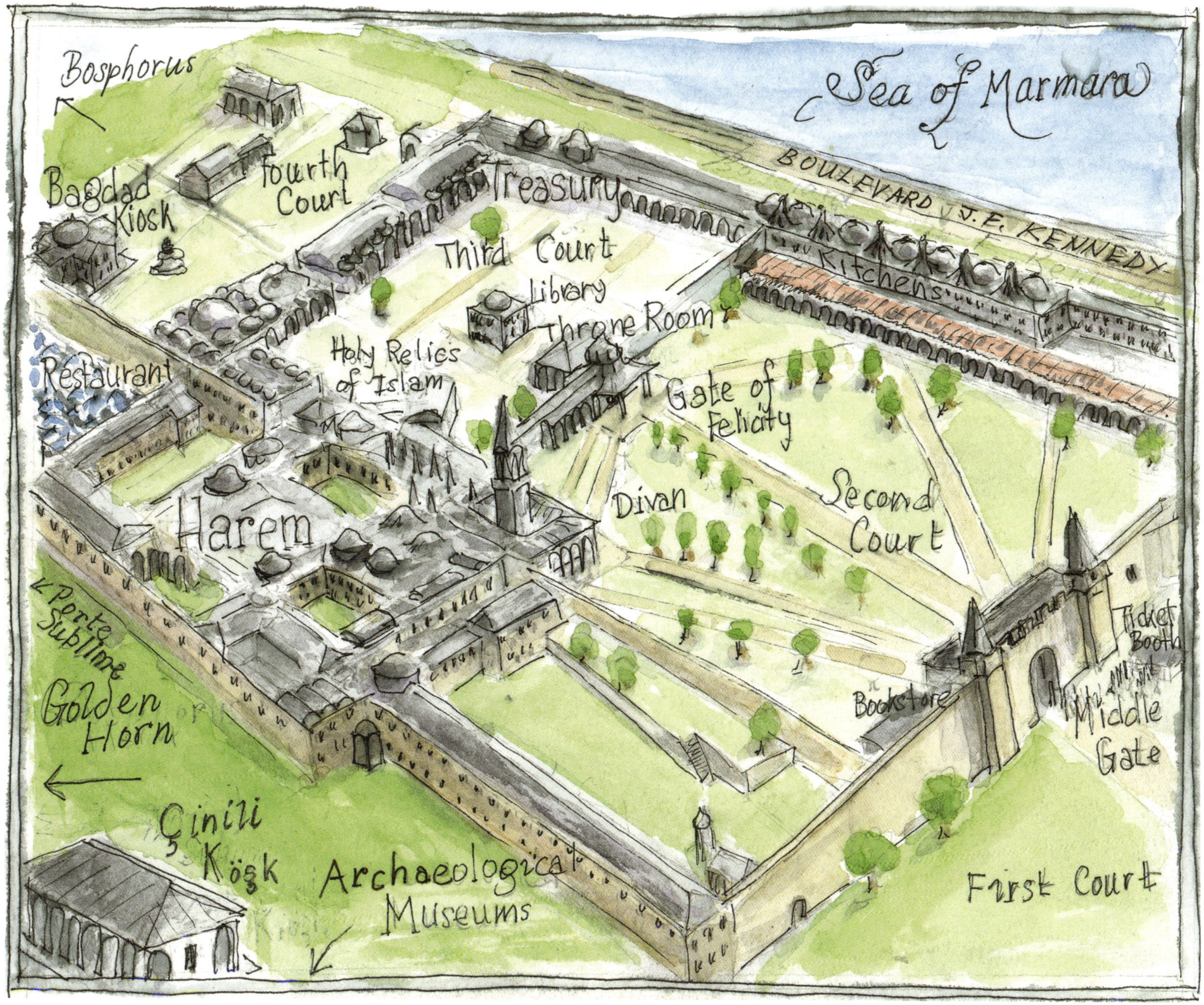
Bosphorus
Sea of Marmara
Fourth Court
Bagdad Kiosk
Treasury
BOULEVARD J.F. KENNEDY
Third Court
Kitchens
Library
Throne Room
Holy Relics of Islam
Restaurant
Gate of Felicity
Divan
Second Court
Harem
Porte Sublime
Ticket Booth
Golden Horn
Bookstore
Middle Gate
Çinili Kösk
Archaeological Museums
First Court

Three Extraordinary Institutions

The Ottoman state was born in the struggle against the infidel. During their migrations across Central Asia, Persia, and Anatolia, the Ottomans had become dedicated, even fanatical warriors on behalf of *gaza*, or holy war. They were settled by the Selçuk sultan in Asia Minor on the eastern marches of the Byzantine Empire. This geopolitical circumstance drew to their ranks* wandering adventurers, warriors, and dervishes who wanted to pursue the holy war against the Christians. The weakness of both the Byzantines and the Selçuks contributed to the rapid rise of the Ottoman state—from a small nomadic tribe to rulers of half the world in 150 years. This rise was due as well to three extraordinary institutions: concubinage, unigeniture, and the Janissaries.

The sultan's concubines, slaves in the harem, became the mothers of sultans. The Ottomans may have learned concubinage from the Persians, but in any case polygamy is a well-established tradition in Central Asia, where traditionally women were acquired through raids—as, for instance, was Genghis's mother. For the Ottoman succession, the family of the mother didn't matter; it was only necessary to be a descendant of Osman. With concubinage, the Ottomans avoided the entanglements of dynastic marriages.

In order to avoid conflicts over the succession as well as weak rulers, very early (1324) they adopted the rule not of primogeniture, but of unigeniture—the rule of fratricide. Upon a sultan's death, the prince who managed to seize the throne first murdered his brothers. These two institutions, plus a third, the Janissaries, were in large part responsible for the astonishing ascendancy of the House of Osman.

The Janissaries, or *Yeni-Ceri*, 'New Soldiers,' were particular to the Ottomans and unlike any type of soldier before or since. No similar institution existed among the Europeans, and the 'irresistible progress'* of the Turks was the result. It was a slave army recruited as young boys through the *devshirme*, or 'boy tax,' levied on Christian families, mostly in the Balkans. Christian by birth, Spartan by upbringing, devout Muslims by conversion, the Janissaries were one of the most amazing military corps in history, combining the discipline of the West with the religious fanaticism of the East.

Starting around 1365, with 12,000 captive Christian youths, the Janissaries obtained over the course of 200 years an almost unbroken succession of victories for the sultan. When these institutions were abandoned, or in the case of the Janissaries became corrupt, the empire began to fail.*

If we say that the Middle Ages began with the fall of Rome, then we must say that they ended with the fall of Constantinople,* the Second Rome. The Second and Third Acts of our play correspond to the Middle Ages in Europe and the rise of Arab and Turkish Islam in the East, beginning with the Hegira, Mohammad's 'flight' from Mecca to Medina in 622. The Fourth Act begins on the afternoon of May 29, 1453, when Mehmet the Conqueror (*Fatih*) entered the city of Constantinople.

The conquest was certainly the main event in Ottoman history, as well as Islam's greatest victory. Even though the Ottoman empire continued to expand throughout the next century and a half, the Conquest represents the real climax of its rise. But it also marks the beginning of its end; and with the discovery of the New World, the principle theater of war shifted from the Mediterranean to the Atlantic as the principle tactical naval weapon shifted from the galley to the weatherly, seagoing ship.

Emblematic of this shift was the first major Turkish defeat,* in 1571 at Lepanto, exactly 500 years after the Turks first made themselves known to the West at Manzikert.

Ertoğrul Gazi Turbesi

Driving a couple of hours southeast of Istanbul, a traveler comes across what might be called Kilometer Zero of the Ottoman Empire: the tomb of Dursun Fakih, the dervish who in 1299 preached the first Friday sermon in Osman's name. Traditionally in Islamic countries the Friday sermon is preached in the name of the ruler: to preach a sermon in his name is to assert his legitimacy to rule. With this sermon, Dursun Fakih proclaimed the beginning of the Ottoman Empire.

In the 19th century, the last sultan to truly rule, Abdül Hamid II, reclaimed the original Islamic title of caliph* in an attempt to bolster his faltering regime. To reassert the legitimacy of his family, he restored—and sometimes built anew—the tombs of his ancestors. Around the little town of Söğüt in northwestern Anatolia, in the center of the pasture lands given to the first Ottomans, Abdül Hamid created an Ottoman necropolis. Not far from Dursun Fakih's tomb is that of Osman's father, Ertoğrul Gazi, a border warlord. All around the green baize cenotaph are little wooden boxes that contain earth from all the countries over which the sultans, Ertoğrul's descendants, once ruled. There are twenty-two boxes, representing the modern nations of the former Eastern Empire.

One of Ertoğrul's descendants, Mehmet the Conqueror, expressed the *gazi* spirit of his ancestors in poetry.

> My purpose is to obey* God's command to wage *jihad*,
> My zeal is for the faith of Islam alone.
> By the grace of God and the brave men of God's army,
> My purpose is to conquer the infidels entirely.
> My trust is in the prophets and the saints,
> My hope of victory and conquest is in God's bounty.
> What if I wage *jihad* with life and fortune?
> Praise be to God, my desire for battle grows many thousandfold.
> O Mohammad, by your own miracles
> Let my power triumph over the enemies of the faith.

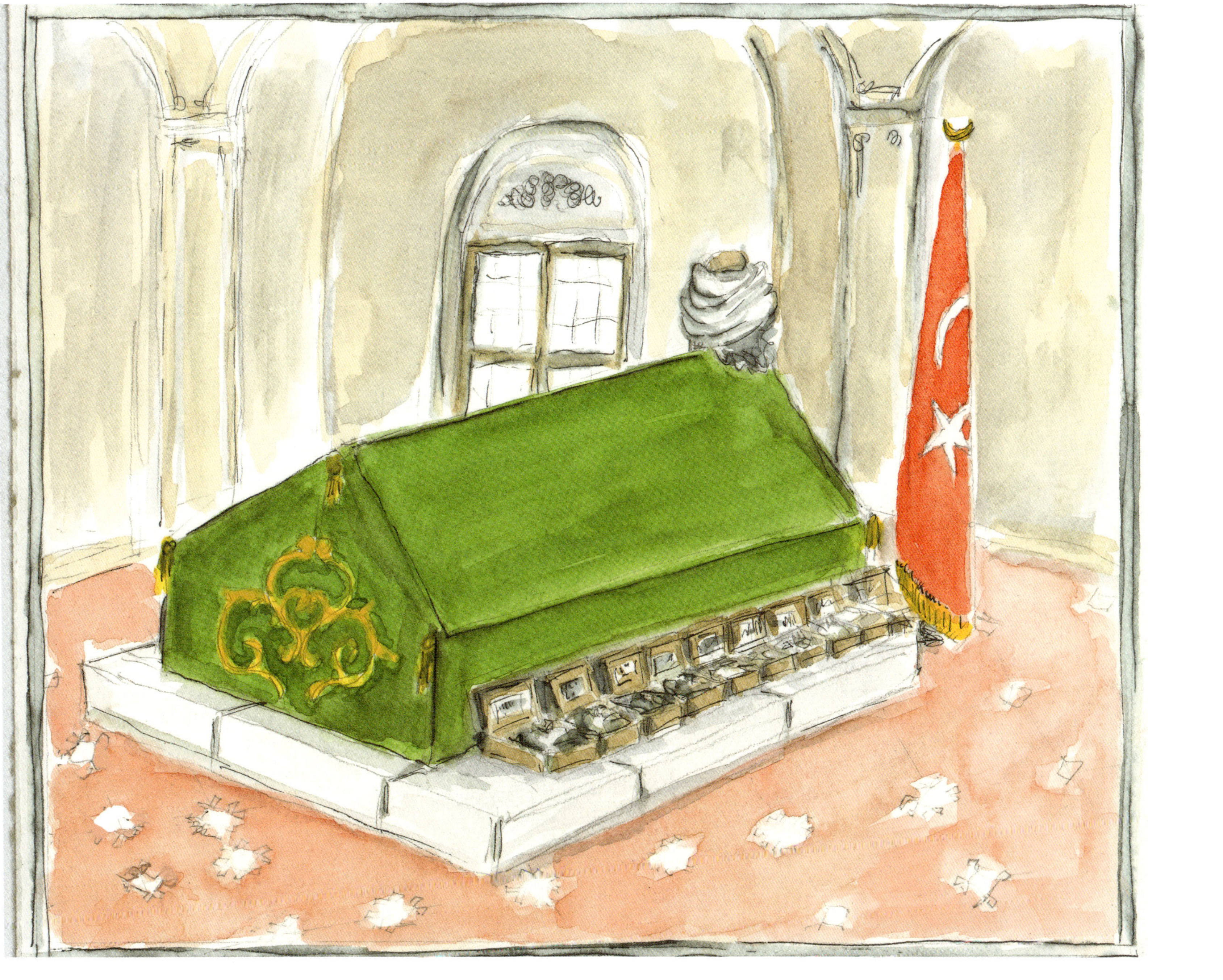

III. The Eastern Question Is Asked

We have a sick man on our hands, a man gravely ill. It will be a great misfortune if one of these days he slips through our hands, especially before the necessary arrangements are made.

—TSAR NICHOLAS I, 1859

THE RISE OF THE WEST

Great 'C'
of
Reconquista
and
Conquista

The Eastern Question began with the rise of the West and Russia, and the decline of Dar al' Islam. Let us now trace the Question's history up to the end of the Cold War.

The energy generated by the struggle to reclaim lost Christian territory in Europe, as well as to regain Jerusalem during the Crusades, became the conquest of the world. These two movements, *Reconquista* and *Conquista*, are closely related, one following from the other. Imagine them having traced a great 'C' across the map of the world, standing for Christianity and Capitalism. The energy generated was that of a tightly coiled spring released.

In 1492, the *Reconquista* came to an end with the fall of the last Moorish state in Spain, Granada. The following spring, the astonishing happened: the existence of a New World was announced to the stunned minds of Europe and Asia, and the *Conquista* of the whole world began. By sailing east, the Portuguese discovered sea routes to the source of all the good stuff coming from the East. By sailing west, Spain discovered a second hemisphere and for a few decades was master of the world. But this dominance was a fleeting delusion.*

The *Reconquista* was an irredentist* movement that extended the boundaries of Europe from Gibraltar in the West almost to the Bosphorus in the East, and which foreshadowed the later European conquest of the world. It was a crusade against unbelievers, a search for booty and plunder, a migration following in the wake of victorious armies, and the subsequent colonization of its newly conquered lands. It laid the foundation of the modern capitalist system.*

At the same time that the Europeans were creating their sea empires, the Russians were creating their land empire, and Dar al' Islam was caught in a vice.

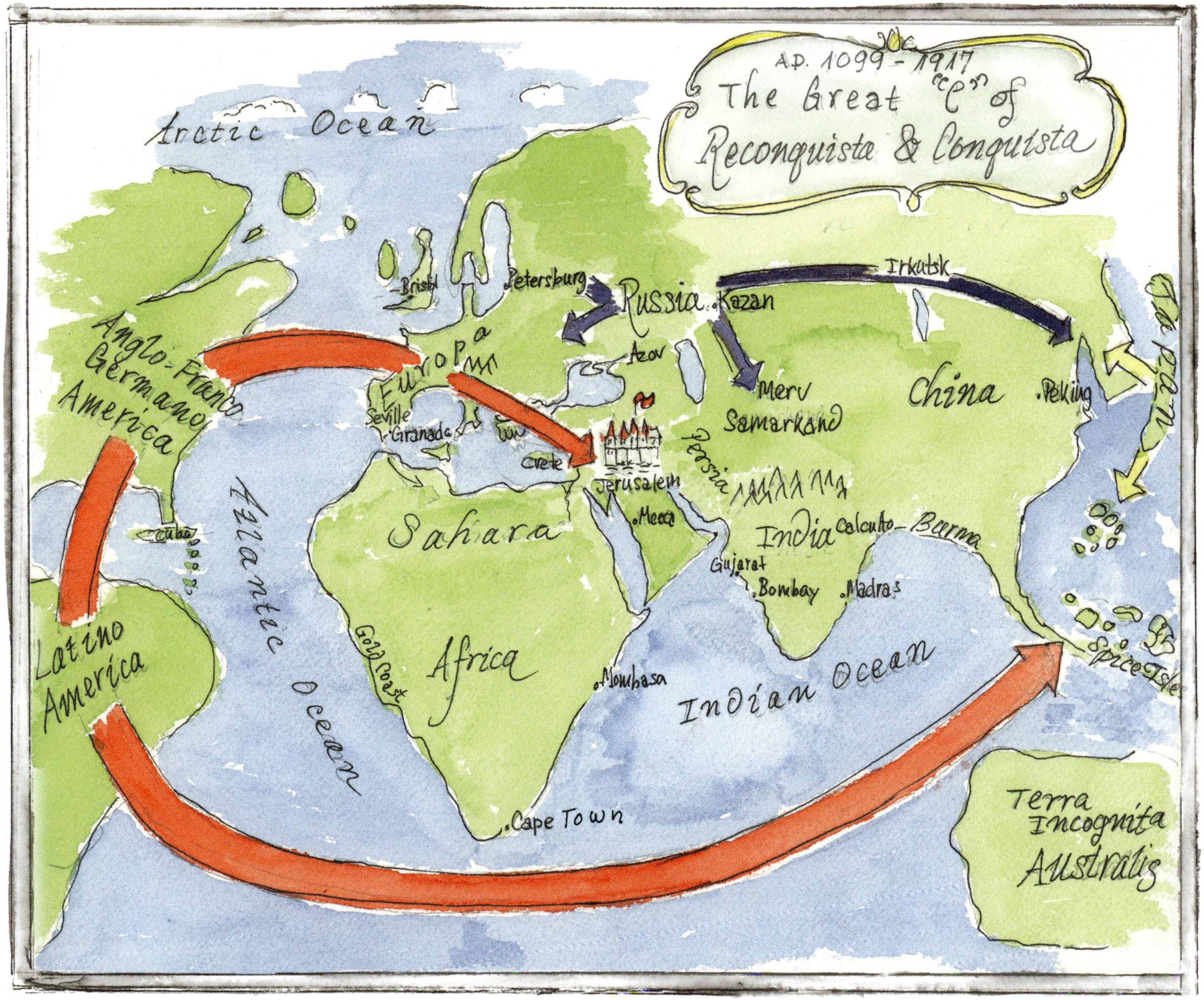
A.D. 1099 - 1917
The Great "C" of
Reconquista & Conquista
Arctic Ocean
Bristol
Petersburg
Russia
Kazan
Irkutsk
Europa
Azov
Merv
Samarkand
China
Peking
Anglo-Franco
Germano
America
Seville
Granada
Crete
Jerusalem
Persia
Mecca
Sahara
India
Calcutta
Barma
Gujarat
Bombay
Madras
Cuba
Atlantic Ocean
Latino
America
Gold Coast
Africa
Mombasa
Indian Ocean
Spice Isle
Cape Town
Terra
Incognita
Australis

Passing of Greek Manuscripts

The conquest of the world by the Europeans was in large part due to the recovery of science. The key to this recovery was the Greek texts in their original language; the key to the Greek texts were the Byzantine scholars* fleeing Constantinople before 1453. From the perspective of my Renaissance studies, it seemed like the touching of two hands—from Ancient to Modern—across the sacred promontory of Greece.

The Italian Renaissance is famous for its paintings and sculpture, but the movement was originally sparked by the revival of the ancient classics. Most important, for the rise of the West, were the Greek scientific, mathematical, and astronomical texts that led to the Scientific Revolution of the 17th century. As Albert Einstein wrote:

> The development of Western science* has been based on two great achievements, the invention of the formal logical system [in Euclidian geometry]…and the discovery of… systematic experiment [at the Renaissance]….

It is said that the only time Isaac Newton ever laughed was when someone asked him of what use could Euclidean geometry possibly be?

The Renaissance was coeval with the Ottoman Empire. Dante sets the beginning of his *Divine Comedy* on the morning of Good Friday 1300, the year after the putative founding of that Empire. The man who initiated the Renaissance, Petrarch, was born two years before the Ottomans won their first victory over the Byzantines at Yalova in 1306. Within two human lifetimes from that date (140 years), the West had regained the ancient texts by virtue of the revival of Greek.

Some sense of the excitement engendered among the early humanists can be gathered from Leonardo Bruni's *Commentaries*:

> Letters at this point* grew mightily in Italy when Chrysoloras of Byzantium brought us Greek learning. Through seven hundred years no one in Italy has been master of Greek letters, and yet all knowledge, that is, all science, is derived from them.

EVROPA
Vienna 1527/1683
ASIA MAJOR
1495
Venice
Azov
Black Sea
Caspian Sea
Florence
1438
Constantinople
1453
Magna Græcia
Troy
Asia Minor
Nicaea
325
Malta 1565
Rhodes
1525
Baghdad
1537
OTTOMAN SEA
Jerusalem 1517
Alexandria
AFRICA
Arabia
Red Sea
Persia

Capital Flows

The rise of the West was concomitant with the rise of capitalism. Where did the capital—the lifeblood of capitalism—come from? The answer is Latin America.

For centuries, Europe had suffered a negative trade balance with the East. The Romans craved the eastern luxuries that came along the Silk Road, and Augustus tried to restrict the cash drain of gold bullion out of the empire. The Portuguese sailed around the bulge of Africa looking to circumvent the Arab lock on the trade of gold coming from Timbuctu.

The quest for precious metals was the principal driving force behind the colonial ventures of the Spanish, culminating in 1545 when a mountain of silver was discovered at Potosí, southeast of Lake Titicaca in Bolivia. In 1560, a new method was discovered for the refining of silver by an amalgam of mercury, and large-scale production began. Over the next 200 years, some 41,000 tons of silver were extracted.

As in one of Don Quixote's delusions of glory, the bullion that flowed past the Torre del Oro on the banks of the Guadalquivir in Seville flowed just as quickly out: to pay for the administration of the empire of the Hapsburgs, for the costly wars against Protestants and Turks, for its ostentatious buildings and monuments, and for the payment of interest on the rapidly mounting debt. By the end of the 16th century, Spain was bankrupt. All the silver in Mexico and Peru could not make Spain a rich country. It was like the Midas touch: something deeply desired,

140

but in reality a curse. The aristocratic warrior culture of Spain did not breed investors of capital, but rather spenders.

Where did the money go? It went north into the hands of their Protestant enemies: into the banks of Amsterdam, Paris, London, and ultimately back to the New World. It capitalized the first corporations, the Dutch East India and the British East India companies, which were both founded two years after Spain's bankruptcy. In the 19th century, British capital financed the industrialization of the United States with bonds underwritten and guaranteed by Junius Morgan and his son J. P. Morgan.

Accustomed to a very short summer growing season and a long, cold winter, northerners were natural savers, as opposed to southerners living around the microclimate of the Mediterranean with its much longer, winter growing season. At the Reformation, north and south split. The north became Protestant while the south fell under the dead hand of the Inquisition and the Index, which stifled scientific development. Think of Galileo. The result was that the north rose and the south declined.

The enormous increase in the money supply from the New World created an inflation* that bankrupted not only the Catholic Hapsburgs, but also the Ottomans. Rising prices are good for rising powers, but spell the doom of declining ones.* From 1650 on, world affairs began to suffer a sea change,

The Turning Point

The turning point in the struggle between Dar al' Islam and Christendom, as well as between the north and south of Europe, takes place in the second half of the 17th century. There are seven key dates in this short span of time, when the foundations of the modern West were laid while at the same time the Turkish advances into Europe were coming to an end.

The Peace of Westphalia of 1648 technically marks the end of the Thirty Years' War, but what it really marks is the end of the 130 years of Wars of Religion that began with Luther's posting his Theses on the church door in Wittenberg. Politically, the Peace represents the end of the Hapsburgs' attempt to suppress the Protestant Reformation and to reclaim for the Church the immense treasure that the nationalist churches of the north had seized. It has been estimated that prior to the Reformation fully half the capital of Europe was tied up in ecclesiastical hands. The dissolution of Church property, together with the bullion slipping through Spanish hands, freed up a tremendous amount of capital.

Westphalia gave birth to the modern nation-state, sovereign within its borders and free from outside interference. These principles of natural sovereignty eventually mutated into the disruptive force of nationalism that institutionalized the continuing fragmentation of the old Roman Empire of the West—and then of the East.*

Twenty-two years after Westphalia, in 1670, Spinoza* published his *Tractatus,* in which he posited the modern concept of the 'inalienable rights' of the individual versus the state: that is, government by the consent of the governed. A government's legitimacy, he asserted, is derived from the people alone. Observing Dutch capitalism, he concluded that individual gain contributes to the general benefit of all, that the sum of all individual goods is the greater good.*

Thirteen years later, on September 12, 1683, the Polish king Jan Sobieski relieved the last Ottoman siege of Vienna. The Turks fled to the southeast, abandoning their camp. That day was the beginning of the end for the Ottomans. When a rising tide is reaching the high-water mark and then begins to recede, who can say which wave will reach farthest up the beach and which will be the last? As it turned out, the siege of Vienna was the last in the succession of Islamic waves to crash against the bulwark of Christendom, starting with Mohammad's death in 632.

Four years after the Siege of Vienna, Isaac Newton published his *Principia*, the mathematical basis of modern science. In the next year, 1688, the long quarrel in England between king and parliament was ended with the Glorious (or Bloodless) Revolution. This was the first time in modern history that a parliament put limits to royal prerogative, establishing the constitution that has become a model for the world.

Sixteen years after the Siege of Vienna, the steam engine was invented in England. With abundant iron and coal, and the technology to mine and transport it, first by canal and then by rail, England was better placed than its ancient rival France to lead the Industrial Revolution. The technological foundations of the modern world were thus laid only a few years after the end of the great Turkish *jihad*. Another bend in the river of history had been reached. Having been so long dominated by the East, the power was now flowing back toward the West. However, into the space left by the declining Ottomans, the Russians began their rise as a new rival in the East by taking the fortress of Azov in 1696. What would be the fate of the Ottoman Empire in the face of Russia's expansion would soon become the Eastern Question.

Seven Key Dates

1648	Peace of Westphalia
1670	Spinoza's *Tractatus Theologico-Politicus*
1683	Siege of Vienna
1687	Newton's *Principia Mathematica*
1688	'Glorious Revolution' in England
1696	Russians take Azov
1699	Invention of the steam engine in England

European Conquest of the World

The eruption of the capitalist West and its conquest of the world was unique in history and vastly exceeded in extent the conquests of Arab and then of Turkish Islam, and that of the Mongols in between. While there were limits to the expansion of the Arabs, Turks, and Mongols, dictated by the physical limits of horses and camels, there have been no limits to a European expansion powered by ships, science, technology, and capitalism. Starting from an equally small base, the European conquest has had a far larger impact, reaching the entire globe—and is now coopting the East.

By virtue of living along the seaboard of the cold, gale-swept North Atlantic, the coastal Europeans developed stout ships that could sail in any sea. While the Spanish were content to plow down the Trade Wind sea lanes with their bullion-laden galleons, the northern Europeans, after first poaching on the Spanish and Portuguese claims, explored and colonized the entire world. One can see the difference between these two cultures projected onto the screen of the New World, evident in the difference between Anglo and Latin America. The frontier between them is the porous and perilous Mexican-American border.

Four Phases of European Expansion

1500s Spain and Portugal
struggle for world domination.

1600s Holland, France, and England
poach on Spanish and Portuguese claims.

1700s France and Britain
struggle for world domination.

1800s Britain triumphant
after Waterloo, but dependent on American oil starting in 1912.

Meanwhile, the Russians were creating a land empire in the Heartland, adding a 100,000 square kilometers every year. Having conquered the vast steppes to the east, they began to push south into Ottoman territory in the Balkans.

In the Tsushima Strait, the rising Japanese Empire put a limit to Russian expansion with a naval defeat in 1904 that provoked the first Russian Revolution of 1905, the precursor to the February Revolution of 1917.

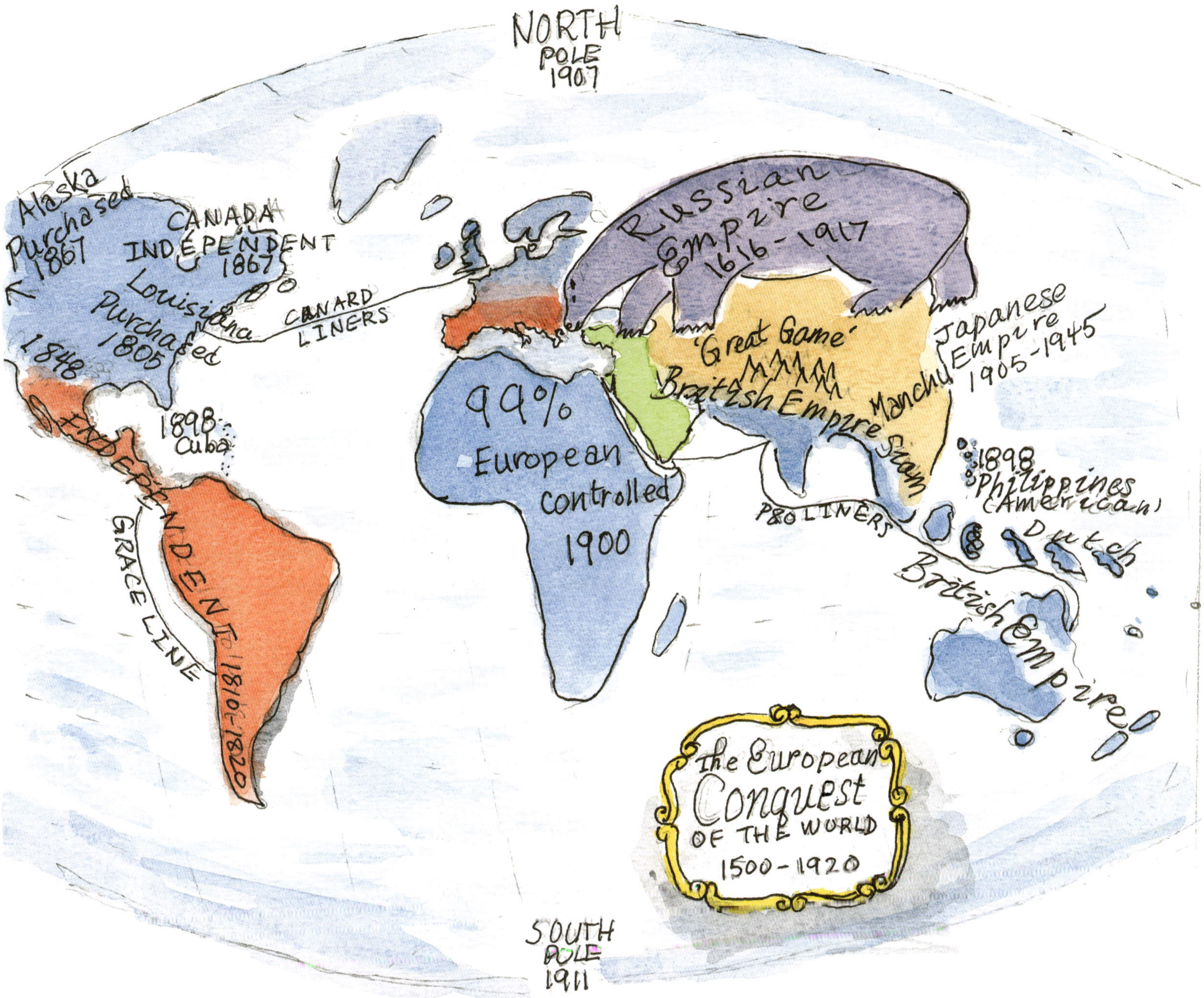

Fall of Dar al' Islam

World conquest became a zero-sum game.* The exploration and exploitation of every corner of the Known World meant that an advance by one power required a retreat by another. As the Europeans were building their capitalistic sea empires, the Russians were building their land empire. As they both advanced, Dar al' Islam retreated. The last colonial prize was the Ottoman Empire, or what was left of it.

The business model of the medieval Islamic slave empire was displaced by the model of the modern corporation, which unleashed the potential of free labor. It was not that the East did not have capitalism; but its capitalists were merchants, not industrialists. Powered by science and technology, industrial capitalism 'unleashed heretofore unimaginable forces.'* From the beginning of the 16th century right up to the present, the rapid pace of scientific and technological advance in the West has been taken for granted. By the time of the Industrial Revolution,* now seemingly freed by science from the immutable laws of Nature, the West had ceased to look back to the past.

The modern corporation institutionalizes these capitalist forces. The joint-stock, limited-liability corporation, invented in Holland and England at the beginning of the 17th century, is what made the explosion of capitalism so powerful. Gunpowder by itself can only make fireworks: put it in a barrel behind a projectile, and you have a gun. The gun was the capitalist system. The powder was the bullion of the New World. The spark was science.

It is a truism demonstrated quarterly in the stock market* that if a business doesn't grow, it collapses. The same was true for the Ottoman economic model. In 1700, the economies of East and West were roughly equal in size, but the Ottoman Empire, whose business model presupposed an ever-expanding tax base, had reached the limits of its conquests,* just as Western capitalist expansion took off.

The net result was that the vast geopolitical entity that had been Dar al' Islam was beleaguered on all sides, surrounded, pushed back, and then crushed.

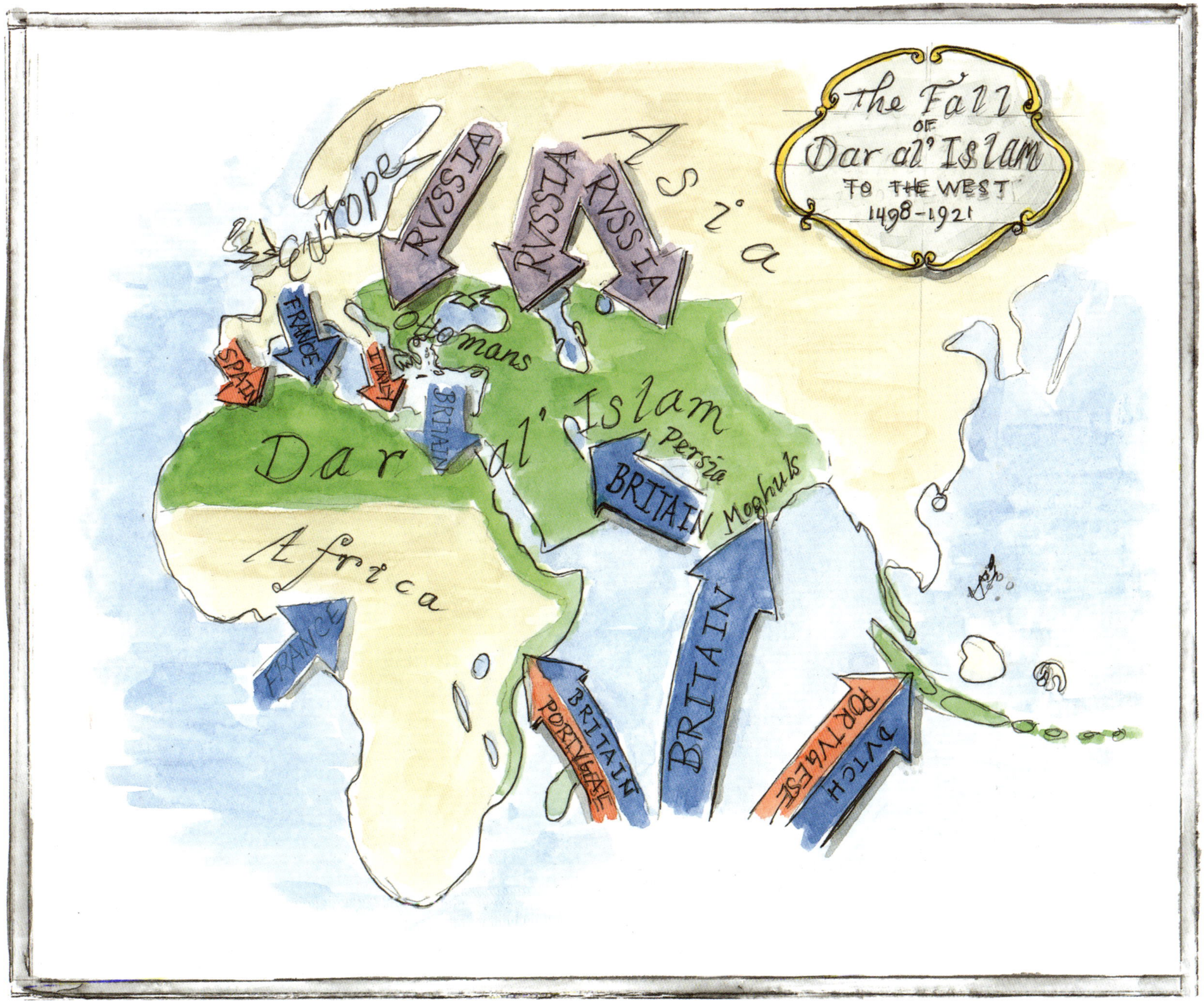

THE EASTERN QUESTION, PER SE

Catherine and Potemkin at Kherson, 1787

RUSSIA'S BREAKOUT from its landlocked situation in the 18th century and its push south into the declining Ottoman Empire threatened not only the Ottomans but also the sea power of Britain. This perceived threat was the Eastern Question, per se. In this chapter, we will discuss this struggle—supposedly settled in 1907 with the partition of Persia and the creation of the modern state of Afghanistan—but was not. Here's when and where the Eastern Question is said by historians to have begun.

In the same year, 1787, that the delegates met in Philadelphia to revise the Articles of Confederation and instead drafted the U.S. Constitution, Catherine the Great and her prime minister and former lover Gregory Potemkin* made a trip to her newly acquired territory in the Crimea with the Hapsburg emperor Joseph II, Mozart's patron, in tow. This was the tour of the famous 'Potemkin villages': prettied-up houses and smiling peasants lined the banks of the route as the party traveled first by luxurious sledges, then by red and gold barges down the Dnieper toward the Black Sea.

In the harbor of Kherson, an old Byzantine trading post, Potemkin assembled Russia's first Black Sea Fleet and had a signpost erected, lettered in Greek, that read, 'To the City,' the Greek source of the name Istanbul.* Here Potemkin proposed to continue two Russian projects envisioned by Peter the Great.

Thirteen years before, in 1774, under the terms of the Treaty of Küçük Kaynarca, the Khanate of Crimea, an Ottoman vassal state since 1478, became independent. In 1783, the last khan ceded the Khanate* to Russia. The Black Sea was no longer an Ottoman lake. Meanwhile, far to the south—on the other side of the Ottoman Empire, beyond the deserts of Persia and the mountains of Afghanistan—the British, having lost their American colonies, were laying the foundation of their future Anglo-Indian Empire.

1787 POTEMKIN & CATHERINE AT KHERSON "TO THE CITY"

ΕΙΣ ΤΗΝ ΠΟΛΙΝ

Russian Bear

Imagine Russia as a great bear with its tongue lapping the waters of the Black Sea, while its right paw reaches for the Mediterranean over the dying Ottoman Empire and its left paw reaches south toward the mountain passes of Afghanistan. At least it seems to have appeared so to the British who were opening up India at the same time that Russia opened a window on the Black Sea. This fear is at the root of the Russophobia that has spooked the West right up to the Ukraine crisis of 2014.

When in 1696 Peter the Great conquered Azov, a fortress at the head of the Sea of Azov, the Russian bear first tasted the waters of the Black Sea—which the sultan had guarded as jealously as the women in his harem. Five years later, Peter opened a 'Window on the West' by taking the future site of St. Petersburg from the Swedes. Eight years later, Russia became a great power with the defeat of the formidable Swedish army at Poltava in modern Ukraine in 1709. Two years later, the Ottomans defeated Peter at the Pruth River, and access to the Black Sea was denied until 1774, when Suvarov's victories over the Ottomans were ratified by the Treaty of Küçük Kaynarca. Russia had finally secured a warm-water port.* All others—St. Petersburg, Archangel, and Vladivostok—are frozen several months a year.

The right paw of the bear represents Potemkin's project to push south into the former Greek empire of the Byzantines. This 'Greek Project,' as it was called, represents an eastern *Reconquista*. The ostensible goal was to regain lost Christian territory in the Balkans. In the 19th century, this project was repackaged as Pan-Slavism, which, according to Engels, was 'nothing more'* than a pretext for taking Constantinople and opening the Straits for Russia's Black Sea Fleet. The left paw, or 'Eastern Project,' represents the push south into the weakening emirates of the old Silk Road, what are today collectively called the 'stans.' Both of these paws, the 'Greek' and the 'Eastern,' were seen by the British as lethal swats at the passage to India and India itself.

Britain had been warily watching Russian expansion since the 18th century. In 1791, William Pitt, the prime minister, tried to pass an ultimatum against Russia as it advanced into the crumbling Ottoman Empire, but the bill failed in Parliament. In the early 1830s, however, Britain's hand was forced when Mohammad Ali, the powerful pasha of Egypt, rebelled against the Ottoman sultan. This resulted in a long and drawn-out conflict that seemed likely to end in defeat for the Turks. The modernized Egyptian forces were far more organized than those of the Ottomans. Horrified at the prospect of a victory for the Egyptians, the British foreign secretary, Lord Palmerston, set to work in August 1839 to persuade France to agree to a treaty by which the two nations pledged to prop up the Turkish sultan. Palmerston—who thought in terms of buffer states—saw the Ottoman Empire as a necessary bulwark against the ambitions of Russia to dominate the Eastern Mediterranean through the Straits of Constantinople.

Control of the Straits had been an issue between East and West since the Trojan War. Troy grew rich controlling the western entrance, across from Gallipoli. Jason had to sail past* it to get to the Golden Fleece, as did the Greek traders to reach the rivers of Russia.

In the Crimean War of the 1850s, Britain and France allied to prevent Russia from seizing Constantinople and the Straits. At the outbreak of the First World War, Russia demanded the Straits* in return for supporting the allies by opening an Eastern Front. If the October Revolution of 1917 had not occurred, Russia would have achieved her millennial dream.

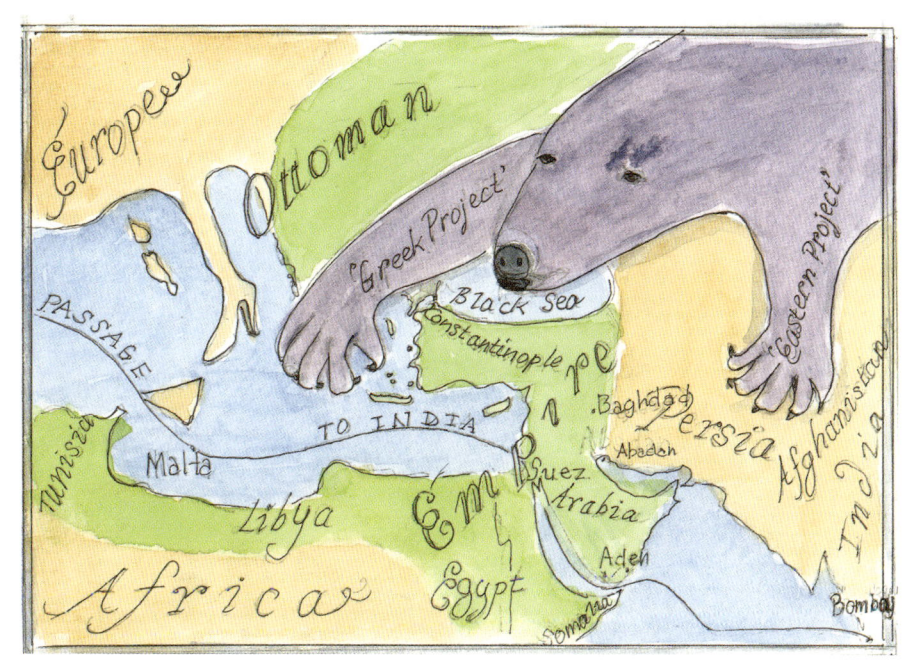

Gates of India The perceived Russian threat to the passage to India became a British obsession. This highly vulnerable link between Britain and the Jewel in the Crown* of her far-flung sea empire ran through the Ottoman Empire, down the Red Sea, and across the Indian Ocean to Bombay. British strategists thought in terms of what might be called the Gates of India:* Gibraltar, Malta, Suez, and Aden. With the outbreak of war in 1914, these gates were extended to include Iraq and Palestine.*

This obsession infused Halford Mackinder's original geopolitical theory of 1904, which would be revived in an altered version* by American planners during the Cold War. Mackinder thought that Russia—in command of the Heartland—was in a naturally far stronger geographical position than any sea power.* With her central railway system,* Russia, like a mechanized Mongol horde, would be able to project power at any point along the arc of her southern borders. On the other hand, the Royal Navy could project power only along the Monsoon Coastlands of the World Island, since the biggest gun on a dreadnought could reach no farther than 11 miles inland.

The navy was Britain's strategic weapon, but navies are huge consumers of fuel. Britain had plenty of coal, but oil is a better fuel for speed and ease of handling. Oil was discovered in 1901 in Persia, a British dependency; and the Anglo-Persian Oil Company (now BP) was formed in 1907 to extract it. The British government owned 100 percent of its shares, and the oil was to be dedicated to the navy. The government's decision to convert from coal to oil in 1912, made oil the world's most strategic commodity.

These fears were exaggerated: a full-scale Russian invasion of India, crossing 1,500 miles of mountains* and deserts, was highly unlikely. If Russia had any object in threatening India, it would have been to distract the British from Baku. Here, where oil had been known* to exist since antiquity in Azerbaijan, the 'Land of Fire,' the first oil well in the world was drilled in 1846. Fears on both sides were played out in the Great Game,* the struggle between Britain and Russia in the mountain passes of Afghanistan.

Russia
"Greek Project"
"Eastern Project"
Bristol
London
Crimea (1855)
Constantinople
Caspian Sea
Baku
"Great Game"
Europe
Balkans
Sarajevo 1914
PRO LINE
OTTOMAN EMPIRE
Mosul 1918
Damascus 1918
Basra 1914
Persia
Oil discovered 1907
Samarkand (1865)
Tashkent
Afghanistan
The Passage to India
Gib
Jerusalem 1917
Trucial States
Suez 1882
"The Gates of India"
Aden
India
Bombay
Africa
Indian Ocean

Fear of the Heartland led Britain into Afghanistan. The last paragraph of my *Labberton's Historical Atlas*, published in 1891, explains why.

Afghanistan

> England succeeded to the inheritance of the Great Mughul, who...never lost sight...that the master of the upper plateau of Afghanistan, commanding access from the passes of the north, is in fact the master of India....If England wants to keep her Anglo-Indian Empire, she ought to pursue the same policy as the Mughul—to take possession of Afghanistan, the true Northwestern Gate of India, of which the key is Herat.

The British vacillated between a 'forward' policy and a policy of 'masterly inaction.' For a period, Britain held Kabul, but in 1842 the garrison was forced out of its cantonment and sent on a 90-mile death march through the passes of the Hindu Kush when 16,000 men, women, and children were annihilated by treacherous tribesmen.

Under the guise of 'private travelers,' agents on both sides had been surreptitiously surveying* lands lying along the greatest mountain range in the world, until then utterly inaccessible to outsiders. As the Russians advanced farther and farther south—taking Tashkent in 1865 and Samarkand in 1868—the buffer between British India and the Russian-controlled zone to the north narrowed in places to less than 50 miles. Celebrated in Kipling's novel *Kim*, this 19th-century scramble for territory was the forerunner of the Cold War, which ended with the Soviet Union's retreat in 1987.

In an attempt to answer the Eastern Question, Afghanistan was created as a buffer zone* by a series of treaties* in the 1890s. Creating the thin Wakhan Corridor, its borders were extended as far as Tibet to ensure that Russian and British claims would not touch at any point. Later, in 1907, Russia and Britain agreed to a partition of Persia into zones of influence, north and south. Afghanistan is a borderland where a defender needs only to not lose a decisive battle and to wait for the invader to go—which public opinion at home will sooner or later force.

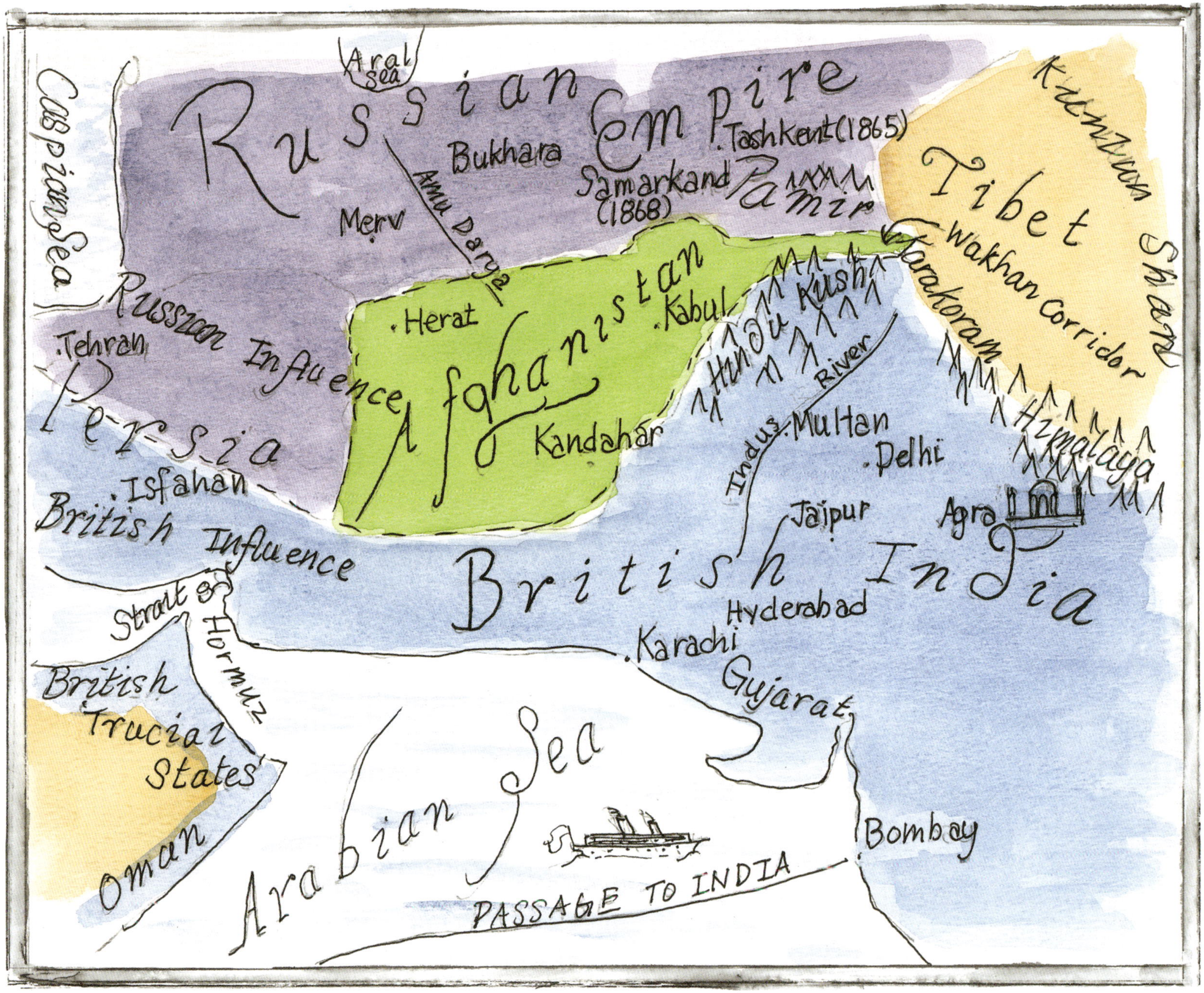

Aral Sea
Russian Empire
Caspian Sea
Bukhara
Tashkent (1865)
Samarkand (1868)
Pamir
Merv
Amu Darya
Tibet
Kunlun Shan
Wakhan Corridor
Karakoram
Russian Influence
Tehran
Herat
Kabul
Afghanistan
Hindu Kush
Persia
Kandahar
Indus River
Multan
Delhi
Himalaya
Isfahan
British Influence
Jaipur
Agra
British India
Strait of Hormuz
Hyderabad
Karachi
British Trucial States
Gujarat
Arabian Sea
Oman
Bombay
PASSAGE TO INDIA

THE EASTERN QUESTION FULL-BLOWN

Political Football   THE DESTRUCTIVE EFFECTS of public opinion on foreign policy* are well known. The Eastern Question is one of the best examples. Polarizing politics in Britain, it became a political football between Gladstone and Disraeli when Turkish massacres in the Balkans in the 1870s elicited Liberal outrage. The Eastern Question now presented itself full-blown and ultimately ended in the First World War with the collapse of empires East and West.

Essentially it came down to a battle between the Liberal, or 'Hellenophile,' party, represented by Gladstone, and the Conservative, or 'Turkophile,' party, represented by Disraeli. Schooled in classical Greek literature, the Hellenophiles had supported the Greek struggle for independence from the sultan in the 1820s; the Romantic poet Byron fought and died for this cause.* The Liberals saw the Turks as hopelessly cruel and lascivious oppressors of the many different peoples under their rule.

Unburdened by such sentiments, the Turkophiles saw the issue in terms of practical politics, or *realpolitik* in Bismarck's term. They were not lovers of the Ottomans per se but saw that—apart from the Russian threat—a thousand seeds of dissension were sown in the collapse of order in the Middle East. The Turkophiles did not seem to particularly object to an occasional massacre* to maintain that order. In 1876, however, a particularly brutal reprisal in Batak, Bulgaria, to suppress an independence movement, forced the abandonment of the British policy of support for the Ottoman Empire.

The same atrocities that were making headlines in London were used by Russia, which had feigned support of the Bulgarian movement, as the pretext to declare war on the Ottomans in 1877. Russian armies rapidly advanced almost to Constantinople, and their gains alarmed Britain.* Claims were adjusted at the Conference of Berlin in 1878.*

BISMARCK: Now, now boys! Let's have a conference in Berlin!
Russia is the rightful heir to the Old Man's estate.
Austria must have Bosnia. We defended Europe for centuries, after all!
Our policy, Mr. Gladstone, has been to support the Sultan, least his empire collapses & falls to the Tsar. We have already had to fight one war; we don't want to fight another.
But Dizzy, have you absolutely no principle? Aren't you outraged by the massacres? The Turks must be sent packing, bag & baggage!! I will insist upon it—ethically.
A POLITICAL FOOTBALL
The Eastern Question

Sandbox of Empire

The last prize of European colonial struggle was now up for grabs. The scramble for it became a free-for-all in what one might imagine as a sandbox of empire.

Britain Everyone blames us, but it was simply beyond our control. We tried to save the Ottomans, but the rise of Germany changed everything. We already had our empire, but the Kaiser wanted to play in the sandbox too…. When the War broke out and the Young Turks, who had seized power in Istanbul, joined the Germans and Austrians, we were forced to attack at Basra to protect our oil refinery on Abadan Island. One requires one's oil, one does … and after the disaster at Al-Kut,* we finally took Baghdad and Mosul. We had promised the Arabs self-rule in return for revolting against the Turks; and a new force, a Jewish lobby, demanded a homeland in Palestine for Jews, and we promised that, too.

France O perfidious Albion, you also promised us Syria, where we have traditions going back to the Crusades. While you were having your colonial holiday in the Middle East, we had the bloodiest war in history in our backyard. So we demanded some kind of compensation… *et évidemment* we wanted our fair share of the oil already known to exist in Iraq.

Austria When my over clever foreign minister* Aehrenthal annexed Bosnia in 1908, the long-expected war almost broke out. With the assassination of my heir six years later in Sarajevo, it really happened.

Russia We demanded Constantinople as our price for opening an Eastern Front, and would have gotten it* if the Bolshies hadn't surrendered and given up my European possessions…. Stalin got them back, Yeltsin gave them up, and Putin is now trying to get them back again.

Germany I just wanted to play with boats and trains. I was just as good as the other boys—better! … But my new navy threatened my uncle the English king, and my railroad to Baghdad threatened my cousin's husband, the tsar. Bismarck had warned me: in a party of five, don't be one of two against three; and never choose Austria over Russia. But somehow that's how it ended up, and we got stuck in the middle, and got encircled…. *Scheiße, eingekreist!* Maybe I shouldn't have fired the old boy.

PLAYGROUND
USA
COLD WAR
FSU
MINE!
MINE!
MINE!
MINE!
MINE!
GERMANY
RUSSIA
AUSTRIA
TRANSYLVANIA
MOLDAVIA
ROMANIA
BULGARIA
SERBIA
Sarajevo
BOSNIA
CROATIA
DALMATIA
ANATOLIA
CRIMEA
ARMENIA
Constantinople & the Straits
OTTOMAN EMPIRE
MACEDONIA
ALBANIA
GREECE
KURDISTAN
IRAQ
BRITAIN
TUNISIA
LYBIA
EGYPT
MAROC & SYRIE
SUDAN
PALESTINE
JORDAN
MECCA
FRANCE
THE LAST OTTOMAN
THE SANDBOX OF EMPIRE
"A PARTY OF FIVE"

In exile in Holland, the Kaiser walks around his estate, muttering to himself in English.*

Full Steam Ahead!

Kaiser So what if I had a chip on my shriveled arm.* I'd show 'em. They all had their empires. We were late getting into the sandbox and we needed our place in the sun. I was destined to rule, not my sick, weak, liberal father. My grandmother Queen Victoria told me to be a good boy and I tried ... but my uncle Bertie* always snubbed me, so I built a yacht to beat him at Cowes and a navy to beat him on the high seas.

When France tried to grab Morocco, I stood up for Moroccan independence. When the Boers stood up against the British, I supported President Kruger in a telegram. When war finally broke out, I gave Austria a 'blank check' for what she wanted to do with Serbia, and I tried to get the Mexicans to attack the U.S. in the rear. Earlier, when Britain abandoned her support of the sultan, I steamed right into the middle of the Eastern Question with my Baghdadbahn*—but this was just the natural continuation of the traditional German push to the east, our *Drang nach Osten*. In between the land empire of Russia and the sea empire of Britain, I would drive my new train empire of German engineering and industry, run by meticulous Swabians.

We needed raw materials for our burgeoning economy. We knew there was oil out there, just bubbling up out of the ground near Mosul. I thought Herr Daimler and Herr Benz could do something with its by-product, gasoline.* Let the Russians have Central Asia, let the Americans have the Midwest, let them all fight over Africa, let Leopold have the Congo, that heart of darkness.* We Germans will have the cradle of the world for our colony. We will send out our archaeologists and philologists—after all, we are the best in the world in these fields!—and they can do a little spying on the side.

I will make friends with the sultan—who could do with a friend—and then I will have all the Mohammedan forces at my disposal; I will build him a railroad with Krupps steel and get him to declare a *jihad* against everyone except us. Only by blood and iron can the Eastern Question be resolved! Full steam ahead!*

Berlin
GERMANY
Poland
Moscow
Full Steam Ahead!
RUSSIA
AUSTRIA
Carpatia
Bulgaria
Ramania
Moldova
Ukraine
Crimea
Azov
RUSSIA
Caspian
Sarajevo
Bosnia
Herzegovina
Serbia
Pola
Black Sea
Oil
Baku
SOCIETE IMPERIALE OTTOMANE DES CHEMINS DE FER DE BAGHDAD
Macedonia
Albania
Constantinople
Colchis
Caucasian Gate
Golden Fleece of Trade
Persia
ITALY
Ithaca
GREECE
Smyrna
Konya
TAURUS
Oil
Mosul
Rhodes
Crete
CYPRUS
LEB
PALESTINE
HAI SPUR
Aleppo
Baghdad
Oil
Basra
PASSAGE TO INDIA
Abadan Island
Suez
Cyrenaica
Libya
Cairo
Medina
Gulf

Origin of the War

Lenin had predicted* that after the 'imperialist' powers had divided up the undiscovered and unexplored parts of the world, a series of world wars would follow. 'What means other than war could there be under capitalism to overcome the disparity between the development of productive forces and the accumulation of capital on the one side, and the division of colonies and spheres of influence ... on the other?' That is one way of seeing the War's origin, one of the most disputed questions in history. More specifically, it could be seen as the inevitable clash between the Great Powers over the remains of the Ottoman Empire: by definition, the Eastern Question.

Since the days of the Teutonic knights, Germany's only option for expansion had been eastward: the *Drang nach Osten,* or drive to the east. This drive conflicted with Russia's ambitions west and south to regain Christian territory in the Balkans. The German plan to extend the Orient Express to Baghdad—the Baghdadbahn with connections at Konya to the Chemins de Fer Ottomanes d'Anatolie—threatened Russian expansionist aspirations. Earlier, in a similar expansionist clash in Africa, the French and British had almost come to blows at Fashoda in 1898, but in the sequel, the German threat made 'strange bedfellows'* of France, Britain, and Russia.

The collapse of Russia toward the end of the war technically ended the Eastern Question, but it asked another question: what would the victors do with the spoils? The victors were Britain, France, Italy, and a new power, the United States, which was as violently opposed, in principle, to imperialism as was Bolshevik Russia, in principle. The twelfth of President Wilson's famous Fourteen Points called for the 'autonomous development' of the provinces of the Ottoman Empire, but their dismemberment into British and French 'mandates' only created new questions. Ironically, this was foreseen by Mark Sykes, the architect of its eventual partition. He had warned the House of Commons in 1914 that the 'disappearance of the Ottoman Empire [will] be the first step towards the disappearance of our own.'

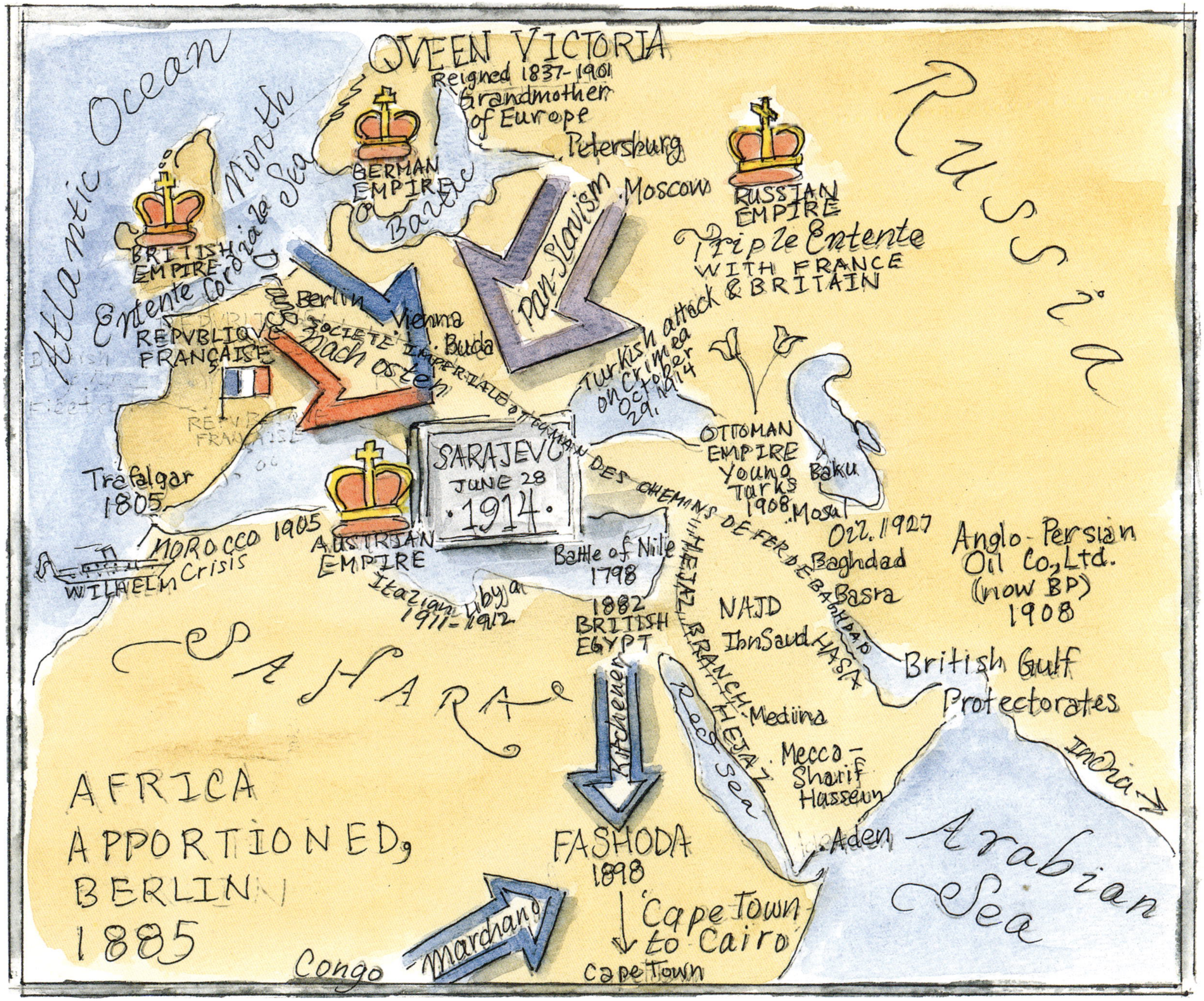
QUEEN VICTORIA
Reigned 1837-1901
Grandmother of Europe
Atlantic Ocean
North Sea
Baltic
Petersburg
Moscow
RUSSIA
GERMAN EMPIRE
RUSSIAN EMPIRE
BRITISH EMPIRE
Entente Cordiale
Drang nach Osten
Pan-Slavism
Triple Entente
WITH FRANCE & BRITAIN
Berlin
Vienna
Buda
REPUBLIQUE FRANÇAISE
SOCIETE IMPERIALE OTTOMAN DES CHEMINS DE FER DE BAGHDAD
Turkish attack on Crimea October 29, 1914
SARAJEVO
JUNE 28
1914
OTTOMAN EMPIRE
Young Turks
1908
Baku
Mosul
Oct. 1927
Trafalgar
1805
MOROCCO 1905
Crisis
WILHELM
AUSTRIAN EMPIRE
Battle of Nile
1798
Italian Libya
1911-1912
1882
BRITISH
EGYPT
HEJAZ BRANCH
HEJAZ
HASA
NAJD
Ibn Saud
Baghdad
Basra
Anglo-Persian Oil Co., Ltd.
(now BP)
1908
British Gulf Protectorates
SAHARA
Kitchener
Red Sea
Medina
Mecca-
Sharif
Hasseun
Aden
India
Arabian Sea
AFRICA APPORTIONED, BERLIN 1885
FASHODA
1898
Cape Town to Cairo
Cape Town
Marchand
Congo

Imagine that an epic poet were to sing of the long-expected doom of the Ottoman Empire, played out in the landscape of Homer, where wily Odysseus was caught between Scylla and Charybdis.

What Was the Cause?

What was the cause that brought the Ottomans into the War
on the German side? What was it that prompted them to take
such a fatal step? Was it Winston Churchill's confiscation
at the beginning of the war of the two brand-new dreadnoughts
being built in British yards for the Turkish navy?
Was it Admiral Souchon's exceeding his orders
and sailing for Istanbul at the outbreak of hostilities,
instead of returning to the Austrian naval port at Pola?

 Was it Souchon's audacity in eluding British pursuit
by sailing his two ships, the *Goeben* and *Breslau*,
into Messina's strait in the fog, and then steaming out
to the east and the Dardanelles* while the British patrolled
to the west of three-cornered Sicily, expecting him there?
Was he inspired by wily Odysseus in the same straits,
when caught between the monster Scylla and Charybdis?

 Was it Enver Pasha who allowed him to sail past Troy
and anchor at Çanakkale, while denying passage
to the two pursuing British dreadnoughts, which had tarried
at Valletta expecting him to double back to the west?

 Or was it the Germans' offer of Souchon's ships
in compensation for the two Turkish dreadnoughts
the British had commandeered that decided the Young Turks
to allow the German ships to stay at Constantinople,
thereby partly compromising Turkish neutrality?
Was it the donning of Turkish uniforms by Souchon

and his crews that pushed events even further toward the brink?

    Was it the subsequent German victory at Tannenberg,*
which deluded the Young Turk leaders into thinking
they could create a 'Pan-Turanian' nation from East to West,
uniting all the Turkic people into one great state?

    Finally, was it Souchon's precipitating war with Russia
by sailing across the Black Sea and shelling Odessa,
Sebastopol, and the naval base of Novorossiysk,
that irrevocably brought the Ottoman Empire
into the War on the side of the Central Powers
in order that the long-expected doom might be accomplished?

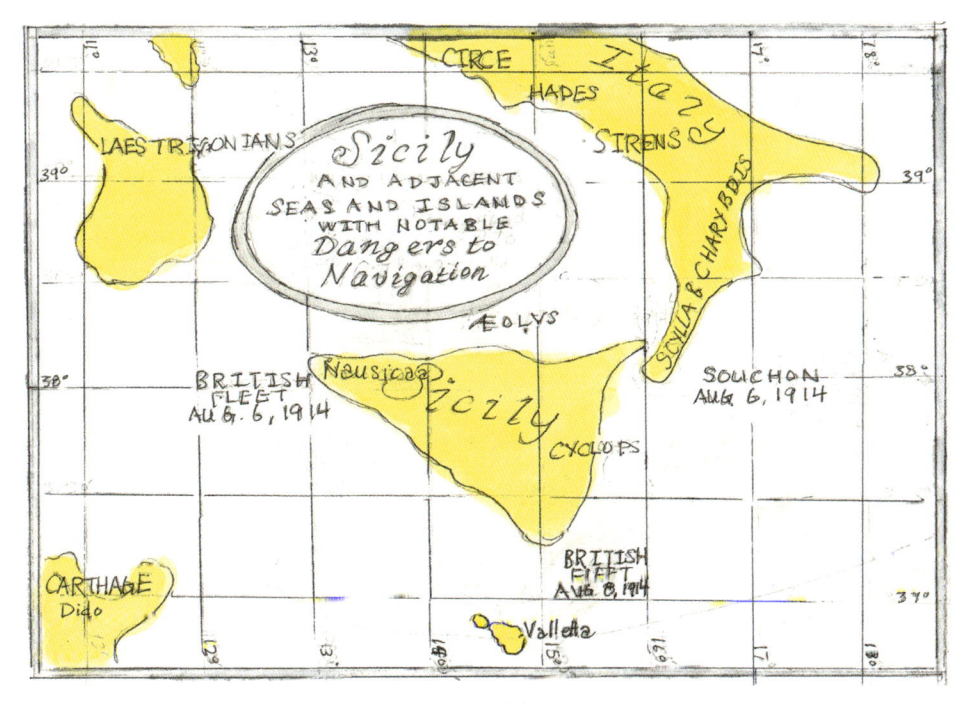

Butcher Block of Empires

After the War, the treaty tables were the butcher blocks on which the carcasses of old empires where carved up by diplomats into new nations. It was also the very end of the colonial expansion of Europe, which started in 1099 with the capture of Jerusalem by the Crusaders and ended in 1947 with Indian independence and the creation of the state of Israel by UN resolution in the same year.

Lenin, of course, was not at the table, nor were Napoleon, the Kaiser, or Hitler.* I have shown them all anachronistically standing and watching enviously or angrily as France and Britain divide the spoils of victory. They could only do this because Russia had temporarily stepped offstage.

While the Great Powers were meeting in Paris, the Bolsheviks were in Moscow starting the Cold War.* They had expected that the workers in the 'bourgeois-imperialist–capitalist' West would rise and extend the Revolution to the whole world. A revolution almost did happen in Germany, but as Lenin is said to have remarked, 'The Germans couldn't even storm a train station without buying tickets first.' Nevertheless, the resulting weakness of the Weimar Republic in the 1920s led shortly to the rise of Hitler, a violent swing to the Left provoking an equally violent swing to the Right.

The Bolsheviks published the secret treaties negotiated during the war between the Great Powers. One treaty would have given the tsar the long-sought prize of Constantinople, demanded for maintaining an Eastern Front. Another of the secret treaties was the Sykes-Picot Agreement of 1916, under which France would have Syria, which at that time included Palestine and Mosul. During the war, Britain had also vaguely promised the Arabs a nation as the price for revolting against the Turks, and with the Balfour Declaration promised Jews a 'homeland'* in Palestine.

All these conflicting promises were sorted out in a series of treaties after the Peace Conference in Paris. At San Remo in 1920, Britain backed away from its promise of an independent state for Arabs when it gave Syria to France. At the Cairo Conference of 1921—Winston Churchill, colonial secretary, presiding—France got half of any oil discovered at Mosul, which was then attached to a British mandate for Iraq. Britain got the other half of the oil and a free hand to create the Jewish homeland in Palestine, and a mandate for Jordan. The infamous Sykes-Picot also had provisions for the partition of the heartland of the Ottoman Empire in Anatolia. Mustafa Kemal had other ideas.

Breaking of Sèvres

The Treaty of Sèvres, the proposed partition of the Anatolian heartland of the Ottoman Empire, was one of the last acts of the European colonial enterprise. The 'Breaking of Sèvres' was Mustafa Kemal's overthrow of this treaty and the start of the breaking of Sykes-Picot.* The occupation of Constantinople by the Allies in 1918 was the reversal of the historical process that began with the rise of Islam in the 7th century. In May 1919, another historical process began: the colonial revolt.

The fragile Treaty of Sèvres—which was supposed to have answered the Eastern Question—had been signed by representatives of the defeated Ottoman Empire in the Paris suburb famous for the manufacture of porcelain. Its terms, dictated by the victors, called for the partition of Anatolia: mandates for Greece, Italy, and France; an international zone of the Straits and Constantinople (then occupied by Allied forces); an independent nation of Armenia;* and for Turkey, a portion of the Black Sea coast and a wedge of territory including the present-day capital, Ankara.

Mustafa Kemal was the hero of Gallipoli, the only undefeated Ottoman general. He was not one of the discredited Young Turks who had brought disaster on the Empire and fled after the War. On May 19, 1919, defying the Great Powers* then meeting in Paris, he landed at the little port city of Samsun on the south coast of the Black Sea. Between that moment and October 29, 1923, when his representatives signed a renegotiated Treaty of Lausanne, he raised an army, ejected the invading* forces of Italy, France, and Greece; exiled the sultan; began the secularization of the state; romanized the alphabet; and forbade the wearing of the fez. In 1924, he abolished the caliphate and exiled the rest of the Ottoman royal family, each with $5,000 and a one-way ticket on the Orient Express. He was Atatürk, 'Father of the Turks.'

On September 18, 1922, the Greeks were driven into the sea at Smyrna and killed as the town burned. For them it was a day of tragedy, their final expulsion from the Ionian coast, the birthplace of Herodotus and Aristotle. For the Turks, it was a day of triumph. Says a Greek friend in Istanbul, 'There is no truth, only versions of it.'

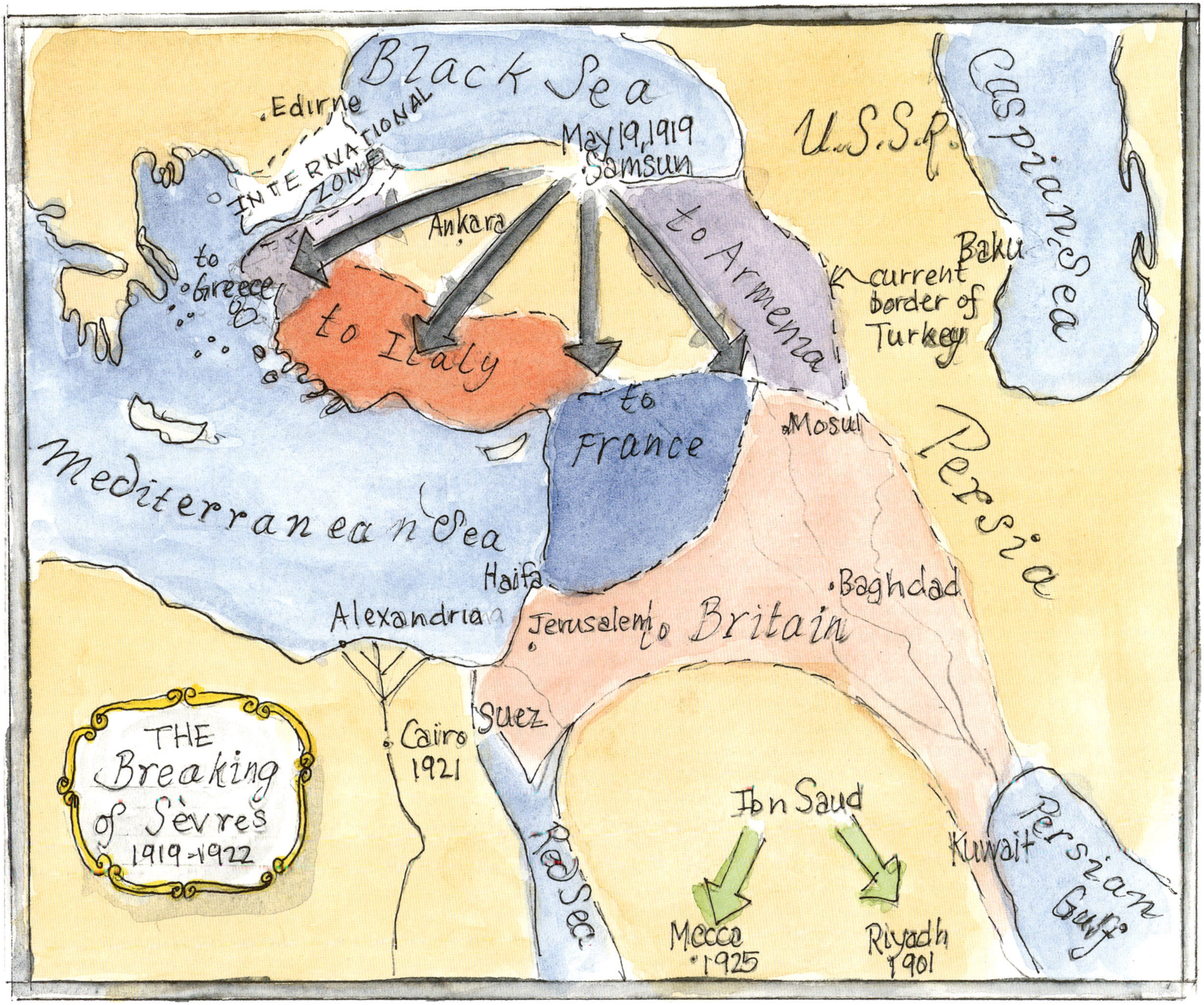
Black Sea
Edirne
INTERNATIONAL ZONE
May 19, 1919
Samsun
U.S.S.R.
Caspian Sea
Ankara
to Greece
to Italy
to Armenia
Baku
current border of Turkey
to France
Mosul
Persia
Mediterranean Sea
Haifa
Baghdad
Alexandria
Jerusalem
to Britain
Suez
Cairo
1921
THE Breaking of Sèvres 1919-1922
Ibn Saud
Red Sea
Kuwait
Persian Gulf
Mecca
1925
Riyadh
1901

Mighty Caesar's Heirs

The House of Caesar had long been in need of demolition and was not fussy about permits or insurance. Neither the fall of the House in the West in 476, with the deposition of the ironically named Romulus Augustulus, nor the fall of the House in the East, with the death of the equally ironically named Constantine IV in 1453, stopped rulers from claiming the deeds to parts of the condemned and fragmented fabric of the ancient structure, as well as the title of Mighty Caesar.* The last ones to do so—the German kaiser, the Austrian emperor, the Russian tsar, and the Ottoman sultan—were all overthrown from 1917 to 1922. The last ruler to claim the title of 'Mighty Caesar' was the also ironically named Sultan Mehmet VI, deposed in 1922.*

The title of Roman emperor has an interesting, if somewhat confusing, history. With the end of the Empire in the West, the Eastern emperor claimed to be the sole possessor of the title. The pope crowned Charlemagne in AD 800 so that there would be a Western emperor, but the Eastern emperor refused to acknowledge this 'cross-gartered German barbarian' as such. With the extinction of the Eastern Empire in 1453, the German Holy Roman emperor claimed to be the only Roman emperor. From then on, the Eastern Empire came to be known in the West as the Byzantine Empire,* but the Byzantines never referred to themselves as 'Byzantines,' but always as Romans. To the Arabs and Turks, they were also the Romans, or Rumi, and their empire was Rum, or Rome. In 1547, the Russian tsars also asserted their rights to the title of Eastern emperor, claiming that Moscow was the Third Rome.

After defeating the Hapsburgs at Austerlitz in 1806, Napoleon abolished the Holy Roman Empire, having earlier (1804) seized the title of emperor for himself. Napoleon III* reclaimed the title in 1852 and then lost it to the Germans in 1871, when Bismarck created the German Empire as the Second Reich. Kaiser Wilhelm II became emperor in 1888. The ironically named* Karl became the last Hapsburg emperor in 1916 and was deposed in 1918. His son served in the European Parliament and died in 2011.

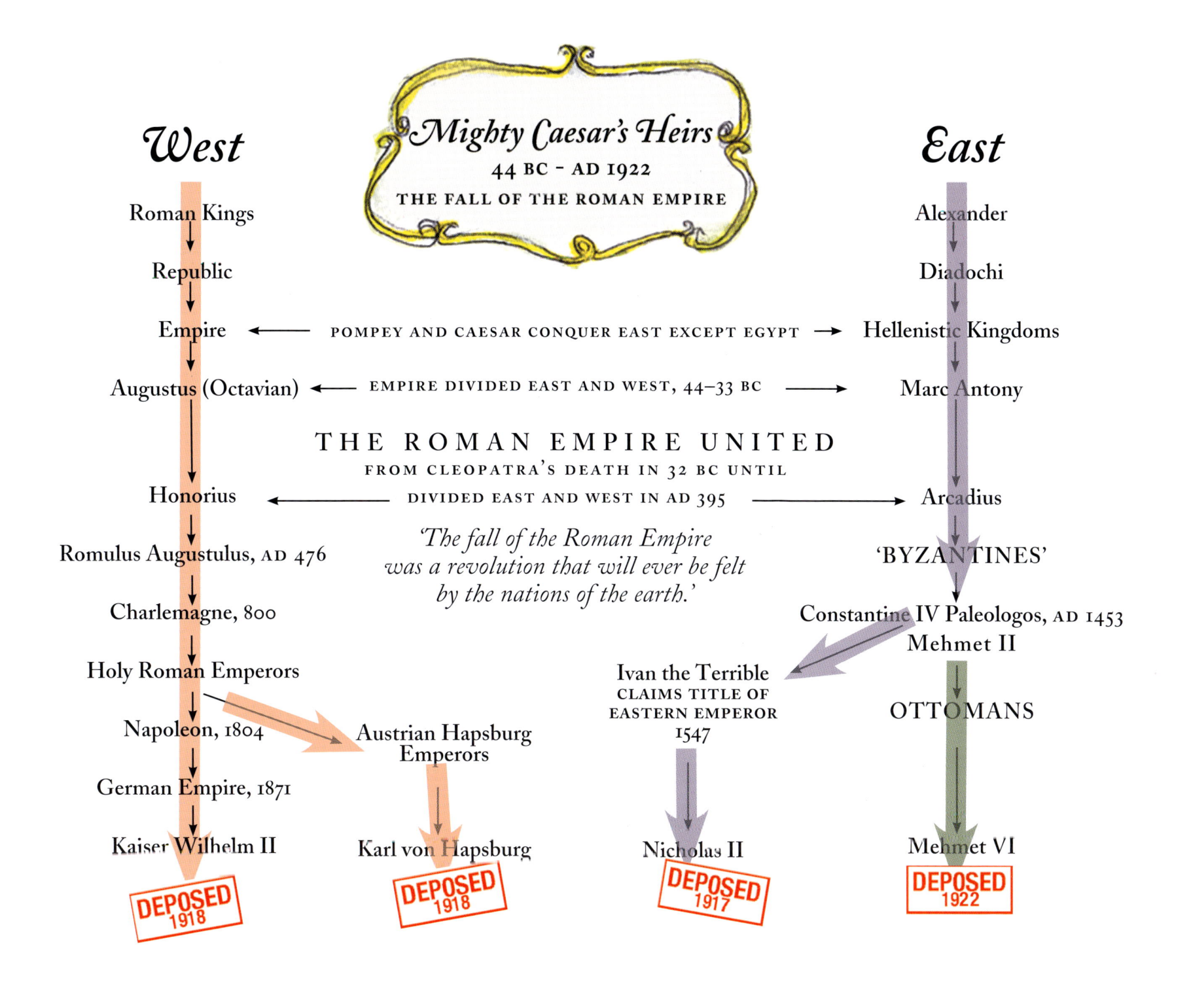

Mighty Caesar's Heirs
44 BC – AD 1922
THE FALL OF THE ROMAN EMPIRE

West

- Roman Kings
- Republic
- Empire ← POMPEY AND CAESAR CONQUER EAST EXCEPT EGYPT →
- Augustus (Octavian) ← EMPIRE DIVIDED EAST AND WEST, 44–33 BC →

THE ROMAN EMPIRE UNITED
FROM CLEOPATRA'S DEATH IN 32 BC UNTIL
DIVIDED EAST AND WEST IN AD 395

- Honorius
- Romulus Augustulus, AD 476

'The fall of the Roman Empire was a revolution that will ever be felt by the nations of the earth.'

- Charlemagne, 800
- Holy Roman Emperors
- Napoleon, 1804 → Austrian Hapsburg Emperors
- German Empire, 1871
- Kaiser Wilhelm II — **DEPOSED 1918**
- Karl von Hapsburg — **DEPOSED 1918**

East

- Alexander
- Diadochi
- Hellenistic Kingdoms
- Marc Antony
- Arcadius
- 'BYZANTINES'
- Constantine IV Paleologos, AD 1453
- Mehmet II
- Ivan the Terrible CLAIMS TITLE OF EASTERN EMPEROR 1547
- OTTOMANS
- Nicholas II — **DEPOSED 1917**
- Mehmet VI — **DEPOSED 1922**

THE COLD WAR

Years Between the Wars

THE FIRST WORLD WAR brought down the lofty tower of the old order. Out of the rubble, two opposing systems for the organization of society—two new orders—presented themselves in the East and the West: Communism and Capitalism. The great struggle between them would have to wait until after the Second World War. Meanwhile, in the years between the wars, the two future superpowers, the U.S. and the Soviet Union, withdrew into isolation. One might imagine them as boxers in a ring* before the fight begins, sitting in their corners.

In Russia, the Revolution had been isolated to 'socialism in one country.' Contrary to Marxist theory, it had taken place in a country without much of an industrial working class. Under the NEP (New Economic Plan), Lenin had to allow a certain degree of small-scale capitalism to keep the economy going. After him, Stalin adjusted reality to suit the theory, forcibly industrializing the country and enslaving millions for his factories. For two decades the country was essentially closed to the outside world.

Rejecting the League of Nations, the U. S. also withdrew into isolation, refusing to take on the role that the country had briefly assumed at the end of the First World War when, like a *deus ex machina*, the new world power had dropped from the sky to resolve the plot and extricate the characters from an impossible situation.

Allied with the West in the Second World War, afterward the Soviets positioned themselves as defenders of what then came to be called the Third World in its struggle against the 'bourgeois-capitalist-imperialist' West. In Cold War terminology, the First World was the West, the sea power that is heir to the Western Roman Empire. The Second World was the Soviet Union, the land power of the Heartland that is heir to the Eastern Roman as well as to the Mongol Empire.

"Before the fight"

THE YEARS BETWEEN THE WARS
1919 – 1947

ROOSEVELT

STALIN

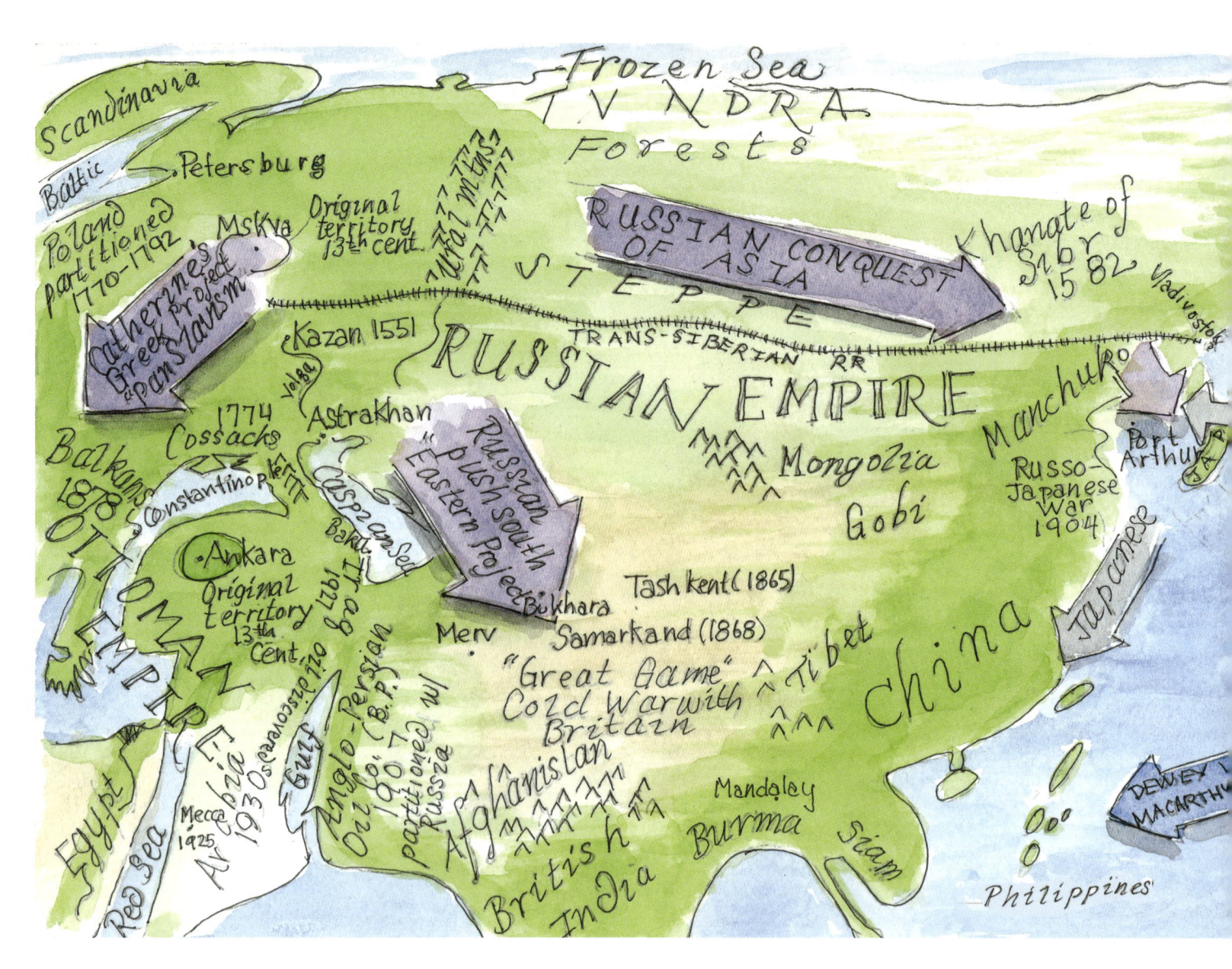

Russia and the United States: Geopolitically

Geopolitically—if not politically—the U.S. and Russia are like a pair of brothers separated at birth. They both are continent-spanning giants; they both command the steppe land in the Northern Temperate Zone. In the 19th century, expanding in contrary directions, east and west, they encounter the same ocean, the Pacific.

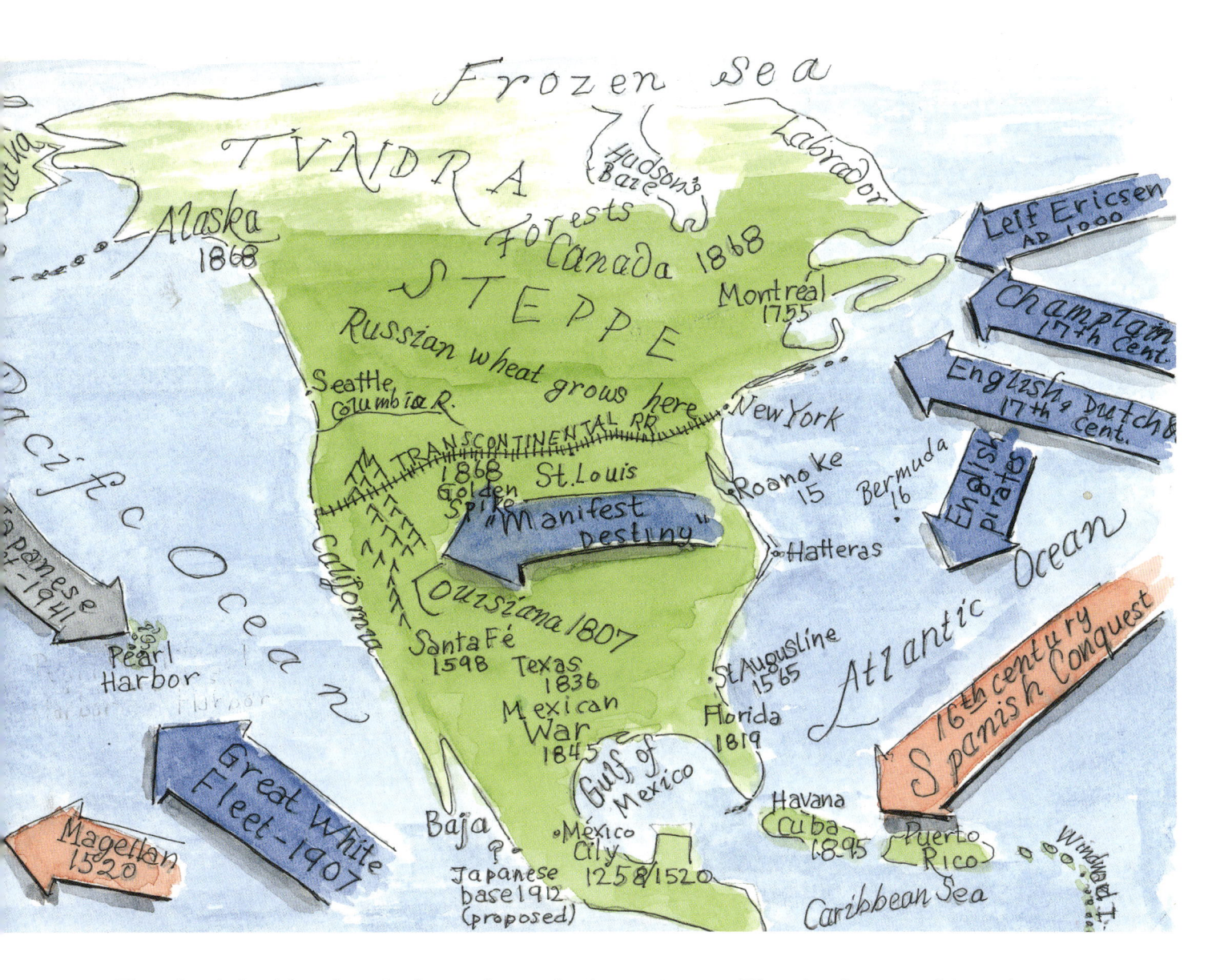

They both build railroads, keys that unlock continents. They both expand into the territories of weak neighbors: Russia into the weak emirates, now the 'stans,' the U.S. into the lands of the native peoples and the former Hapsburg Empire in Mexico. Vladimir Nabokov celebrated this strange kinship in his novel *Ada*.*

Russia and the United States: Politically

Ideologically, Russia and the U.S. couldn't be more different, on the surface. Below the surface, however, there exist parallels. For example, except in the sense of having style, 'class' is a bad word in the U.S., and yet that word united the U.S. and U.S.S.R., for both proposed to create classless societies that would incorporate the workers into a system from which, under the old order, they had been excluded.

Karl Marx read history as a socioeconomic struggle in Hegelian terms* of thesis, antithesis, and synthesis; but his reading of the future was faulty. One of the three founders of the modern discipline of sociology,* Marx extrapolated backwards from his own time in the mid-19th century, when society was indeed cut into a thesis and antithesis: the 'haves' and the 'have-nots.'* Perhaps he was tempted by the logical fallacy,* *post hoc ergo propter hoc*—the false argument that, because something took place before something else, the first was the cause of the second.

In any case, however interesting his reading of European history may be, the dialectic famously did not work out as he predicted. The revolution took place in a largely rural pre-industrial society, the state did not 'wither away,' and Lenin's 'dictatorship of the proletariat' under Stalin quickly turned into the dictatorship of the party. In the end, instead of the workers of the world defeating the bourgeois capitalists, the capitalist system defeated the 'failed workers' state.'* Into the resultant power vacuum in the East, an entirely unexpected antithesis has flowed, the revolt of Islam.

The capitalist system has succeeded far better than communism at what the latter proposed to do: provide the greatest good for the greatest number of people. Capitalism achieved the transfer of the ownership of the means of production to the workers through IRAs, insurance, pension plans, mortgages. With its lure of material goods, the capitalist system tends to coopt its enemies, thesis gobbling antithesis. As Marx wrote in 1848, 'The Revolution is dead. Long live the Revolution!' The revolution never succeeded: the Paris Commune, the Soviet Union, the Chinese Experiment all failed—yet the idea of the revolution still lives on in the Fifth International.*

HISTORY AS CLASS WAR

16th
FEUDAL LORDS & CHURCH v. KING & BOURGEOISIE

Wars of Religion

17th
ABSOLUTIST 'WESTPHALIA' STATE v. RISING BOURGEOISIE, EARLY CAPITALISM

Quis regis...

DUTCH EAST INDIAMAN

Glorious Rev.
French Rev.
American Revs.

18th
Louis XIV

NATIONALIST BOURGEOIS QUASI-DEMOCRATIC STATE v. NEW WORKING CLASS — 1st & 2nd INTERNATIONALS

"Rights of Man"

Communism & Socialism

The flag of the revolution

19th
"Satanic Mills"

Rev's of 1848
RUSSIAN REVOLUTION
2 WORLD WARS

20th
CAPITALIST BOURGEOIS DEMOC'C WEST v. COMMUNIST STATE CAPITALIST TOTALITARIAN EAST

'Free World'   'Soviet Bloc'

Cold War

"TRIUMPH" OF CAPITALISM
GLOBALIZATION
"FUNCTIONING CORE"
"LESSER INCLUDEDS"

WORLD REVOLUTION
TERRORISM
ANTI-GLOBALIZATION
"5th INTERNATIONAL"
NON-INTEGRATION GAP

21st
Symbols of world trade or the 'red apple'?

New War

CAR BOMB

Passing of the Baton

In the succession of states, there is no question that the U.S. inherited the leadership of the West.* One might imagine this as the passing of a baton from one runner to another in a relay race, across the Atlantic from an aging Europe to a young and relatively inexperienced United States. As the new leader of the West, the U.S. inherited the role of being anti-Communist and thus, by Soviet definition, imperialist.*

After the Bolsheviks seized power in Russia in 1917, they expected the revolution would spread to the West. When this did not happen, it became apparent that the revolution was not the international revolution of Marxist theory, having been limited to 'socialism in one country.'* In reaction, Lenin founded the Third International, or 'Comintern,' to spread the revolution to the colonies (and after the Second World War to the former colonies) of the imperialist powers from which they derived so much wealth. The Comintern was the natural continuation of Potemkin's project* of Russian expansion. These former colonies of the Western powers now came to be known as the Third World, and the Great Game of the 19th century continued to be fought as the Cold War of the 20th. Defined as the containment of Russian expansion, the Cold War can be seen as the continuation of the Eastern Question, a Great Game II.

Communism proved far more exportable to the East than to the West, and merged with the anticolonial movement. Anticolonial leaders and the Soviets shared a common goal and had a common enemy. The founding of the Comintern was essentially a declaration of war on all existing governments. Officially abandoned at Tehran in 1943, Nikita Khrushchev re-embraced it in 1961, pledging support for 'wars of national liberation' throughout the world beginning with China, the first Comintern country.

The struggle of the West now became a counter-Comintern project: to prevent the spread of the revolution in the Third World.

It is generally accepted that the baton was passed at the time of the Suez Crisis of 1956. In that year, President Nasser nationalized the Suez Canal; Israel invaded Egypt; Britain and France sent armed forces to retake the canal; and the United Nations forced them to withdraw. Citing the principle of 'noninterference' in the affairs of other nations, President Eisenhower threatened to destroy the British currency by dumping the pound on the currency market. Afterward, the British Foreign Office cabled the State Department in Washington saying, in effect, 'It's all yours, boys.' This was the last time* that the former 'Great Powers' resorted to gunboat diplomacy; now it was the U.S.'s turn to surreptitiously work toward the same ends. In fact, it had already done so three years earlier, in 1953. Because of the threat of both the nationalization of the Anglo-Persian Oil Co. (now BP) and of Soviet influence, in its first successful coup the CIA had overthrown the prime minister of Iran, Mohammad Mossadegh.

Thus, three years before Suez, the force of events had already constrained the U.S. to abandon its own stated principles* of self-determination and noninterference. The contradictory actions of 1953 and 1956 seem to exemplify *the* classic moral conflict* between what is 'right' and what is expedient.

This conflict has bedeviled American foreign policy since the end of the Second World War: in Korea, Vietnam, Latin America, and now in the Middle East. This is the same conflict that bedeviled Britain in the 19th century and led it happily to pass the baton in the 20th.

A Delicate Balance Upset

Whatever else it might have been, the Cold War represented an effective balance of power. Like two fat boys on a seesaw, no matter how big they were, they balanced. Even with an arms race, the Cold War constituted peace and could be fought by proxy with conventional weapons. As an extra benefit, it provided a great background for spy novels. But when one of the boys fell off, the other went flying.

The abject failure of communism and the triumph of capitalism has left seemingly only one system for the organization of society. To be a sole superpower, without check or restraint on its policies, is a perilous role to play—as Thucydides demonstrated* in the second book of history. Without the collapse of the Soviet Union, the U.S. probably could not have invaded Iraq or Afghanistan. As Vladimir Putin said in 2014, "After the dissolution of bipolarity on the planet, we no longer have stability."

One has to be careful when one kills a dragon: its blood can kill you. The Soviet Union collapsed in 1991 but, like a dead dragon, it spilled the poisonous blood of world revolution. It is one of the turning points of history: the beginning of what one might call a New War.

The 17th-century British political philosopher Thomas Hobbes characterized the Roman Catholic Church as the ghost of the Roman Empire, 'entombed on the throne thereof.' Just so the ghost of the Comintern—the spirit of world revolution against the capitalist West—lies like the body of a dead dragon over the world.

The death throes of the Soviet Union began in the mountain passes of Afghanistan. The withdrawal of Soviet forces in complete failure in 1987 led to the fall of the Berlin Wall two years later and then, in 1991, to the collapse of the Soviet regime.

The U.S. had supported the insurgents, among them Osama bin Laden. As a former U.S. ambassador* to Pakistan wrote, 'The Afghan war did for militant Islam what the Spanish Civil War did for the Communists. It gave the veterans an esprit de corps, it radicalized them and gave them a sense of further mission, and with the Soviets gone, the freedom fighter's mission now turned westward.' As Benazir Bhutto,* former president of Pakistan, wrote, 'They had defeated one superpower. Why not another?' Thus were sown the seeds of the New War, a Great Game III.

Fate
Power
Vacuums
the Dusty
Old Oriental

It is said that President George H. W. Bush averted and that his son brought on the overthrow of Saddam Hussein, but neither could the father avert nor the son bring on something other than what Fate—or historical necessity—decrees.

Without the power vacuum left by the collapse of the Soviet Union in 1991, the U.S. could never have invaded Kuwait to eject Saddam's troops during the Gulf War in the early 1990s; nor could she have engaged in Yugoslavia to stop the bloodshed in the same decade; nor supported the democratic movements in Georgia, Armenia, and Kurdistan; nor brought her fleet into the Black Sea; nor could she have invaded Afghanistan or Iraq in 2001 and 2003.

Into the new power vacuum left by the weakness of the Iraqi state and a civil war in Syria, Sunni Isis (the Islamic State of Iraq and the Levant) and Shia Iran have moved. With the collapse of power in Kiev, Russia has moved into Crimea. Into the vacuum left by the overthrow of Gaddafi, terrorist cells have risen in Saharan Africa. After the death of the dictator Tito, Yugoslavia broke up.

Without the demise of the Ottoman Empire, the West could not have created the modern 'mess' of the Middle East nor retaken Palestine. With the vacuum left in Istanbul after the revolt of the Young Turks in 1908, Austria annexed Bosnia, which led to the First World War seven years later. Into the vacuum left after the decline of the Arabs in the 11th century and before the rise of the Ottomans, the Crusaders moved into Palestine and Syria. Into the vacuum left by the declining Western Roman Empire moved the barbarians—the Goths, Visigoths, and Vandals—with well-known effect.

A millennium and a half before,* a vacuum arose on Assyria's western periphery with the collapse of the Mitanni state in present-day northern Iraq and Syria—a vacuum into which Assyria moved in 1200 BC and into which Isis moved in 2014.

Great powers create and sustain order, promoting stability and toleration. Perhaps they were created by conquests and sustained by oppression, but their fragmentation creates disorder, strife, war: what Fate oft times decrees.

Fate, in the form of a cleaning lady, power vacuums the dusty old oriental.

IV. New Conflicts, Old Questions

*…historians are like deaf men answering
questions that no one has asked.*

— LEO TOLSTOY

THE EAST STRIKES BACK

Revolt of Islam

IMAGINE THE WEST as a triumphant Crusader who has been surprised—like Roland in the narrow pass of Roncesvalles—turning his back on his defeated and forgotten foe. The Saracens have found renewed confidence in their faith and a new weapon, 'a sword of oil.'* New conflicts ask old questions.

The Revolt of Islam* grew out of the 20th-century anticolonial struggles that were fostered by the revolutionary movements spread throughout the world by the Comintern. The roots of Islamic renewal and radicalism, however, can be traced back to the 18th century, when a purifying antiforeign movement in Arabia called Wahhabism became allied with the Ibn Saud family. In the 19th century, Jamal-ad-Din al-Afghani (1838–1897) was 'less interested in theology* than he was in organizing Muslim response to Western pressure.' Al-Afghani's movement was taken up by Sultan Abdül Hamid II, who invited him to Constantinople. The sultan, who had reasserted his title of caliph, sought to use al-Afghani for pan-Islamic propaganda.

In India, revolt began with what the British called the Great Mutiny of 1857, but which Indians call the First War of Independence. Originally a united Hindu-Muslim movement, it later split along religious lines, a split that led to the Partition of India in 1947 and the creation of Pakistan in the same year. With the breakup of the Ottoman Empire, Turkish nationalists, Arab nationalists, Islamists, Zionists, and Baathists, all acting under the rubric of self-determination, brought the East to its greatest state of fragmentation in 3,000 years. At the Versailles Peace Conference, the leader of the Khilifat, the Indian pan-Islamic movement, stated before Lloyd George, 'Recent actions* of allied powers are likely to give rise to feelings that will be difficult to restrain, and which would be very dangerous to the peace of the world.'

THE REVOLT OF ISLAM
Ahhh! Mission Accomplished!
O foolish knight Dost thou think that I have forgotten thee!
OIL

Struggles between nations are often struggles for limited resources. The 'geo' in geopolitics means in Greek the earth, the geology of what's in or on top of it—or in the strata of what might be imagined as an Oil Farm.

Oil Farm   Only two events in the history of mankind are comparable to the discovery of gold and silver in Mexico and Peru after 1520. The first was the discovery of oil in Russia and in the United States* in the mid-19th century; the second was its discovery in the Middle East in the 20th—first in Persia, then in Iraq, Arabia, and Libya. In all these instances, unimaginably vast treasure was found buried in the earth.

In the First World War, 'the Allies floated to victory* on a wave of oil,' wrote the British foreign secretary Lord Curzon. He predicted that those who controlled the oil would rule the world. Most of this oil was supplied by the United States. The Second World War was certainly decided by oil. The soon-to-be superpowers won because they controlled it; Germany and Japan lost because they failed in their objectives* to get it.

The economy of the world is dependent on a stable price of oil and is therefore dependent upon a relative degree of peace in the Middle East. For instance, the Strait of Hormuz—dubbed the 'jugular vein of the West'*—must be kept open to fuel the global economy. In order to keep peace and stability in the region, the U.S. consumes huge amounts of oil for its military. In an anti-imperialist age, the U.S. thus once again has been drawn into fighting imperialist wars—against its stated principles.

Since the Standard Oil Company of California acquired its profitable concession in Saudi Arabia in 1933, Middle East oil has played a crucial role in America's geopolitical strategy. After 1945, motivated more by strategic interests than by its needs for fuel, the U.S. pursued a policy to exclude the Soviets from the Persian Gulf.

After the fall of the Soviet Union, the U.S. continued to protect Middle Eastern oil resources to undercut ambitions for regional hegemony of local powers such as Iraq and Iran. Protecting the flow of oil to global markets serves as a means of maintaining American strategic superiority, especially versus China.

To counter American dominance over the Middle East, Saddam Hussein tried to use Iraq's rich oil resources in the same way, as a strategic tool. In the early 1970s, Iraq nationalized U.S. petroleum interests and partnered with the Soviet Union to develop Iraq's oil capacity. In 1990, Saddam used Kuwait's perceived overproduction* as the pretext for his ill-fated invasion of Kuwait. Thirteen years later, with the U.S.'s ill-fated invasion of Iraq, he was overthrown, captured, tried, condemned, and hanged.

The geopolitics of natural resources come down in the final analysis to the classic economic issue of supply and demand: whoever has the surplus of supply over demand has the political advantage. In the 1970s, U.S. demand* exceeded its production. Without a surplus, the country lost its bargaining position with oil-producing nations. New domestic supply has shifted the position, and falling prices have shifted it again.*

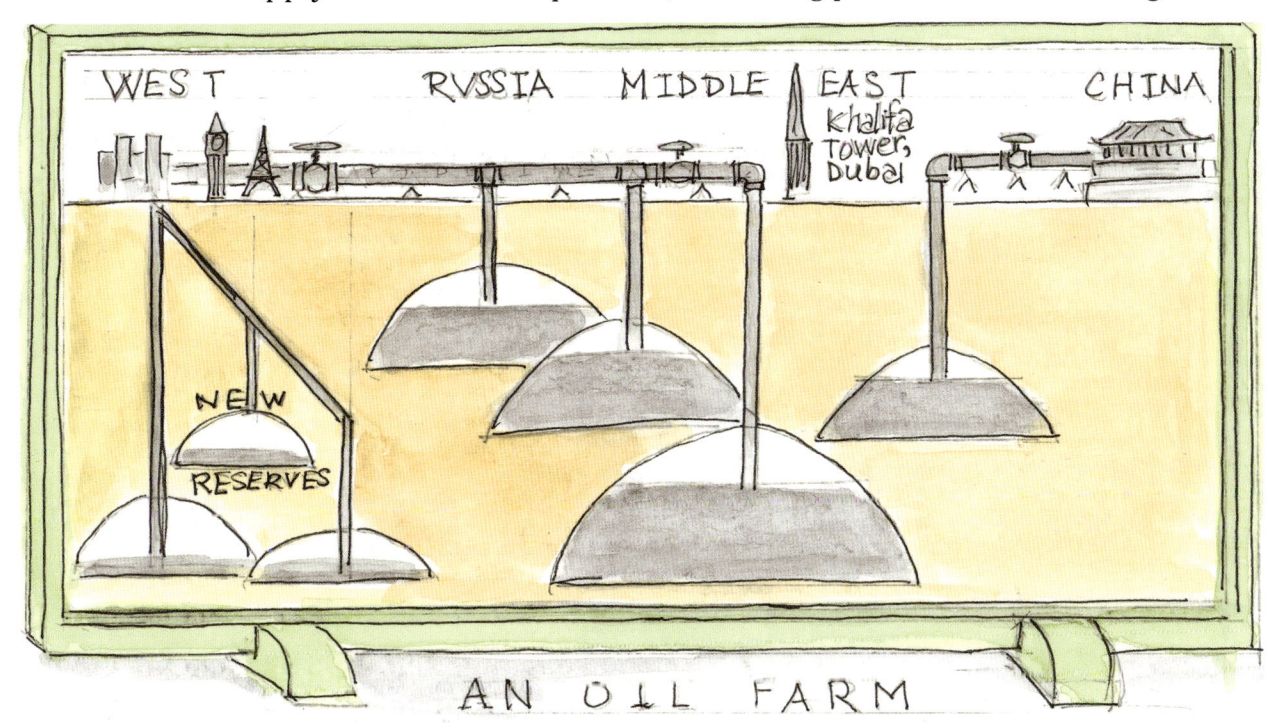

AN OIL FARM

World Traders and Raiders

No wonder the terrorists of 9/11 hit the 'World Trade' Center: world trade is the lifeblood of the modern global economy, its sine qua non, what defines it existentially. The attack was a highly symbolic act: a strike at Islam's new Red Apple* with the West's own machines loaded with the fuel that is at the center of geopolitical struggle today: a nexus of oil, globalization, and transnational terrorism.*

The ancestors of these terrorists had been the original world traders—and raiders—the great merchant capitalists, for the Arabs were traders as far back as the Silk Road. Mohammad himself had been a trader and a raider. By virtue of the central geopolitical position of Dar al' Islam in the World Island, Muslims controlled world trade from the 7th to the 16th century. Like the Mongols, they were by nature nomadic and therefore natural traders. The political unity of the Caliphate of Baghdad, and later of the Ottoman Empire, was essential to this control of goods. Iraq was a clearinghouse of trade, its *plaque tournante*. For centuries, Dar al' Islam controlled and profited from the trade between Europe and the Far East.

But then, as we have said, everything changed. The Spanish and Portuguese did an end run around this barrier, and world trade was diverted to run south of the great Capes in the Antipodes. Later, the northern Europeans built the machine of industry, fueled with raw goods from the growing colonial world, which in turn provided a market* for finished goods. In 1912, the machines began to run on oil. Just as people began to worry about how long it would last, oil was discovered in Iraq in 1927,* and the gravity of economic power began to shift imperceptibly eastward.

Like the first caliphs in the 7th century who went from being desert nomads to fabulously wealthy rulers in 40 years by relieving the Byzantines and the Persians of their money as legitimate booty,* just so the Arab oil-producing countries have gone from being desert nomads to fabulously wealthy rulers by relieving the West of its petrodollars—a new form of booty or tribute. Meanwhile, the West struggles with diminishing returns from the golden-egg-laying goose of capitalism.

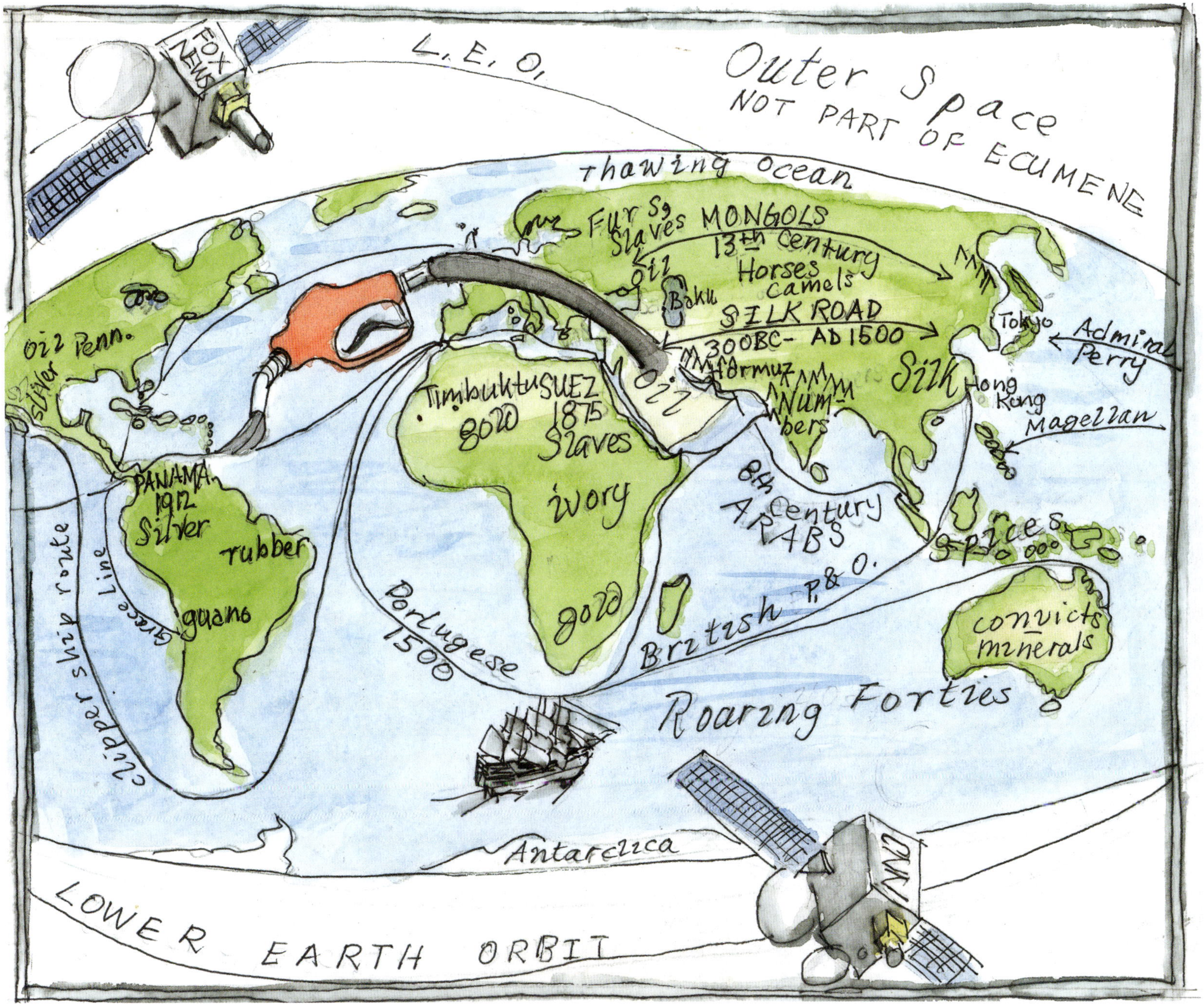
FOX NEWS
L.E.O.
Outer Space
NOT PART OF ECUMENE
thawing ocean
Fur &
Slaves
MONGOLS
13th century
oil
Horses
camels
Baku
SILK ROAD
300BC- AD1500
Tokyo
Admiral
Perry
Hormuz
Silk
Hong
Kong
Magellan
Num-
bers
oil
Oil Penn.
Silver
Timbuktu
gold
SUEZ
1875
Slaves
ivory
gold
8th century
ARABS
spices
PANAMA
1912
Silver
rubber
guano
grace line
clipper ship route
Portugese
1500
British
P. & O.
convicts
minerals
Roaring Forties
Antarctica
LOWER EARTH ORBIT
CNN

Killing the Golden Goose

A boardroom somewhere high up in a steel-and-glass tower.

Chairman Gentlemen, we are meeting today to discuss what to do about the slow growth of output from the goose of the economy. I will entertain suggestions from the various departments.

Securitized Mortgage Dept. Perhaps we should slice up the different income streams into tranches, package them as equities, and sell them into the secondary and tertiary markets.

Options Dept. Let's sell deep-in-the-money naked calls on the goose. Goose prices will never drop.

Chief Risk Officer But that will expose us to potentially unlimited losses, as in shorting the market.

Hedge Fund Dept. There are no downside risks. It is clear that capitalism and the free-market economy is the model of the future. There will only be extreme volatility as trading volume expands in derivatives, and therefore capital will keep growing. All we need is volatility. It does not matter if it goes up or down. We still make money.

Risk But the capital is now flowing eastward, as the retained earnings of three centuries are being siphoned out in a trade imbalance. We are in the same precarious position that the Hapsburgs were in, having a hugely negative cash flow while borrowing heavily from their rivals.

Credit-Default Swaps Dept. Don't know which bank Hapsburgs was, but our department can guarantee that there will be no exposure.

Private Equity Dept. Let's buy up under performing geese, load them up with debt, lay off the workers in the factories, take out our capital, and then let them sink or swim in the free-market economy.

Risk But what about our moral responsibility—and our own necks? As John Maynard Keynes pointed out, workers only tolerate us to rule over them as long we don't eat the whole economic cake, but rather reinvest our profits in businesses that will employ them.

Trading Dept. Oh, that's all old-fashioned stuff. We can calibrate risk automatically, dialing it down with low volatility, cranking it up with high beta, or opting in for pure volatility plays. Change your brain. We just need access to all the funds of the bank.

Risk Well, of course it's more profitable, but again high-speed trading exposes us to flash crashes … and the risk of more regulation.

Regulatory Dept. Oh, don't worry about them. We're way too big to fail … and even if they do, it will serve only to reinforce special protection for derivatives. And if it all blows up, they'll have to bail us out.

Risk Not necessarily. What about Lehman Brothers?

Interest-Rate Swaps Dept. Lehman schlehman. We can protect against any contingency, and can do a fixed-for-floating rate on any basis point you want above or below LIGOR [London Inter-Goose Rate] against the same or different currencies…

Risk You guys are creating financial weapons of mass destruction that are going to blow up in our faces, and destroy the goose of capitalism that lays the golden eggs. Don't exceed the limits!

Chairman Well, you boys have all had your say. I'm still in charge, and I say let's just kill the damn thing, take the golden eggs, and get the hell out of here!

Risk (*sotto voce*) "'Vengeance is mine,' saith the Lord. 'I shall repay.'"

THE EASTERN QUESTION, AGAIN

Geopolitics 'THE EASTERN QUESTION, AGAIN' is a headline in the old newspaper* that gave me the title for this book. That word 'again' reminds one that this question is ever with us, now as well as in 1887. We return again and again to the same question. Beyond the question of what would happen to the Ottoman Empire, the East has always been a question. It is a geopolitical question. We have identified three geopolitical dynamics—*Desert & Sown*, *East & West*, and *Order & Fragmentation*—between which poles history unceasingly oscillates, returning again and again to the same questions. But now the axis between those poles has shifted, again.

Halford Mackinder imagined the World Island rimmed by 'Monsoon Coastlands.' Nicholas Spykman* called them the 'Rimlands.'* Extending Spykman's ideas to the New World, we include Latin America in these Rimlands. During the Cold War, the Rimlands were called the Third World and are now called the Developing World.

Mackinder imagined a 'broad river' of mountains and deserts cleaving the world north from south, connecting it east to west. We call this broad river the Great Border of the World. From the 16th through the 19th century, mastering the desert of the sea, the Europeans conquered and exploited the Rimlands, while Russia conquered the former desert of the Heartland. In the Cold War, this turned into a struggle between the First and Second worlds to conquer and exploit the Third. Now after the fall of the Soviet Union, the struggle has become one between the Developed World to the north and the Developing World to the south. Dividing them is again the great border,* a semipermeable membrane through which, as in the phenomenon of osmosis, 'transference occurs owing to the presence of a greater pressure on one side of the membrane or the other': the pressure of the desert on the sown.

First World
Second World
Gulf of NATO
The Great Border of the World
85% WORLD POPULATION
RIMLANDS
BY 2050
Outlying Islands
Roaring Forties

Desert & Sown

Our first geopolitical dynamic is that of *Desert & Sown*: the struggle of tough mobile tribesmen, living in the parched lands, trying to either migrate into or conquer the sown, the prime agricultural regions of the Mediterranean, the World Egg. As with the dynamic of *East & West*, this was the result of the climatology of the earth. With the European conquest of the world, the sown conquered the desert. In the 19th century, the age-old human opposition of poverty and wealth manifested itself yet again as a confrontation of 'haves and have-nots'* within the sown.

Here is a 21st-century version of *Desert & Sown* as seen by a Pentagon consultant.* Studying recent global conflicts and mapping the places where the U.S. has exerted force, he draws a distinction between a 'Functioning Core' of globalization and a 'Non-Integrating Gap' of those outside who are struggling against or trying to get into this core. Now, however, the desert is enfolded within the sown, as it is indeed in the megalopolises of the Developed World with alienated segments of society plotting and conspiring against the society in which they live: for example, the two brothers from Chechnya—one of them was named Tamerlan—who detonated homemade pressure-cooker bombs hidden in backpacks at the finish of the 2013 Boston Marathon.

Geographically speaking, what then is this 'Non-integrating Gap' but that band of deserts and mountains cutting the World Island in half—the great border—that divided the Known World of the ancients from Africa, India, and China? Through it ran the Silk Road, the trade link between these two 'world systems,'* which was first controlled by the Persians, then by the Selçuk Turks, then by the Mongols, and then finally by the Ottomans, who controlled the ports on its western end. All of these empires both protected and profited from the trade. In the 16th century, the Europeans did an end run around this Islamic block and established direct contact with Africa, India, and China, settling surplus populations, converting 'heathens,' and exploiting resources—the three motives for colonization. With the rise of the economic power and independence of the Far East in the postcolonial period, it has again become the great border of the world where nations scramble for oil.

In the history of *Desert & Sown*, there have been four periods.* First, people go into the desert in search of minerals, using horses. Second, horsemen migrate or invade in waves into the sown. Third, with the discovery of the sea routes and Russian expansion into the Heartland, the sown conquers the desert. And finally, as here with no more deserts to conquer, the desert is enfolded within the sown.

East & West

Our second dynamic is *East & West*: the premise that because of the climatology of the earth, most of human history has been played out on a stage that runs in a narrow band between a freezing north and a burning south. Inextricably interwoven with this dynamic is that of *Desert & Sown*, our first dynamic, because the desert lay mostly to the east of the sown, the World Egg of the ancient world.

To the 19th-century American mind, history seemed to have been moving ever westward* from its beginnings in Mesopotamia, through Greece, to Rome, to northern Europe, and finally across the Atlantic to North America. At the end of the 20th century, to some* it seemed as if history had come to an end with the U.S. When the Soviet Union collapsed in 1991, the Western capitalist system was triumphant at the finish of what was apparently the last great struggle of *East & West*: the Cold War. The hand of history, however, kept on writing across the Pacific, moving ever westward to China, which has created a system of capitalism 'with Chinese characteristics.'

Herodotus gave the uppercase letters to the words 'East' and 'West,' and saw this opposition intertwined with another, one between tyranny and freedom. But it has never been that simple. Large-franchise democracy has existed in the West for barely two centuries—elsewhere not at all. 'In the East,' said Recep Erdoğan, the president of Turkey, 'democracy is a bus you get off when you have reached your destination.'

One theory* holds that as the wealth of nations rises, democracy rises too, but that is not necessarily so either. Most countries claim to be democratic republics of this or that, but the newfound riches have generally ended up in the pockets of oligarchs. Without the spread of wealth, 'democracy' is an empty word. The real struggle seems less between tyranny and freedom than between stability and chaos.* In truth, a rough-and-ready form of democracy has always existed in the East. The Chinese sage Confucius thought that the state is a ship and the people are the water on which it floats. The water will let the ship float only if it sails in accordance with the water's will.* If the ship tries to sail against the water, it will sink.

In the 14th century, Ibn Khaldūn identified the dynamic of *Desert & Sown*, linking it to another, the succession of states: the rise and fall of powers in the same place. In doing so, he broached the question of the legitimacy of power, which is further connected to our geopolitical dynamic of *Order & Fragmentation*. If people reject the rule of a supranational order under an emperor or sultan, the result is fragmentation.

Now we have more than fragmentation, but the 'state itself confounded to decay.'* The concept of the national state sovereign within its own boundaries* is crumbling, being replaced by failed states, or what one might call NGOs of a different order: international terrorist organizations that have no place at treaty tables. Whether in Egypt, Libya, Syria, or post-Soviet Ukraine, recent history is littered with failed states and broken dreams of new democratic beginnings. The forces of the old order retreat, regroup, and capitalize on the instability of the new. New questions get old answers.

Order & Fragmentation

Our third dynamic has been the oscillation between *Order & Fragmentation*. For centuries, the Ottoman Empire imposed order in the Middle East. Over the course of the 19th century, it slowly disintegrated. In 1921, the West imposed its own fragmented nature on the lands of the defeated Empire. Today, after the 'Arab Spring' and the rise of Isis (Islamic State of Iraq and the Levant), people ask, What will happen next?

Empires are out of fashion these days, but they did have their uses. The Persians, Alexander, the Romans, and lastly the Ottomans created zones of order and toleration in which many different peoples, speaking many different languages,* lived in a homeland without interior borders. Perhaps a league like the U.N.—headquartered in Istanbul and with Western, Russian, and Saudi support—could help to restore order.

Fragmentation has its own price, which is strife. The overthrow of Saddam Hussein removed a buffer to the natural expansion of Shia Iran. The weakness of the Iraqi government established by the U.S. led to the rise of Isis. The example of the Arab Spring emboldened rebels in Syria, but Western fear of arming them as well as Russia's support of Bashar al-Assad led to a stalemate of which Isis took advantage. Arab turmoil has made Israel reckless and complacent. The weakness of African states north and south of the Sahara has allowed *jihadi* to seize control of northern Mali. Somalia is a failed state. The border between Sudan and South Sudan* is one of the 'most dangerous'* in the world. Sinai is becoming another base for *jihadi*.

Halford Mackinder saw in the map of the world a shape he called the 'Arab Eagle,' but which might more accurately be called a Muslim, or even an Ottoman eagle since its head, body, and right wing are composed of the lands over which the sultan-caliph once ruled, the Shadow of the Almighty Dispensing Peace in this World.* For 2,300 years, this empire represented the force of order in this geopolitical zone, a fact of which Ankara is not unaware.* 'We are not aspiring to become an imperialist power,' a senior Turkish official asserted in 2012, 'but history and geography are chasing us.'

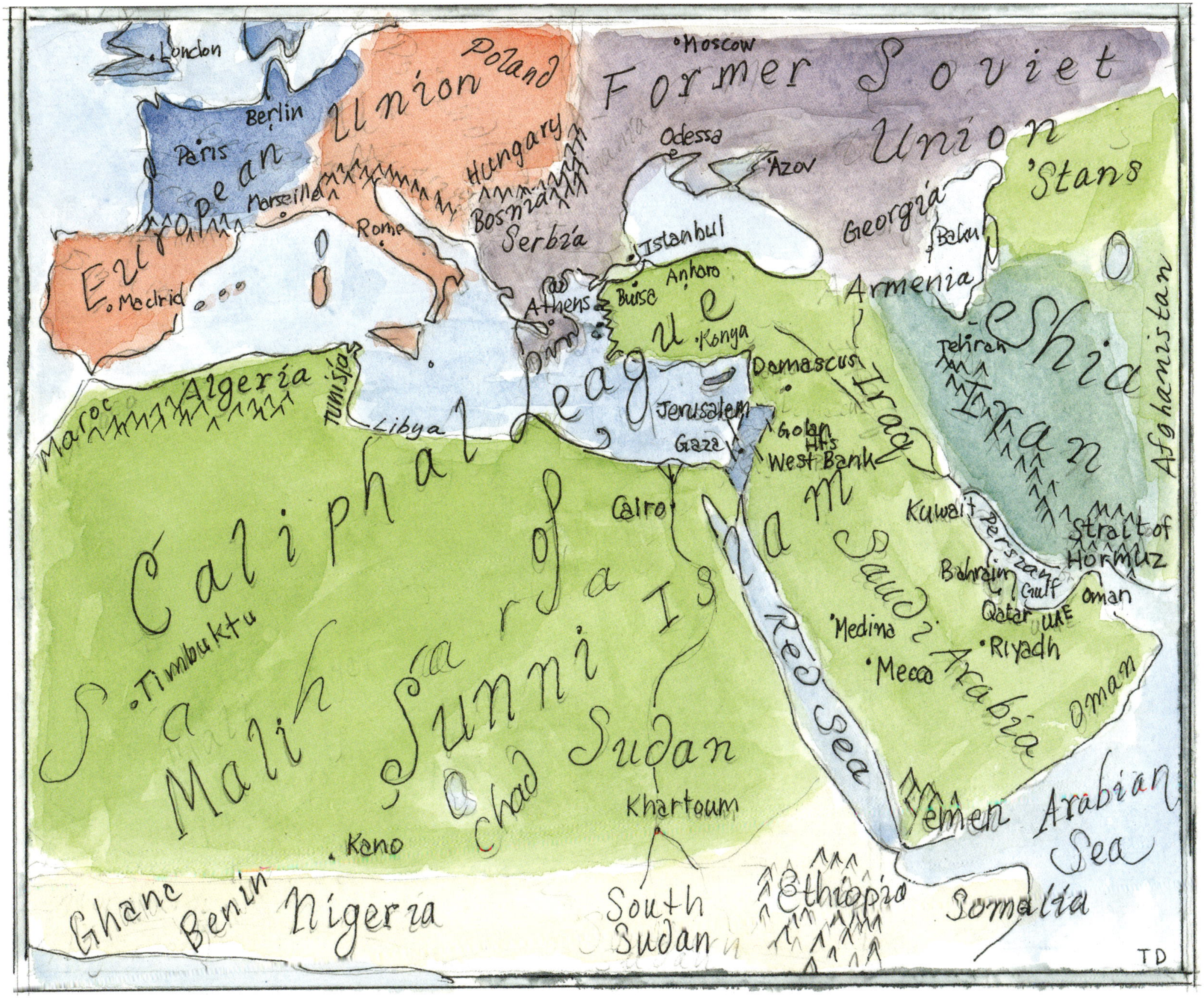
London
Berlin
Paris
Poland
Moscow
Former Soviet Union
European Union
Hungary
Marseille
Bosnia
Serbia
Rome
Madrid
Odessa
Azov
Istanbul
Georgia
Baku
Armenia
'Stans
Athens
Ankara
Konya
Damascus
Tehran
Shia
Iran
Afghanistan
Algeria
Maroc
Tunisia
Libya
Jerusalem
Gaza
Golan Hts
West Bank
Iraq
Kuwait
Persian Gulf
Strait of Hormuz
Bahrain
Qatar
UAE
Oman
Cairo
Caliphal League of Sunni Islam
Saudi Arabia
Medina
Mecca
Riyadh
Red Sea
Timbuktu
Mali
Chad
Sudan
Khartoum
Kano
Yemen
Arabian Sea
Ghana
Benin
Nigeria
South Sudan
Ethiopia
Somalia
TD

IMPERIA IRREDENTA

Persia/Iran EVEN THOUGH 'thrones are shattered, and empires are shaken,'* many in the East still dream of states so far unreedemed (*irredenta*). One such is Persia, or Iran, the successor of the first world empire. Syria and Israel also dream of regaining territory. Irredentism is counter-fragmentation—in the Middle East, counter-Sykes-Picot.

From its very beginning, the history of Persia/Iran has witnessed a pattern of wave upon wave of invasions—from the Indo-Europeans to the Europeans—alternating with periodic ejections of these invaders and revivals under a succession of dynasties. The Parthians fought off the Romans. The Samanids ejected the Arabs. In 1501, the Safavid Shah Ismail converted the country to Shiism, so that Persians could be Muslims in a way that retained their traditional distinction from the Sunni Arabs and Turks. Persians always return to being Persians.

Before Shah Ismail's death in 1524, another wave was already encroaching. In 1515, the Portuguese had seized Hormuz; in 1616, the English landed at the little port of Jask on the Persian Gulf; in 1717, the Russians demanded Baku on the Caspian; in 1907, the British and Russians partitioned Persia into zones of influence; in 1943, Roosevelt, Churchill, and Stalin overthrew Reza Shah, replacing him with his son;* in 1953, the CIA engineered the overthrow of Prime Minister Mossadegh and reinstalled the Shah. That covert action has been called* 'the first step towards the Iranian catastrophe of 1979'—the Ayatollah's Islamic Revolution that threw out the latest invaders.

If a modern nation is 2,500 years old, its people have a different perspective on history. If that nation once had been a vast empire, its people have a different perspective on their geopolitical role as a world power. In order to be a full-fledged world power today, possession of a nuclear weapon* is a sine qua non.

Armenia
Azerbaijan
Uzbekistan
Turkmen.
Turkey
Greece
Persian Empire
Syria
Lebanon
Israel
Iraq
Susa
Persepolis
Libya
Egypt
Arabia
Afghanistan

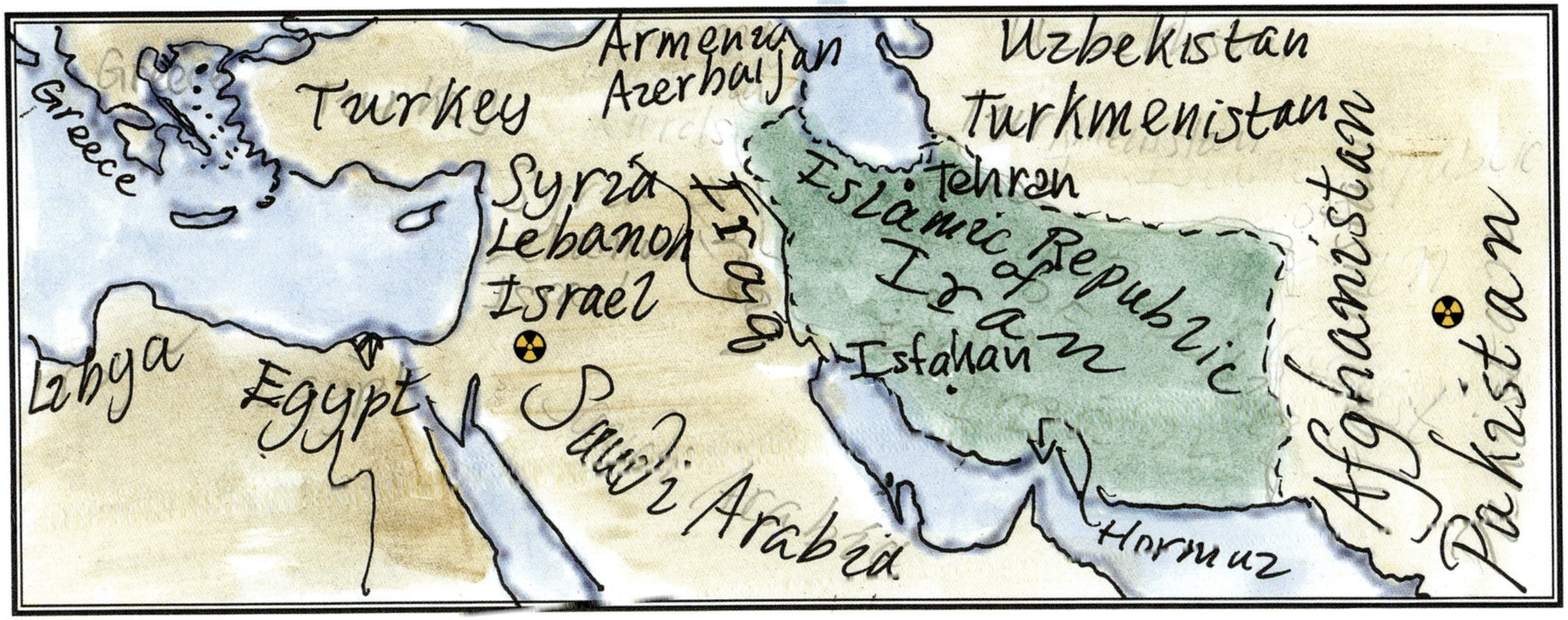
Armenia
Azerbaijan
Uzbekistan
Turkmenistan
Turkey
Greece
Syria
Lebanon
Israel
Iraq
Tehran
Islamic Republic of Iran
Isfahan
Libya
Egypt
Saudi Arabia
Hormuz
Afghanistan
Pakistan

Here we are back in the Fertile Crescent, where this story began. Earlier, we called it a cockpit of conflict. It still is. Nations there see it as entirely their own. Their overlapping irredentist dreams are tantamount to sacred vows of mutual obliteration.

Syria/ Isis/ Israel

At Syrian border crossings today, one encounters a map of Syria on which no Israel appears, and the current borders between Lebanon and Turkey, the Golan Heights and Gaza Strip, are marked as temporary internal borders within a 'Greater Syria.'* The dream of such a 'Greater Syria' was shattered in 1920, the 'Year of Catastrophe' (*Am al-Nakba*), when the promised independent Arab state of the British was turned over to the French under the terms of Sykes-Picot, modified after the war to give the British a free hand to create a Jewish homeland in Palestine. Today Isis,* a classic Islamic rebel state,* is fighting for an ancient concept of the region, stretching from southern Turkey, the homeland of the Hittites, through Lebanon, Israel, the Palestinian Territories, and Jordan. Both Isis and Syrian dreamers see the present-day borders of the country as illegitimate imperial divisions imposed on the region as part of the settlement of the Eastern Question under the secret Sykes-Picot agreement, as well as under the UN Resolution of 1947 that created the state of Israel.

On the other hand, some in Israel, and even in the U.S., dream of a 'Greater Israel' whose borders are essentially coterminous with those of a 'Greater Syria.' This is eretz yisrael, the Promised Land of Genesis (15:18), stretching from 'the river of Egypt* to the great river, the river Euphrates.' Some believe that in order to survive, Israel must become an imperial regional power by weakening and promoting the fragmentation of the surrounding Arab states, which will then in theory succumb to Israeli hegemony.

However unlikely, however much a fantasy of neocons and Zionists, whether real or imputed by anti-Semites, all these conflicting dreams—with the West supporting Israel and Russia supporting the Assad regime in Syria—demonstrate that the Eastern Question has not yet been consigned to the 'trash can of history.'*

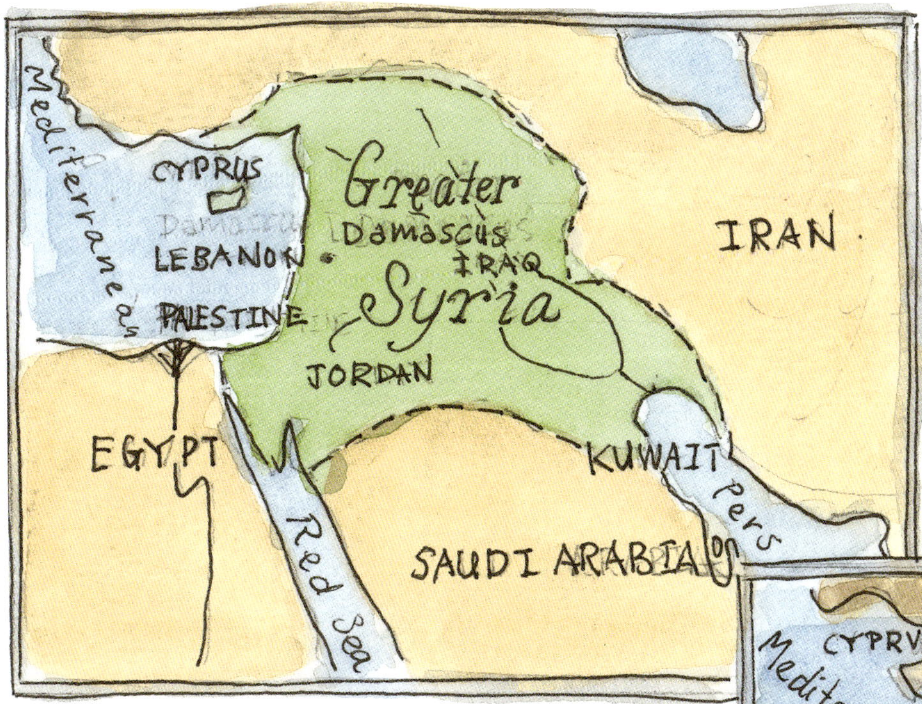
Mediterranean
CYPRUS
LEBANON
PALESTINE
Greater
Damascus
IRAQ
Syria
JORDAN
IRAN
EGYPT
KUWAIT
Pers
Red Sea
SAUDI ARABIA

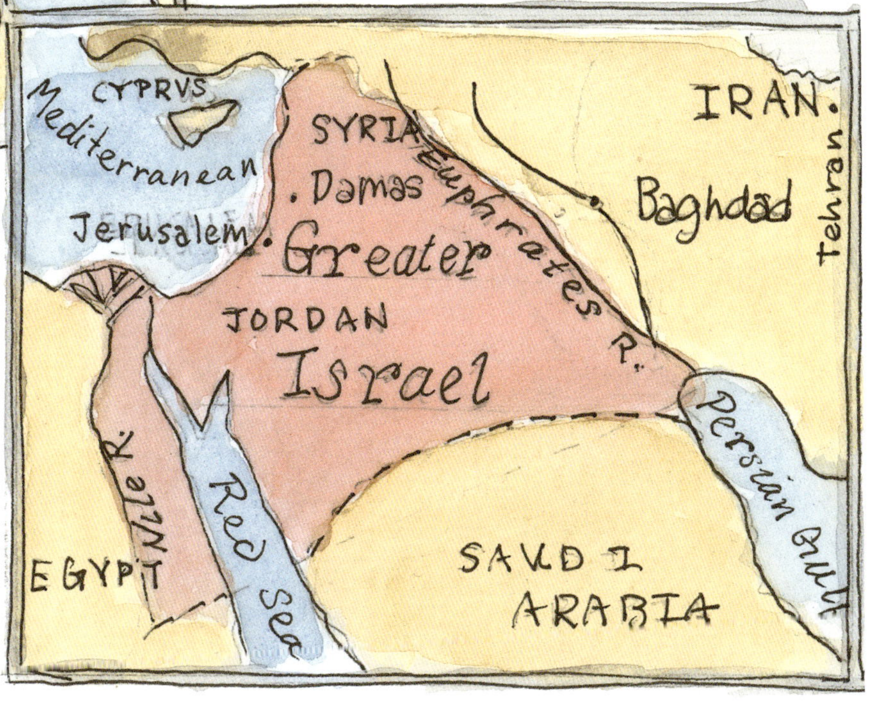
CYPRUS
Mediterranean
SYRIA
. Damas
Euphrates R.
Baghdad
IRAN.
Tehran
Jerusalem
Greater
JORDAN
Israel
Persian Gulf
Nile R.
EGYPT
Red Sea
SAUDI
ARABIA

Ukraine, 2014

The Ukraine crisis of 2014 was irredentism in action and demonstrated in a dramatic fashion our three geopolitical dynamics, at ground zero of the Eastern Question.

Peter the Great briefly opened the Eastern Question in 1696 by taking Azov. In 1699,* the first Russian ship passed the strait of Kerch to sail on the sultan's private lake; but at the battle of the Pruth River in 1711, the Ottomans defeated him, and he had to give Azov back. The Question was postponed for three quarters of a century, until the time of Potemkin. In 2014, Russian forces pushed westward along the north coast of the Sea of Azov past Taganrog, Peter's original naval base.

Here we see the dynamic of *Desert & Sown.* These were once the lands of the Don Cossacks* and Crimean Tatars, the last remnant of the Mongol Golden Horde. Their khan was a descendant of Genghis himself. In 1783, these lands became Russian. In 1954, Khrushchev, a Ukrainian, transferred them to the Soviet Socialist Republic of Ukraine, as it was called when part of the U.S.S.R.

Here we see the dynamic of *East & West.* Ukraine is the wide borderland* between them. Its very name means just that, the march between two great geopolitical characters—the Catholic West and the Orthodox East. Here in 1709 was fought the battle of Poltava, where Peter the Great defeated the invading Swedish army of Charles XII. With this victory, Russia stepped onto the stage of world power. Here in 1944 between Korsun and Cherkassy, two Ukrainian Fronts of the Red Army encircled a German army group which had penetrated thus far into Eurasia. The crisis in 2014 clearly reveals as in an X-ray image the crack in the bone between East and West.

Here we see illustrated the dynamic of *Order & Fragmentation.* Kiev is the 'Mother of All Russian Cities,' and from here began the eventual unification of the Russian Empire. In 1918 and again in 1991, the Empire fragmented. Now after two decades of order, Russia again is trying to reunify, and the West is once again threatened by Russian expansion. As Vladimir Putin put it, 'The infamous policy of containment continues today.' In the Ukraine crisis of 2014, Western Russophobia met Russian irredentism.

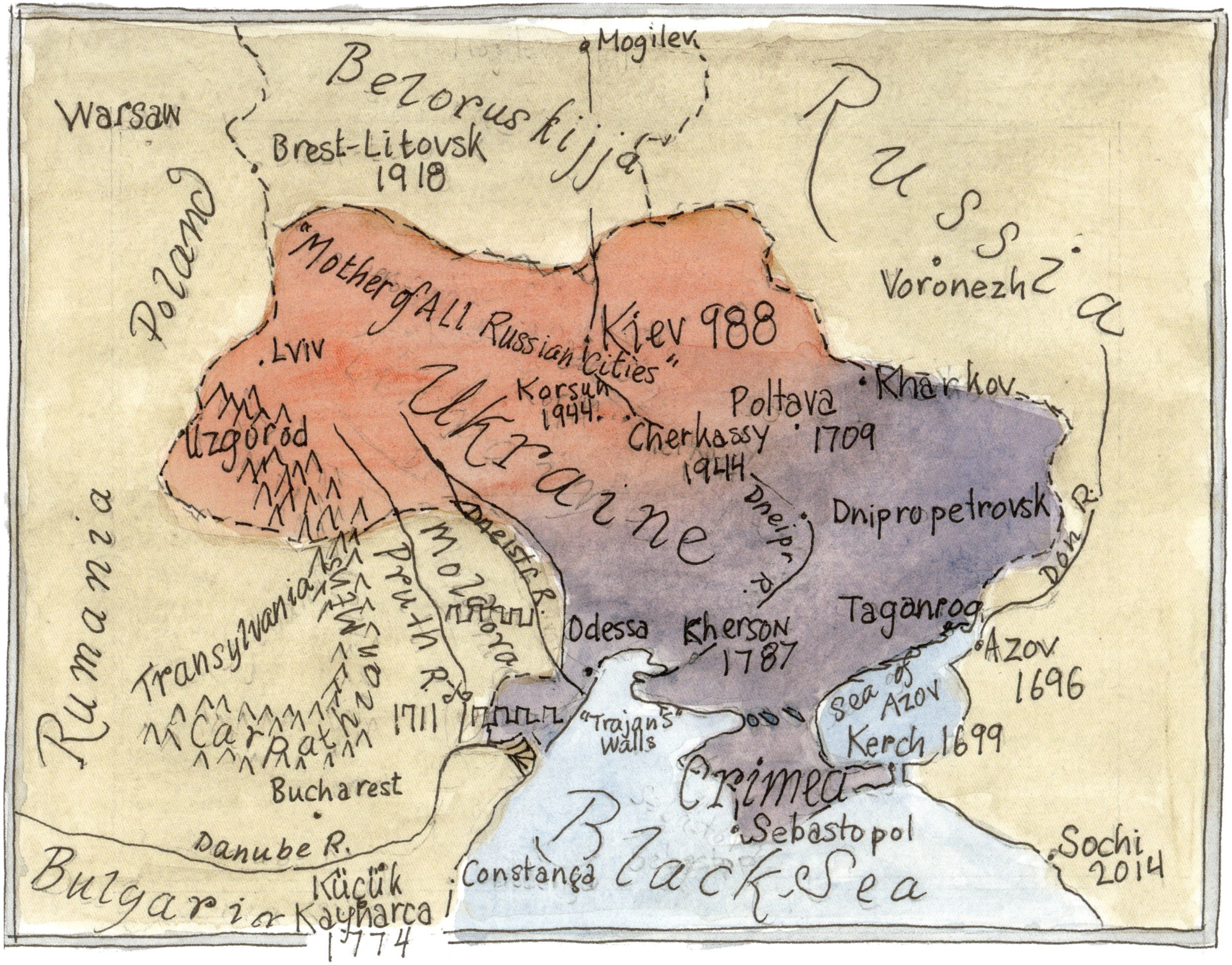

Mogilev
Belorus kijja
Warsaw
Brest-Litovsk 1918
Russia
Poland
Voronezh
"Mother of All Russian Cities"
Kiev 988
Lviv
Ukraine
Kharkov
Korsun 1944
Poltava 1709
Uzgorod
Cherkassy 1944
Dneipr R.
Dnipropetrovsk
Rumania
Dneistr R.
Moldavia
Pruth R.
Don R.
Transylvania
Taganrog
Odessa
Kherson 1787
Azov 1696
Sea of Azov
1711
"Trajan's" Walls
Kerch 1699
Carpathians
Crimea
Bucharest
Sebastopol
Danube R.
Black Sea
Sochi 2014
Bulgaria
Küçük Kaynarca 1774
Constança

A Geopolitical Theater in the Round

On the hundredth anniversary of the outbreak of war in 1914, what will happen in the former lands of the sultan is still very much in question. The *commedia della storia* is still playing in the sandy arena of this geopolitical theater in the round.

It is still the same old drama. The same geopolitical characters are still there: Russia, the West, the Former Ottoman Empire, albeit fragmented into its former provinces, and Persia/Iran. Using proxies, Obama, Merkel, Cameron, and Hollande play the role of the West; Putin plays the role of the East; the Iranian ayatollahs play the role of Shia Persia, and the Sunni Arabs play themselves, fighting in these same lands where the Trojans fought the Greeks, the Greeks fought the Persians, Homer wrote the first epic, Herodotus the first history; where the Byzantines fought the Turks at Manzikert in 1071, and the Turks defeated the Crusaders in 1187.

Russia still presses westward, reacquiring former imperial territory. Persia/Iran still presses into the borderland of Iraq. The Arabs still press north out of the desert, armed with the old-time religion but now with a new weapon. Rebellions and civil wars continue to torment the F.O.E. in Tunisia, Libya, Egypt, Syria, Kurdistan, and Gaza. *Jihadi* still flow in from all directions, just as in the old days when the Arabs and Turks were the original Islamic rebel states. Now, a modern Islamic rebel state has moved into northern Iraq and Syria, a place prone to power vacuums since at least the end of the 2nd millennium BC, about the time of the legendary siege of Troy.

Iran surreptitiously supports Assad. The Saudis and Qatar surreptitiously support Isis. The West's tentative support of the Syrian rebels comes face-to-face with Russia's unwavering support of Assad. Ankara refuses to help the fight against Isis unless the West helps overthrow Assad. The Kurds demand help from Ankara, threatening rebellion within Turkey. Isis on the Turkish border is face-to-face with NATO as the battle rages on in the cockpit of conflict between the Zagros and Taurus mountains.

What will happen? people ask, just as they did in the 19th century when the Eastern Question perplexed the finest diplomatic minds of Europe.

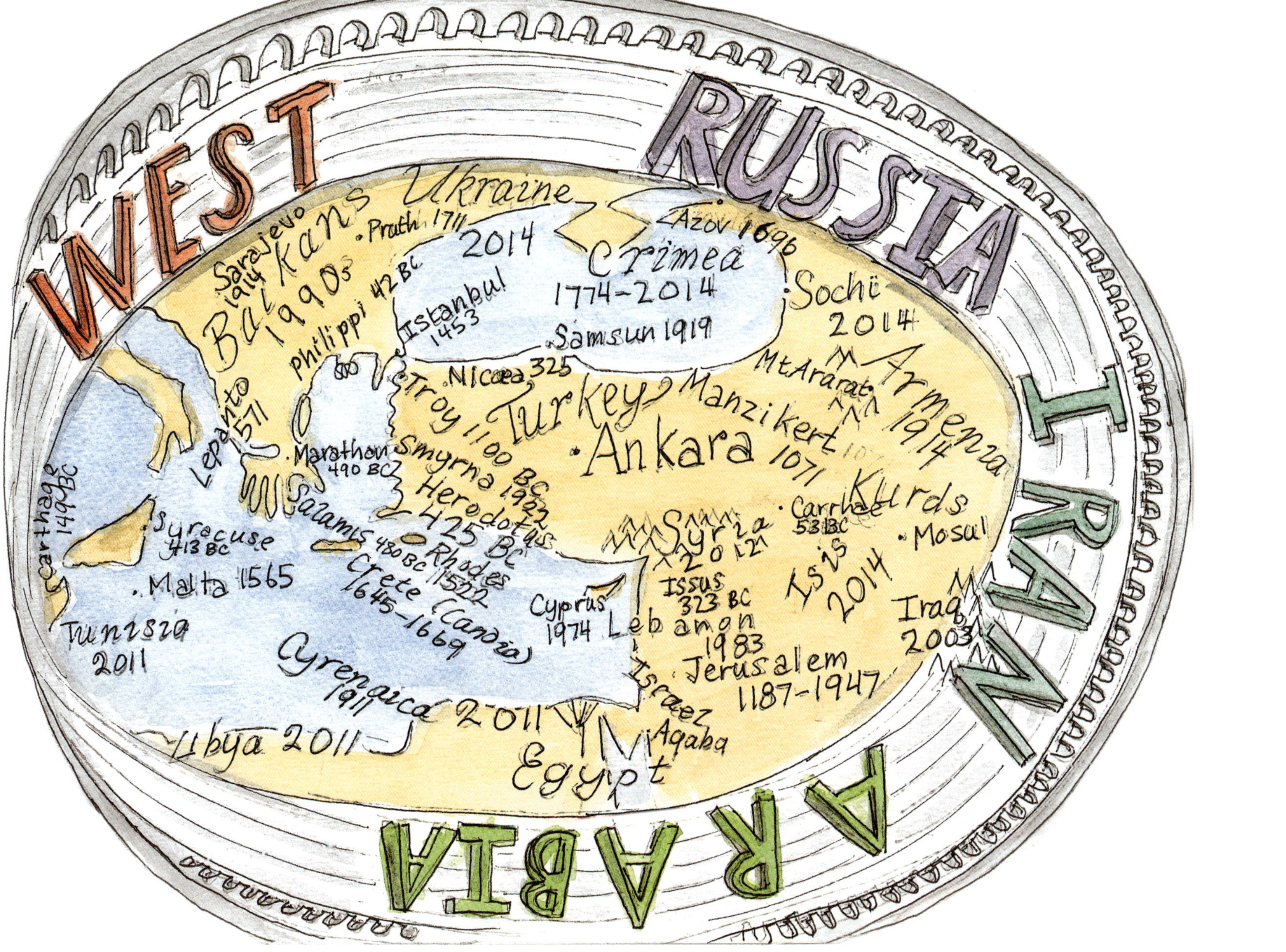

WEST
RUSSIA
IRAN
ARABIA
Balkans 1990s
Ukraine
Sarajevo 1914
Pruth 1711
2014
Azov 1696
Crimea 1774-2014
Sochi 2014
Istanbul 1453
Philippi 42 BC
Samsun 1919
Nicaea 325
Mt Ararat
Armenia 1914
Turkey
Manzikert 1071
Ankara
Troy 1100 BC
Lepanto 1571
Marathon 490 BC
Smyrna 1922
Herodotus 425 BC
Salamis 480 BC
Rhodes 1522
Carthage 149 BC
Syracuse 413 BC
Malta 1565
Crete (Candia) 1645-1669
Kurds
Syria 2012
Carrhae 53 BC
Mosul
Isis 2014
Issus 323 BC
Cyprus 1974
Lebanon 1983
Iraq 2003
Tunisia 2011
Cyrenaica 1911
2011
Jerusalem 1187-1947
Israel
Aqaba
Libya 2011
Egypt

Dreams from My Fathers

White House Situation Room, late one night, 2014: The national security advisers and Pentagon chiefs have gone home, but President Barack Obama stays on, pondering the decisions he must now make for himself. Tired after having listened to their arguments, he falls into a deep sleep and dreams that sitting in the armchairs around the big, shiny oval conference table are some of the cleverest statesmen in history, assembled there to advise him.

Bismarck Mr. President, don't let the ghosts of the Eastern Question and the Cold War fool you into making an enemy of a natural ally. Don't be led into a two-fronted struggle, against both Russia and the Islamic *jihad*. Let Russia pursue her legitimate interests in her proper geopolitical sphere. Cleave to Russia, my son. That was always my policy; the abandonment of it led to the War in 1914.

Potemkin His Excellency is right, Mr. President. Ever since General Suvarov defeated the Ottomans two years before you Americans declared your independence from Britain, the lands of the Crimean Tatars and Don Cossacks have been Russian. Her Imperial Highness Catherine gave them to me to rule, and I founded Odessa and built our Black Sea Fleet. Historians say that the taking of these Ottoman tributary states first posed the Eastern Question. However that may be, these lands are as Russian as Kansas and California are American.

Palmerston Well, I admit we in Britain were worried about His Highness's policy of advancing south. It threatened our passage to India; so I initiated the policy of supporting the Ottoman Empire as a buffer state. It turned out that our fears were groundless. Now, the situation appears to be utterly the reverse, especially in this new hybrid, nonlinear type of warfare with rogue states. Turn the Eastern Question on its head: instead of struggling against an irredentist Russia, allow her to pursue her interests as Prince Bismarck suggests, but meanwhile secure her assistance against the troubles breaking out all over the sultan's former domains as a counterbalance in the East, her zone. Let Russia and the West empower Turkey to control the expansion of the new *soi-disant* Islamic State that has moved into the power vacuum lying between a failed Iraqi state and a weakened Syria.

Machiavelli The noble lord is a wise man, Mr. President. As he told Parliament in 1844, Britain has no permanent enemies, no permanent friends, only permanent interests. A prince cannot be squeamish when it suits his ends to switch sides. In Renaissance Italy, they always did.

Saladin Peace be upon you, Mr. President. It was I, Salah ad-Din, to whom Allah—blessings be upon him—gave the honor of ejecting the Crusaders from Jerusalem and the heretical Shias from Egypt. Now, my people are defending their lands against another wave of Crusaders—Jews and Christians—and are struggling against an illegitimate order imposed by Western colonialists on Dar al'Islam, the House of Peace. Their struggle is just. They are unconquerable.*

Metternich Order, Mr. President, cannot be imposed from above nor from without. At the Congress of Vienna in 1815, I set the 'Concert of Europe'* to playing, but its harmonies were broken by the clangor of nationalism and the Eastern Question. The order I established maintained peace more or less for almost a hundred years, until the outbreak of the War in 1914. Liberals claimed that it was repressive, but peace has its price. In the end, if people do not accept a given order a revolutionary situation* necessarily results—as I learned to my cost in 1848 when I had to flee Vienna.

Trotsky Exactly so, Mr. President. In those same hundred years of peace of which Prince Metternich so proudly speaks, Russia groaned under an autocratic order that people—workers and peasants, liberals and socialists—increasingly refused to accept. As much as we thought our revolution would create a new world order, it quickly turned into a bureaucratic tyranny. It failed, and the capitalists won. Clearly, we were on the wrong path. But the revolution is permanent.* People will always struggle against an illegitimate order. There will always be revolution, Mr. President. Revolution is the inspired frenzy of history.*

Michelle Obama (*entering*) Oh, here you are! Why are you up so late? You fell asleep. You need some rest. Come on … let's go upstairs. There's no one here. They've all gone home.

Oxbows in Time

Today we are haunted by many ghosts of defunct empires—a long succession of failed states—not only in Syria but also in Egypt, where in 1958 Gamal Abdel Nasser tried to create a United Arab Republic, re-creating Pharaoh's empire, or in Iraq, where Nuri as-Said dreamed of re-creating the Babylonian Empire. Nor were these entirely dreams. It was not much more than 80 years ago that—amazingly enough—there still existed the remnants of a vast empire of which these were mere provinces. Another province was Bosnia, where young men dreaming of a Greater Serbia assassinated the heir of the Austro-Hungarian Empire, the Hapsburg Archduke Franz Ferdinand, at Sarajevo in 1914, thus striking the spark that set fire to the House of Mighty Caesar.

Houses rise and fall, empires are brought together and break up, the desert presses on the sown, the sown presses on the desert, the East presses on the West, the West presses on the East in geopolitical dynamics that reflect the underlying duality of Nature, oscillating between limits like the oxbows of an old river meandering in thousand-year swings across the landscape of Time, continually folding back on itself.

If you would like to know the sequel of this story, you will find it in the daily news, in which the present reflects the past, and the past like an antique mirror reflects back to the present a mottled and dark image of itself, as here in another piece from one of those old newspapers* that hung in frames on the wall of our printing shop.

> Venice, May 13 [1789]—The new Sultan has made no alteration in the councils of the Turks: The Reis Effendi [the Ottoman foreign minister] has declared to the Ambassadors of France and Spain [the West], who are very pressing in their offers of mediation, that he has orders not to listen to any propositions concerning peace, unless the preliminaries were on an entire restitution of all conquests [those ratified by the Treaty of Küçük Kaynarca in 1774]; the renunciation of the supremacy of the Empress of Russia [Catherine the Great] over the Tatars, and the independence of the Crimea.

1000 YEARS

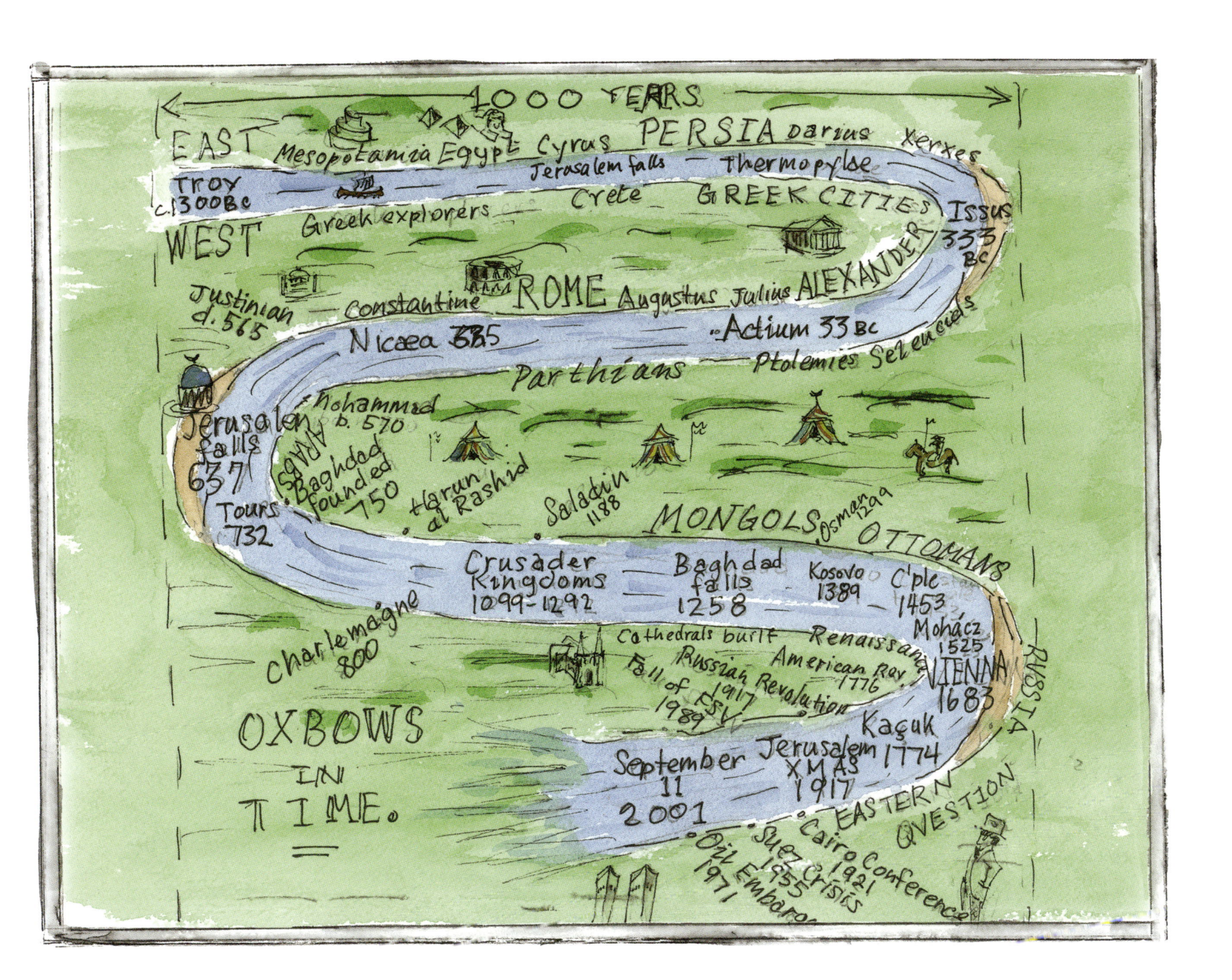

EAST — Mesopotamia · Egypt · Cyrus · PERSIA · Darius · Xerxes
Jerusalem falls — Thermopylae
Troy c.1300 BC · Greek explorers · Crete · GREEK CITIES · Issus 333 BC
WEST

Justinian d. 565 · Constantine · ROME · Augustus · Julius · ALEXANDER
Nicaea 385 · Actium 33 BC
Parthians · Ptolemies · Seleucids

Jerusalem falls 637 · Mohammed b. 570 · ARABS · Baghdad founded 750 · Harun al Rashid · Saladin 1188 · MONGOLS · Osman 1299 · OTTOMANS
Tours 732
Crusader Kingdoms 1099–1292 · Baghdad falls 1258 · Kosovo 1389 · C'ple 1453 · Mohácz 1525

Charlemagne 800 · Cathedrals built · Renaissance · American Rev 1776 · VIENNA 1683 · RUSSIA
Russian Revolution 1917
Fall of FSU 1989

OXBOWS IN TIME

September 11 2001 · Jerusalem XMAS 1917 · Kaçuk 1774
Cairo Conference 1921 · Suez Crisis 1955 · Oil Embargo 1971 · **EASTERN QUESTION**

THE EASTERN QUESTION *A Chronology*

497 BC Battle of Marathon: East attacks West
333 Battle of Issus: The West strikes back
301 Cleopatra's death; Roman Empire completed
AD 33 Death of Jesus (commonly accepted)
324 Constantinople founded as 'New Rome'
395 Division of Roman Empire East and West
451 Battle of Châlons
453 Death of Attila
476 Last Roman emperor in West deposed
570 Birth of Mohammad; England Christianized
632 Death of Mohammad
637 Arabs take Jerusalem
732 Battle of Poitiers: limit of Arab advance
750 Baghdad founded as capital of Caliphate
800 Charlemagne crowned emperor
861 Norman kingdom of Kievan 'Rus' established
988 Kiev accepts Christianity
1055 Selçuk Turk Alp Arslan sultan of Baghdad
1064 Orthodox and Catholic churches split
1066 Norman Conquest of England
1071 Battle of Manzikert
1095 Pope preaches First Crusade
1099 Jerusalem falls to Crusaders
1187 Saladin retakes Jerusalem
1204 Fourth Crusade plunders Constantinople
1242 Mongols penetrate suburbs of Vienna
1248 Mongols invade territory of Kievans
1258 Mongols sack Baghdad
1261 Constantinople retaken by Byzantines
1291 Crusaders lose last stronghold (Acre)
1299 Osman throws off Selçuk yoke
1304 Birth of Petrarch: beginning of Italian Renaissance and rise of the West
1348 Black Death: end of Mongol Empire
1389 Battle of Kosovo
1438 Study of classical Greek begun in the West
1448 Russian Orthodox Church splits from Greek Orthodox
1453 Ottoman conquest of Constantinople
1479 Ivan the Terrible throws off Tatar yoke
1492 Granada falls; Columbus sails
1507 Copernicus: beginning of Western science
1517 Luther posts his theses at Wittenberg
1526 Battle of Mohács; first siege of Vienna (1527)
1620 Pilgrims land at Plymouth Rock
1648 Peace of Westphalia
1683 Second Turkish siege of Vienna
1711 Last Ottoman victory, at Pruth River
1713 Peace of Utrecht
1774 Treaty of Küçük Kaynarca: beginning of Eastern Question
1795 Napoleon invades Egypt
1853 Crimean War: Britain and France prevent Russia from advancing on Constantinople
1869 Suez Canal opened
1877 Turkish massacres in Balkans

1878	Congress of Berlin convened by Bismarck; Ottomans lose Bulgaria, Romania, Serbia, &c.	**1920**	U.S. Senate rejects League of Nations (March); refuses to take Armenian 'mandate'
1884	Conference of Berlin: Africa divided	**1920**	San Remo Conference: France given mandate for Syria in return for letting Britain keep Jerusalem and Mosul, plus 50% of oil (April)
1905	First Moroccan Crisis: first of series of crises over the Eastern Question		
1908	First Bosnian Crisis: Austria annexes Bosnia	**1920**	Battle of Maysalun: Arabs defeated on road to Damascus by French troops; Faisal flees to Britain (July)
1912	Ottomans lose almost all European territory		
1914	Austrian archduke shot at Sarajevo (June)	**1920**	Treaty of Sèvres signed by emissaries of sultan
1914	Ottomans attack Russia; British troops begin attack on Basra (Nov.)		
1915	Anglo-French force lands at Gallipoli (Feb.)	**1921**	Cairo Conference (March): Faisal to be king of Iraq; brother Abdullah to be king of Jordan; Britain gets mandate for Palestine, free hand to create a Jewish 'homeland'
1915	Russians demand Constantinople (March): 'Eastern Question must now be confronted'		
1915	British promise Arabs independence (Oct.)	**1924**	Atatürk abolishes caliphate; death of Lenin (Jan.)
1916	Sykes-Picot Agreement (May)		
1917	Baghdad falls to British troops (March)	**1925**	Ibn Saud takes Mecca; Sharif ejected (Oct.)
1917	Balfour Declaration; Bolsheviks seize power in Petrograd (Oct.)	**1927**	Oil struck at Kirkuk; 'Red Line' Agreement
		1938	Oil discovered in Saudi Arabia
1917	Gen. Allenby enters Jerusalem (Christmas)	**1946**	Churchill gives 'Iron Curtain' speech
1918	Wilson's 14 Points: 'self-determination' asserted as a principle of peace (June)	**1947**	End of British rule in India; state of Israel created by UN Resolution
1918	ANZAC troops take Damascus (Sept.)	**1953**	Mossadegh overthrown; Shah reinstalled
1918	Arab government in Damascus (Oct.)	**1956**	Suez Crisis: America now leader of the West
1918	Arabs promised free elections (Nov.)	**1970**	End of U.S. oil surplus
1918	November 11: Armistice Day	**1973**	Yom Kippur War; Oil Embargo
1919	'Feisal-Weizmann Accord' (Jan.)	**1979**	Shah overthrown in Islamic Revolution; Soviets invade Afghanistan
1919	First Comintern Congress in Kremlin (March)		
1919	Mustafa Kemal Atatürk lands at Samsun (May)	**1987**	Soviets retreat, defeated by *mujahideen* with U.S. support
		1989	Fall of Berlin Wall
THE YEAR OF CATASTROPHE (*Am al-Nakba*), 1920–21		**1990**	Saddam invades Kuwait
		1993	First attack on World Trade Center
1920	Faisal elected king of Syria (March)	**2001**	Second attack (Sept. 11)

NOTES

COCKPIT OF CONFLICT, p. 4
Fertile Crescent ... is a term popularized by Henry Breasted of the University of Chicago in his textbooks *Outline of European History* (1914), *Ancient Times*, and *A History of the Early World* (1916).
cry 'Havoc' ... Shakespeare, *Julius Caesar*: ANTONY '... domestic fury and fierce civil strife / shall cumber all the parts of Italy; / blood and destruction shall be so in use / and dreadful objects so familiar / that mothers shall but smile when they behold / their infants quarter'd with the hands of war; / all pity choked with custom of fell deeds: / and Caesar's spirit, ranging for revenge, / with Ate by his side come hot from hell, / shall in these confines with a monarch's voice / cry "Havoc," and let slip the dogs of war...'
some three millennia ... roughly 3700–550 BC.

PERSIANS, ALEXANDER, ROMANS, p. 6
Persian assault on Greece ... Why did the Persians attack the Greeks? Herodotus says that the motive was revenge for Greek support of the Lydian revolt against Persian rule. It is also said that the Persian objective was to circle to the west of the Black Sea so as to attack the Pontic Scythians in their rear, in revenge for Cyrus's death at the hands of the Massagetae Queen Tomyris, who had put his head in a skin full of blood. Of necessity such an expedition meant crossing the Hellespont from Asia to Europe, from East to West. An advance into Scythia would mean that Greece would be in the rear and have to be secured.
freedom versus tyranny ... In Herodotus, two Spartan emissaries are asked by a Persian satrap why they will not submit to Persian rule. They reply, 'You are speaking of what you do not know. You only know tyranny and slavery. If you were ever to taste of freedom, you would fight for it with sword and axe and your very life.'
circle of conquest ... Gibbon, *Decline and Fall*.
insensibly melt ... *ibid*.
transforming the old Roman republic ... Here, because our focus is the Eastern Empire, we pass with barely a sidewards glance over one of the most remarkable periods of history: the end of the Republic and the beginning of the Empire.

OLD WAR/COLD WAR/NEW WAR, p. 10
While the Romans ... Gibbon, *op. cit.*
Great Schism ... Emissaries of the pope laid a bull excommunicating the entire Eastern Empire on the high altar of Hagia Sophia. Even today, symbolic efforts are still made to heal the breach. In 2014, Pope Francis traveled to Jerusalem to meet the Patriarch of Constantinople, head of the Greek Orthodox Church. The real purpose of the visit was forgotten when the pope seized the opportunity to upbraid Israel for its human rights violations.

THE LIBRARY, p. 12
maps and drawings ... The drawings are the result of a ten-year process of finding a means to express ideas that 'like sparks into my mind did fly' (Bunyan).
Herald Tribune ... Oct. 4, 1887, then the European edition of *The New York Herald*, which merged with the *Tribune* in 1924. The publishing of a Paris edition of the principal New York paper is emblematic of the rise of the U.S. to world power. Her newly rich citizens were traveling abroad in greater numbers and buying from the declining aristocracy of the Old World the artworks—another emblem of world power—now in major American museums.

MUSEUM OF HISTORY, p. 16
tapestries ... such as the tapestries made from Rubens's cartoons in the Descalzadas monastery in Madrid, Spain, or the same artist's series in the Louvre celebrating the life of Marie de Medici, or the Hall of Maps in the Vatican.
The tradition of ... Karl Marx.

GEOPOLITICAL DYNAMICS, p. 18
rules ... laws ... 'There are laws governing events: some we are ignorant of, others we are groping to. The discovery of these laws becomes possible only when we finally give up looking for such causes in the will of one man, just as the discovery of the laws of the motion of the planets was possible only when men renounced the conception of the earth as stationary' (Tolstoy, *War and Peace* [Penguin edition, p. 1168]).

This is Tolstoy's theory of history: that no individual, such as a Napoleon, controls events. He is only doing history's bidding at the command of the combined will of millions.
Aristotle ... Galileo ... Thomas Kuhn, *The Structure of Scientific Revolutions* (1962).
between the poles ... These oscillations represent not so much 'duality' but a balance between extremes. Nature craves such balance, always returning to it after a disturbance.

One of the earliest philosophers, Pythagoras, made a table of opposites: finite/infinite; odd/even; one/many; right/left; rest/motion; straight/crooked; light/darkness; good/evil; square/oblong. Some sources add male/female. Empedocles added another, love/strife. Heraclitus divided Nature into matter and the force that flows through it, animating it. He saw that force as a dynamic of opposites achieving a balance, a stasis. Chinese philosophy organizes objects and qualities under Yin and Yang. Hegel has his thesis and antithesis; and a third, synthesis, representing the balance achieved out of the opposition of the two.

COMMEDIA DELLA STORIA, p. 20
Sicilian puppet theater ... arose in a place swept for centuries by the tides of history. It combines an energetic irreverence with a deep understanding of political power.

A visitor from Sicily took one look at this puppet standing on my work table and without pausing to think belted out this line from one of the plays: 'Roland with one blow killed three hundred Saracens! (*Orlando con un solo golpe mato a tre centi Saraceni!*)'
Song of Roland ... 'All along the pilgrimage routes that crisscrossed Christendom, leading to and from Compostella, Mont St-Michel, and Canterbury, these verses were in the minds and mouths of all, echoing in every castle, in every monastery and abbey, on every battlefield from the Welsh Marches to the Dead Sea. No modern opera, musical, or movie ever approached the popularity of the *Chanson*. None has ever expressed anything like the same completeness of society that produced it. Chanted by every minstrel—known by heart, from the beginning to end, by every man and woman and child, lay and clerical—translated into every tongue, more intensely felt, if possible, in Italy and Spain than in Normandy and England—perhaps most effective, as a work of art, when sung by the Templars in their great castles in the Holy Land ...'(Henry Adams, *Mont-St-Michel*).

'The outline of the poem moves from the particular to the general, from a national war to the world war of Cross and Crescent. At the end, there looms up behind the figures of the French champion [Roland] and the Spanish [Saracen] king the more august images of Emperor and Emir, West and East, Christendom and Islam. The world opens up before our eyes: we look beyond Saragossa to Alexandria and fabled Babylon. And now embattled alongside the French, for the first time we see the "Frank," and hear the voice of all Christendom' (Dorothy Sayers, intro., *The Song of Roland*).

commedia dell'arte... comes out of Roman comedy, ultimately out of ancient Greek farce. Stephen Sondheim honored this ancient tradition in his musical *A Funny Thing Happened on the Way to the Forum*.

tragical-comical-historical... Shakespeare, *Hamlet*. As Engels wrote to Marx, 'It really seems as if old Hegel in his grave as World Spirit directing history has ordained that it should be unrolled twice over, once as a great tragedy and once as a wretched farce.'

HISTORIAN'S COLORS, p. 22
born in the purple... or *porphyrogenitos*, that is, born in the Porphyry Chamber, the birthing room of the Great Palace in Constantinople.

MACKINDER'S WORLD ISLAND, p. 26
sea power could not... Even though the sea power feared the land power of the Heartland, the Heartland itself feared being landlocked and denied access to the sea. A navy was the ultimate world weapon, at least according to the American geo-stratagist Admiral Alfred Mahan, author of *The Influence of Sea Power on History*. Peter the Great was fascinated with anything to do with the sea and the West, apprenticing himself as a shipwright in Holland. His first little boat is preserved like a sacred relic in St. Petersburg.

DESERT & SOWN, p. 28
To the north... Halford Mackinder.

EAST & WEST, pp. 30–31
Nicholas Spykman... See note p. 242.

Can you not understand... Michael Grant, tr.
Greek passion for balance... reflected in Greek grammar, which has—in addition to singular and plural—a discrete grammatical number, the dual.
Terra Australis... or Unknown Southern Land. This is where we get the name for the continent of Australia—even though that name should more properly be applied to Antarctica, the rump of Aristotle's vast southern continent.
rising and setting... the general origin of 'East' and 'West' in many languages. For instance, the name for the West (meaning Morocco, Algeria) in Arabic is *Maghreb*, the land of the setting. The eastern seaboard of the Mediterranean (Syria, Lebanon, and Israel) is the Levant, or in French, the rising. In Turkish, however, directions are indicated by color. The Black Sea is black because it is north. The flag of Turkey is red because it is the westernmost of the Turkic countries.
There are no North... Joseph Conrad, *The Mirror of the Sea*.

ORDER & FRAGMENTATION, p. 32
has been called... by Arnold Toynbee.
Bedouins... 'Bedouins are more disposed to courage than sedentary people. The reason for this is that sedentary people have become used to laziness and ease.

'They are sunk in well-being and luxury. They have entrusted the defense of their property and their lives to the governor and ruler who rules them, and to the militia which has the task of guarding them. They find full assurance of safety in the walls that surround them, and the fortifications that protect them. No noise disturbs them, and no hunting occupies their time. They are carefree and trusting, and have ceased to carry weapons. Successive generations have grown up in this way of life. They have become

218

like women and children, who depend upon the master of the house. Eventually, this has come to be a quality of character that replaces natural disposition.

'The Bedouins, on the other hand, live apart from the community. They are alone in the country and remote from militias. They have no walls or gates. Therefore, they provide their own defense and do not trust it to, or rely upon others for it. They always carry weapons. They watch carefully all sides of the road. They take hurried naps only when they are together in company or when they are in the saddle. They pay attention to the most distant barking or noise. They go alone in the desert, guided by their fortitude, putting their trust in themselves. Fortitude has become a character quality of theirs, and courage their nature' (Ibn Khaldûn, *The Muquaddimah* [Bruce B. Lawrence, ed.]).

'The harder the life, the finer the person,' wrote Wilfrid Thesiger (1910–2003), the desert traveler who twice crossed the Empty Quarter (*Rub al Khali*) of Arabia.

not related by blood ...which Ibn Khaldûn says is unnatural. It is natural for children to submit to a father, and for fathers to submit to the village headman, and for the village headman to the tribal council and chief, to whom they are all related by blood; but to submit to another tribal ruler requires that he have some higher order of legitimacy.

This King Timur ... quoted in Fischel, *Ibn Khaldûn and Tamurlane*, p. 47. Ibn Khaldûn 'saw in the Central Asian world conqueror a Turko-Mongol vindication of his own thesis, to wit, that civilization is always and everywhere marked by the fundamental difference between urban and primitive, producing a tension that is also an interplay between nomad and merchant, desert and city, orality and literacy' (Bruce B. Lawrence).

NOMADS, p. 34
contrary to their nature ... So thought Ibn Khaldûn.
defined by the means ...The words Goth and Tatar in their respective languages mean 'horse' or 'horseman.'
only treasure ... Titus Burkhardt, *Art of Islam: Language and Meaning* (1976).
extraordinarily rich ground ... Bernard Lewis.
Mongols are outmoded ... The last horse people, the Comanches, were still a formidable force up to the 1870s. They were a Stone Age people living into the time of railways and canals, precision machinery and factories. They occupied the wide borderlands of the Great Plains, between the declining Spanish Bourbon, later Mexican empire, and the rising power of the U.S. They held both at bay until the Treaty of Guadalupe Hidalgo (1848) manifested the 'destiny' of American dreams, and opened the Plains to the buffalo hunters who destroyed the lifeblood of the Comanches.

In the end they were left with only one foe, the federal government, which, with the Civil War over, had plenty of soldiery with which to subdue the last of the real raiding nomadic horse people (S. C. Gwynne, *Empire of the Summer Sun*, 2010).
no more Tamerlanes ... This is the widely accepted view, but a case might be made that the last great invader was Mohammad Shaibani Khan, a direct descendant of Genghis. He was defeated in 1510 by the Persian Shah Ismail.

HORSES, CAMELS, SHIPS, p. 36
became sea nomads ... As Thucydides writes, 'The first question that you ask people coming from the sea is, "Are you pirates?"'

In addition to establishing a Norman dukedom in France, from which they attacked England in 1066, the northern sea nomads, the

the Turkish nomadic tribes turned westward.
declining Byzantine Empire... This, of course, was not the end for the empire, and it kept declining for another 400 years. It is often argued by historians that the real cause was not the defeat at Manzikert and the emperor's death in the battle, but palace intrigue and infighting.
Latin Kingdoms... consisted of the Kingdom of Jerusalem, the County of Tripoli, the Principality of Antioch, the Principality of Armenian Cilicia. They are indicated on the map as the Latin kingdoms, even though there was only one kingdom, the Kingdom of Jerusalem.

Eventually the Crusaders were evicted in 1292 with the loss of Acre. One of their orders, The Knights Hospitaller of St. John of Jerusalem, fled to Rhodes, from where Suleyman the Magnificent chased them in 1525 to Malta—for which they became known as the Knights of Malta. Later, they turned the island into a fortress to protect the West from the Ottoman advance.

Napoleon evicted the Knights from Malta on his way to Egypt in 1795. The British evicted the French, and it later became one of Britain's gates of India. Britain's refusal to give it back to France under the terms of the Treaty of Amiens (1802) led to Napoleon's renewing the war with Britain, and his decision to sell Louisiana to the U.S. in 1803 to fund that war.

The Knights of St. John are now a fashionable charity that supports hospitals in Jerusalem, the order's original function.
Jerusalem... Saladin had earlier ejected the Shia Fatamids from Cairo. For Sunni Islam, he is thus a double hero because he defeated two heretical powers.

MONGOLS, p. 58
Genghis... was born on the Altai Plateau in what is now called Mongolia in 1162, the year before work began on Notre Dame in Paris.

Ayn al-Galat... the 'spring of Goliath,' in 1260. Ayn al-Galat is in the valley of Jezreel, near the Sea of Galilee, where Saul is supposed to have been defeated and killed by the Philistines, and not far away is where the Crusaders were defeated by Saladin at the Horns of Hattin in 1188.
typhoon... From the Japanese point of view it was a 'divine wind,' or *kamikaze*. In the Second World War, the Japanese suicide bombers were so named in hopes that they would be another wind that would drive off the invader.
service of the Great Khan... Gibbon, quoted by Jack Weatherford, *Genghis Khan and the Making of the Modern World* (2005). This book, a few lines of which I have paraphrased, has been very useful.

RUSSIAN FAÇADE, p. 60
successor of the Mongol Empire... The Mongol occupation left a deep mark on Russia. Wrote Pushkin in a letter, 'It was Russia who contained the Mongol conquest within her vast expanses. The Tatars did not dare cross our western frontiers and so leave us in the rear. They retreated to their deserts, and Christian civilization was saved. To this end we were obliged to lead a completely separate existence which, while it left us Christians, almost made us complete strangers in the Christian world.... The Tatar invasion is a sad and impressive history.... Do you not discern something imposing in the situation of Russia, something that will strike a future historian? Do you think he will put us outside of Europe?' (quoted by Figes, *Natasha's Dance* [2002]).

'Scratch a Russian and you will find a Tatar,' Napoleon once said. Some of the most well-known names in Russian history have Tatar origins: Karamzin, Turgenev, Akhmatova, Chaadaev, Godunov, Bukharin, Rimsky-Korsakov. Vladimir Nabokov even claimed that his family descended directly from Genghis Khan himself, who 'is said to have fathered the Nabok, a petty Tatar prince in the twelfth century who married a Russian damsel in an era of intensely artistic Russian culture.' Vladimir Ilyich Ulyanov, or Lenin, was descended from a Kalmyk tribesman from Astrakhan.

European-style façade... The historian V. O. Kliuchevsky described the Russian state as 'an Asiatic structure, albeit one that has been decorated by a European façade.'

Italian architects... For instance, Francesco Bartolomeo Rastrelli (1716–1788) designed the Winter Palace in St. Petersburg and the Catherine Palace in Tsarskoye Selo (now Pushkin). The walls of the Moscow Kremlim were built by Italian masters in the 15th century, all of whom were called Freyazin, Russian for Italian.

no trace now remains... even though, according to Ibn Battuta, it took a day to ride the circuit of the wall on horseback. Most likely it was a vast city of yurts. There were, in fact, two Sarays: the first founded by Batu Khan upriver from Astrakhan on the Volga; the second by Berke, farther to the north, east of the present city of Volgograd (Stalingrad) (*Voyageurs Arabes*, Editions Gallimard [1995]).

reproached them for... R. D. Charques, *A Short History of Russia* (1956). This book, a few lines of which I have paraphrased, has been very useful.

The autocratic power... *ibid.* The historian Alexander Herzen claimed that Tsar Nicholas I was 'Genghis Khan with a telegraph.' Likewise, Stalin was 'Genghis Khan with a telephone.'

SUCCESSION OF STATES, p. 62

accepted Christianity... Looking for a religion with which to unite his people, Vladimir the Great, Grand Prince of Kiev, sent out emissaries to inquire about the various religions of the world. Rejecting Judaism and Islam because of dietary restrictions, he chose Eastern Orthodox Christianity because of the reports of the dazzling worship his emissaries saw celebrated at Hagia Sophia. 'We knew not whether we were in heaven or on earth, for surely there is no such splendor or beauty anywhere upon the earth.'

Patriarchate of Moscow... The original Patriarchates of the Eastern Orthodox Church were Jerusalem, Alexandria, Antioch, and Constantinople, all under Islamic control at this time, or shortly to be. To have a Patriarchate in Moscow free from Islamic control gave the tsars the seal of religion. Ruling over a Third Rome gave them the seal of political legitimacy. Winning battle after battle against infidels — adding 100,000 square kilometers per year — and recovering lost Christian territory, gave them the seal of victory, Ibn Khaldūn's *farrh*.

Sophia Palaiologina... Russian feminine of Paleologus, the dynasty that ruled Byzantium from 1261, when they ejected the Crusaders, to 1453. Ivan the Terrible's nine-year-old son Dmitri, the last descendant of the Rurikid and Byzantine dynasties, was murdered in Uglich in 1591, presumably on the order of Boris Godunov.

subdued the lands... Trotsky in his *History of the Russian Revolution* (1930) writes: 'Russia was formed not as a national state, but as a state made up of nationalities....The expansion of the state was in its foundation the expansion of agriculture, which with all its primitiveness showed a certain superiority to that of the nomads in the south and east. The bureaucratic-caste state, which formed itself on this enormous and continually broadening basis, became sufficiently strong to subjugate certain nations to the west possessed of a higher culture but unable because of their small numbers or condition of inner crises to defend their independence (Poland, Lithuania, the Baltic States, Finland, Ukraine). To the seventy million Great

Russians constituting the main mass of the country, there were gradually added about ninety million "outlanders" sharply divided into two groups: the western peoples exceeding Russia in their culture, and the eastern standing on a lower level. Thus was created an empire of whose population the ruling nationality constituted only 43 per cent. The remaining 57 per cent were nationalities of various degrees of culture and subjection, including Ukrainians 17 per cent, Poles 6 per cent, White Russians 4.5 per cent.'

Both projects... also had a religious motivation: in the West to reconquer former Christian territory, and in the East to convert the Muslim tribes of 'the stans' to the Orthodox faith.

CROSS AND CRESCENT, p. 64

pushed back... ultimately in the West as far as the Strait of Gibraltar and in the East almost to the Strait of Constantinople. Until the late 19th century, most of the Balkans were still under Ottoman control. It was this 'European Turkey' that was at the heart of the Eastern Question before the First World War.

Can anyone tolerate... There are several different reported versions of this famous sermon. This is that of Martin of Tours.

TWO GREAT JIHADS, p. 66

jihads... There are two types of *jihad*, a word that does not occur in the Qur'an. In one of Mohammad's sayings (*hadith*), he remarked to his wife on returning from battle against the Meccans, 'I return from the lesser *jihad* to the greater.' Presumably he meant from the struggle with the enemies of the Faith to the struggle with one's self.

The two arrows marked *Reconquista* and *Pan-Slavism* represent the later pushback of Christendom.

The dates for Jerusalem refer to its conquest by the Arabs, the Crusaders, the British, and finally the founding of the state of Israel by UN resolution. The Ottomans captured the city in 1517 with their defeat of the Egyptian Mamluks, who had controlled both Jerusalem and Mecca. The two holy cities were taken in the same year that Luther posted his theses in Wittenburg, starting the Protestant Reformation. The date 1820 refers to the beginning of Greek struggle for independence from the Ottomans.

Within three years... John Julius Norwich gives us this swift chronology.

HOLY ROMAN EMPIRE, p. 68

enemy territory... from which came slave raiders. A Spanish idiom meaning 'Be careful, there are enemies around': ¡Hay Moros en la costa! (Or, literally: There are Moors on the shore!)

Charlemagne would have been... Henri Pirenne.

his kingdom split in half... originally into *Francia Orientalis*, or Eastern Frankland, now modern Germany; and *Francia Occidentalis*, Western Frankland, now modern France.

a linguistic and climatic divide... Culturally we might say that the south experienced neither the Reform nor the Enlightenment, but shared the inheritance of the Renaissance with the north. Russia experienced neither Renaissance, nor Reform, nor—in spite of Catherine's attempts—an Enlightenment.

The Cyrillic alphabet, invented by Byzantine missionaries to translate the scriptures for the Slavs, further cut Russia off from the West.

original European Union... West Germany, France, the Benelux countries, and Italy. This is why *The Economist* titles its column on European affairs 'Charlemagne.'

The original European Union did not include East Germany because when the Union was created, East Germany was on the other side of the Iron Curtain, which lay along the Elbe. Crossing that river before the war, Konrad Adenauer, the future West German chancellor, is said to have exclaimed, "Ach, Asia!" (quoted in Anthony Bailey, *Along the Edge of the Forest* [1983]).

The map is of the later, larger Holy Roman Empire with its eastern border on the Oder farther to the east, including East Germany. It lasted much longer as a political entity than Charlemagne's kingdom, up until Napoleon abolished it and seized the title of emperor for himself in 1801, a millennium after Charlemagne had been crowned Roman emperor by the pope.

Charlemagne's father, Pepin, conquered Lombardy and created the Papal States as a protectorate. The two political parties of Medieval Italy, the Guelphs and the Ghibbelines, were respectively for pope or emperor. Exiled from Florence in the struggle, Dante dreamed that one day both powers—the Church and the Empire—would be united in a European union.

Ibn Khaldūn remarks that, as opposed to Dar al' Islam, Europe was not united because it did not have the religious duty to fight a *jihad*. However, Europe was certainly brought together—even if not politically united—to fight the counter-*jihad* of the Crusades, as celebrated in the old chansons, and after them in the epic poems of Tasso and Ariosto. See note p. 228.

harassed Christendom... Edward Gibbon.
the 'Moor-killer'... The real St. James most likely perished—if he had even been still living—when the Romans suppressed the Great Revolt in Judea, AD 66–70. His transformation into the patron saint of the Crusades came out of the same religious imagination that accounts for the many apparitions of the Virgin in different places, or the 'translation' of her house to Loreto in Italy after the East fell to Islam.

PENINSULARITY OF EUROPE, p. 70
A victorious line of march... Edward Gibbon.
almost the entire peninsula... with the exception of an independent Fascist power in Spain and neutral Switzerland and Sweden.
most of Russia in Asia... See note p. 222. As heir to the Mongols, Russia is an Asian power.

EASTERN BORDERS OF EUROPE, p. 72
uti posseditis... A good example of *uti posseditis* was the Line of Contact along the Elbe where the armies of East and West met in 1945: On orders from Truman, and against the advice of Churchill, the Allies withdrew to the line farther west agreed to at Yalta.
A man seems to take... Stoye, *The Siege of Malta*. The same might be said of today's Third World that 'with no great variety but under some conformity extends' all over Latin America, Africa, and Asia.
football field of the Balkans... The Huns under Attila penetrated as far as Châlons. At the Mincio River outside Milan, they were supposedly turned back by Pope Leo. The Cossacks camped in Paris, but had been invited as part of the Allied forces that had defeated Napoleon at Waterloo.

EIN FESTE BURG, p. 74
Ein Feste Burg... A mighty fortress, as in Luther's hymn. It is appropriate that the northern European Protestants saw themselves in a fortress. Luther, after all, was hidden in a fortress by his protector, the Elector of Saxony.
a renegade Hungarian... It is ironic that he was the namesake of Pope Urban II, who preached the Crusade in 1095.
Long War... Technically speaking, this 'Long War' lasted for a relatively short period of time (1593–1606), but I use it here in an extended sense referring to the long struggle fought

between Islam and Christendom—what Gibbon calls the 'Great Debate.' A website called 'The Long War Journal' reports on the war against terror, an extension of the long struggle.

TWO-FRONTED WARS, p. 76
Drabness was... Fredric Morton, *A Nervous Splendor* (1980). A true Hapsburg, Franz Josef II saved paper by cutting off the unused portion of letters he received.
series of brilliant marriages... A saying has it: *Bella gerant alii, tu felix Austria nube.*—Let others wage war: thou, happy Austria, marry.
defeat of the French at Pavia... capturing King Francis I, who had incited Suleyman to open an eastern front. At the battle of Mohács, Charles V's brother-in-law, Louis of Hungary and Bohemia, was killed. The Hapsburgs thus inherited these lands. There is a Hungarian saying, 'More was lost at Mohács,' meaning worse things have happened.
defender of the Roman Church... Napoleon is said to have remarked that if Charles had chosen to support the Protestant cause at the Diet of Worms in 1521, the history of the world would have been utterly different.
sea battle off Lepanto... very near where another great sea battle, Actium, was fought between the combined fleet of Antony and Cleopatra and that of Octavian (later Augustus). These two places, Actium and Lepanto, lie along the border between the Eastern and Western empires, the Adriatic Sea. Lepanto was the last significant sea battle fought with galleys.
Don Juan of Austria... *Vivat Hispania! / Domino Gloria! /* Don John of Austria / Has set his people free! (G. K. Chesterton)
el manco... literally, the maimed man. His left arm was rendered useless. It was amazing that he survived at all.
'What the survivors would remember—as far as they remembered anything from the flash-lit moments of battle—was the noise.... Behind the volcanic detonation of the guns came other sounds: the sharp snapping of oars like successive pistol shots, the crash and splinter of colliding ships, the rattle of arquebuses, the sinister whip of arrows, cries of pain, wild shouting, the splash of bodies backwards into the sea ... thick and red with blood' (Roger Crowley, *Empires of the Sea: the Siege of Malta and the Battle of Lepanto*, [2008]).
Persia alone... quoted in Wheatcroft, *op. cit.*

HAPSBURG MILITARY FRONTIER, p. 78
exact anniversary... in the Eastern Julian calendar. Using the Western Gregorian calendar, the Austrians were apparently unaware of the unhappy conjunction.

THE WORLD EGG BROKEN, p. 80
Sicilian puppets... See p. 20 and note p. 217.

ACT TWO, p. 84
vasty wilds... Shakespeare, *The Merchant of Venice*. The background of the play is Venice's lucrative but dangerous trade with the Ottoman Empire. The city was often accused by the Church of playing a double game between East and West, being more interested in commerce than Christianity. Venice's precarious position in between two hostile behemoths—the Ottomans and the Hapsburgs—and dependent on both for trade, led to the development of the modern diplomatic system of permanent embassies that also serve as permanent bases for espionage.

ACT THREE, p. 86
ghost of the Roman... Hobbes (*Leviathan*): 'The Papacy is not other than the Ghost of the deceased Roman Empire, sitting crowned upon the grave thereof.'

ACT FOUR, p. 90
Red Apple... The 'Red Apple' is a term used in Islamic history referring to the future conquest of the great Christian city, and used in the phrase, 'Next year in the Red Apple.' For almost a thousand years, it was the as-yet-unconquered city of Constantinople. After 1453, it became Vienna, or even Rome. It is said that it may have originally been inspired by the shining golden dome of Hagia Sophia. In 2001, it might be said, with a certain exaggeration, to have been New York.
slaves of all the Slavs... The Slavs were slaves to begin with and by definition: the Viking slave trade in them led to their being called 'Slavs.'

ACT FIVE, p. 92
it was reported... *N.Y. Times*, Sept. 3, 2012.
antimissile defenses... as well as one offensive weapon, the 30,000-pound MOP, or 'Massive Ordinance Penetrator,' developed by Boeing specifically to destroy the Ferdow nuclear facility (*Wall Street Journal*, May 5, 2013).
edge of the Western world... Scott Bates, a friend of the present writer formerly in the State Department, wrote in an e-mail from Baghdad in 2008 that he felt as if he were standing on the edge of the Western world.
Euripides' Bacchae... According to Plutarch, Crassus' head was brought in to the court during a performance of the play to replace a prop for the head of the character Pentheus.
Lord Palmerston... (1784–1865) British foreign secretary and prime minister

THE PETRI DISH, pp. 102–103
This schism... Braudel, *The Mediterranean Sea*.

BATTLE OF ISSUS, p. 104
where the East... Milton, *Paradise Lost*.
artisan of the world... Titus Burckhardt, *op. cit*. Alexander figures just as largely in Eastern as he does in Western history. An American officer, Major Stoney Portis, deployed in Nuristan, Afghanistan, in 2009 observed, 'The blond and redheaded Nuristanis who dotted the mountainsides took pride in the idea that they descended from Alexander's Greeks and outlasted conquerors for millennia (*N.Y. Times*, Nov. 23, 2014).
his sister became a mermaid... Mary Renault, *The Nature of Alexander*.

VOYAGES OF SAUL OF TARSUS, p. 106
But who celebrates... Certainly the significance of that journey has not been lost on the citizens of Kavalla, Greece (ancient Neapolis), where Paul first set foot in Europe. On the façade of a church—formerly a mosque—near the port there is a modern (1989) mosaic in Byzantine style showing Paul stepping across from Asia to Europe.
vernacular Greek of traders... or *koine* Greek, the lingua franca of the Byzantine Empire, also called Alexandrian Greek.

The Christian Old Testament is based on the *Septuagint*, the Hebrew scriptures translated into Greek in Alexandria under the Ptolemies. It was translated into Latin by Jerome, who also translated the Greek scriptures, combining both into the Old and New Testaments of the Latin 'Vulgate' Bible, later translated into the modern European languages at the Reformation.
be known only... If it were not for Plato, Socrates would be known only as a corrupter of Athenian youth

Mohammad, on the contrary, was Jesus, Paul, and Constantine in one person. He was not only the Prophet, but evangelist (receiving the text, the Qur'an, directly from the archangel Gabriel), apostle, and military leader, the 'commander of the faithful.' We know more about him than about any other founder of a world religion.

EPIC AS HISTORY, p. 108
first sentence of his book... 'These are the inquiries of Herodotus of Halicarnassus, which he publishes to preserve the remembrance of the great and wonderful actions of the Greeks and the barbarians... and to put on record what were the grounds of their feuds.'

Our word 'history' comes from Herodotus' use here of the word *historia*, or 'inquiries' in Greek. To the Greeks, anybody not Greek was a 'barbarian,' literally a 'foreigner.'
at Gallipoli... where, in 1915, Australia and New Zealand began to see themselves as *not* British. The biggest national holiday in both countries, ANZAC Day, celebrates that sense of national independence.

GREEK LETTERS, p. 110
knowledge of Aristotle... Mixing sources, the Arabs added a dash of Platonism to their Aristotelian philosophy. Averroës (Ibn Rushd), born in Cordobá in 1126, contributed an 'indispensable' commentary.
Greek... died out... Many of the classical Latin texts, as well as the Greek, were thought to have been lost. The recovery of both was the spark that started the European Renaissance. Without Greek, Latin literature would be a house without a foundation.

RELIGION AS POLITICS, p. 112
spread of Christianity... The dates on the map refer to the various conversions of the north to Christianity, and to the Arab conquests of North Africa, Israel, and Persia. Black arrows are the Jewish diasporas.
Islam is politics... Khomeini was asserting the right of the *ulema*, the religious leaders, to rule politically. This is contrary to Shia doctrine, which holds that their rule must wait until the Hidden Imam, the Mahdi, returns to restore the rule of justice in the world and not until then.
pagan tribes of northern... the ancestors of the nations of northern Europe
Declaration of Independence... 'When in the course of human events, it becomes necessary for one people to dissolve the political bands which have connected them with another, and to assume among the powers of the earth, the separate and equal station to which the Laws of Nature and of Nature's God entitle them, a decent respect to the opinions of mankind requires that they should declare the causes which impel them to the separation.

'We hold these truths to be self-evident, that all men are created equal, that they are endowed by their Creator with certain inalienable rights, that among these are life, liberty and the pursuit of happiness.

'That to secure these rights, governments are instituted among men, deriving their just powers from the consent of the governed. That whenever any form of government becomes destructive of these ends, it is the right of the people to alter or abolish it, and to institute new government, laying its foundation on such principles and organizing its powers in such form, as to them shall seem most likely to effect their safety and happiness.

'Prudence, indeed, will dictate that governments long established should not be changed for light and transient causes; and accordingly all experience hath shown, that mankind are more disposed to suffer, while evils are sufferable, than to right themselves by abolishing the forms to which they are accustomed.

'But when a long train of abuses and usurpations, pursuing invariably the same object evinces a design to reduce them under absolute despotism, it is their right, it is their duty, to throw off such government, and to provide new guards for their future security.'

JERUSALEM THE GOLDEN, p. 114

***Gerusalemme liberata!*...** Tasso's *Gerusalemme liberata* and Ariosto's *Orlando Furioso*, the two great epic poems of Italian Renaissance literature, celebrate the struggle of Islam and Christendom. As with the Sicilian puppets, the stories are taken from the *chansons de geste*, like the *Song of Roland*, but romanticized with love interests.

At the end of the Passover Seder service, it is traditional to say, 'Next year in Jerusalem.' Even though Jews can now live in Jerusalem, the phrase refers to an ideal Jerusalem: a city with the Temple, the Sanhedrin, and a Jewish monarch.

General Allenby... Lloyd George dubbed Allenby's conquest of Jerusalem 'the last and most triumphant of the Crusades.' In July 1920, when the French general Henri Gouraud took charge of Damascus, he is said to have walked up to Saladin's tomb next to the Grand Mosque, kicked it, and exclaimed, 'Awake, Saladin, we have returned. My presence here consecrates the victory of the Cross over the Crescent.' After an earlier visit in 1898, Kaiser Wilhelm had the tomb restored in a gesture of friendship to Sultan Abdül Hamid.

THREE MAJOR LANGUAGE GROUPS, p. 116

obliteration of the Greek culture... Greek is, of course, still spoken in Greece. With Italian, it is the basis of the nautical vocabulary of the Mediterranean as it has been since Hellenistic times, or before, following on Phoenician. This 'obliteration,' as I call it, is at the heart of the mutual animosity of Greeks and Turks today.

The original Indo-European-speaking people were long supposed to have been the nomads of the Pontic steppe north of the Black Sea—the desert. A new (2012) theory holds for an earlier, Anatolian origin among the first agriculturalists—the sown.

PERSIAN LETTERS, p. 118

Mahmoud of Ghazna... laid the foundation of Muslim rule in what is now Pakistan. He is known in Persian poetry as the lover of a Turkish soldier named Ayaz. 'To make Mahmoud's eye happy on Ayaz's foot once more' is to grant the lover the fulfillment of his wishes. The main subject of Persian poetry is unrequited love. The identity of the loved one is left ambiguous: he can be God, the 'granter of desires,' or the prince, whom the poet hopes will shower pearls on the head of the singer of his praises, or an earthly lover, sex undisclosed. Since women were off limits unless the poet wished to be murdered by a father or brother, the safer poetic object of desire is a boy with the down just starting on his lip and cheeks: a 'green beard.' There is a pun—Persian poetry delights in puns—on the word 'down,' or *khatt*, which can also mean the calligraphy in which the poem is written.

There is a jewel-like quality about Persian poetry, whose verses are said to be 'pearls strung on the thread of the rhyme.' The American poet James Russell Lowell uses this image in his very Persian poem 'Rubayyat of Edward Fitzgerald': 'these pearls of thought in Persian Gulfs were bred, / each softly loosened as a rounded moon, / the diver Omar plucked them from their bed, / Fitzgerald strung them on an English thread.'

Persian poets had a fascination with precious and semiprecious stones like the red carnelian of Yemen, a country that for the poets had a magical mystery, often counterpoised with the materialism of the Maghreb, the West (Tunisia, Algeria, and Morocco). Carnelian symbolizes the lips of the beloved, nightingales the yearning lover, and roses the loved one, the object of desire. Like 'love' and 'dove,' or 'burn' and 'yearn,' in English, rose (*gul*) and nightingale (*bulbul*) make an easy rhyme (Schimmel, *The Two-Colored Brocade* [1992]).

RUMI'S TOMB, pp. 120–21
Fitzkhayyam... Edward Fitzgerald's translation of the *Rubayyat of Omar Khayyam* is said to be at least as much the creation of Fitzgerald as of Khayyam.

ARCHITECTURE, EAST AND WEST, p. 122
Hagia Sophia... the oldest church in Christendom, and for a millennium—until the building of St. Peter's in Rome—the largest. Mehmet made it a mosque, Atatürk a museum. Ibn Battuta asserts that it was built by Solomon's cousin, as was the Ka'aba believed to have been by Abraham and Ishmael.
the sunbeams, all we know... George Bradley, 'An Arrangement of Sunlight at Hagia Sophia.'
supports invisibly flow down... William MacDonald, *Early Christian & Byzantine Architecture*.
a circle whose circumference... St. Augustine.
Edirne... the ancient Adrianople, founded by Roman Emperor Hadrian. Edirne was the Ottoman's second (after Bursa), and first European capital. The Selimiye Mosque was completed by Suleyman's son Selim with the booty from the conquest of Cyprus in 1571, five months before the battle of Lepanto.

   Born a Greek in 1490, Sinan was taken as part of the 'boy tax' (*devshirme*) and trained as a Janissary. His skill as a military engineer attracted the interest of Sultan Suleyman, who in 1537 appointed him as head of the office of royal architects. He died in 1588. He was a contemporary of the Venetian painter Titian (1488/90–1576).
There might be no other... Titus Burckhardt, *op. cit.*

TIME AND SPACE, p. 124
Time in the form of... Burckhardt, *ibid.* I do not mean to imply that there is no sense of time in Islam. Mosques often have large tall-case clocks and an official position of timekeeper. The hours of prayer are most carefully observed. My point is that the mosque is not oriented temporally to an astronomical event, but rather spatially to a geographical center.
Easter... It is said that the name comes from that of the Teutonic goddess Eostre, whose feast day was the vernal equinox.
This house... Burckhardt, *ibid.* Originally Mohammad had directed his followers to pray in the direction of Jerusalem, as in the synagogues of the Diaspora. When the Jewish community of Medina refused to recognize him as a prophet, he changed the direction of prayer (*qibla*), to Mecca. Bernard Lewis called this Mohammad's 'most creative religious act.'

THE OTTOMAN RHINOCEROS, p. 126
pirates... Being horse people, the Ottomans preferred to hire pirates as their chief naval operatives, such as Barbarossa and Turgut Reis. Turgut died at the siege of Malta in 1565. With the weakening of the Ottoman Empire, the North African pirates continued to raid shipping in the Mediterranean until finally suppressed by the U.S. Marines in 1815.
damasked blade of jihad... See note p. 231.
Royal authority... Ibn Khaldūn quotes the Sassanian ruler Khosraw I (531–579). He also quotes Aristotle: 'The world is a garden the fence of which is the dynasty... The ruler is an institution supported by the soldiers. The soldiers are helpers maintained by money. Money is sustenance brought together by the subjects. The subjects are servants protected by justice... and through it the world persists. The world is a garden...' Ibn Khaldūn goes on to say, 'The author [Aristotle] was proud of what he had hit upon....'

   It is certainly a truth that the state is founded on the army. A former French ambassador remarked that Pakistan is 'an army in search of a country.' Generals may wear suits, but they extend an iron hand from a pinstriped sleeve.

TOPKAPI PALACE, p. 128
fountain *...* This fountain was hated and feared as a symbol of the power of the sultan. High officials and members of the royal family were executed by the head gardeners (*bastançi*) using the famous 'silken cord.' Their heads were subsequently displayed outside the gate. One always praised God's mercy and the sultan's clemency before kneeling to the executioner.
a young man *...* quoted in Wheatcroft, *The Ottomans: Dissolving Images* (1996). This book, a few lines of which I have paraphrased, has been very helpful.

THREE INSTITUTIONS, pp. 130–31
drew to their ranks *...* The same could be said of Isis in 2014, located on the borders of weak states and drawing to its ranks *jihadi* from all over the world.
irresistible progress *...* Gibbon.
began to fail *...* with Suleyman's marriage to Roxanne, which began the period of the 'rule of women.' After Suleyman, who inherited the throne without contest, Ottoman princes were brought up in the harem and ceased to command provinces and armies, ruling thenceforward through grand viziers. The Janissaries had long outlived their usefulness when they were suppressed by Sultan Mahmud II in 1826 in the 'Auspicious Incident' when more than 6,000 were executed.
the fall of Constantinople *...* anticipated in the 30th Surah of the Qur'an, Al-Rum: 'The Roman Empire has been defeated....'

Upon entering Hagia Sophia in May 1453, Mehmet is said to have quoted the Persian poet Saadi, who died in 1291 (a year before the Crusaders lost their foothold at Acre): 'The spider weaves the curtains in the palace of the Caesars / The owl stands watch upon his ramparts...'

The death of the last Byzantine emperor is described in a Turkish chronicle of the next century in classic Ottoman style: 'The blind-hearted emperor became aware that [the Turkish besiegers] had found a path within the walls. He... rushed from his palace... and encountered a small number of heroes who were busy, with minds at ease, collecting plunder... and the sickle of his saber reaped the harvest of their lives. One feeble 'azab was lying on the ground suffering the life dissolving torment of his wounds. That monarch of evil-custom, raising his sword against that one who was soon to be a wanderer from existence thought to destroy the last spark of his being. Then that helpless one, struggling with but half his life, through the aid of the Granter of Desires, tore down the enemy of the Faith and brought down on his head the damasked blade of *jihad*. He cut off his head and confounded the emperor's followers' (quoted in Wheatcroft, *op. cit.*).

The Byzantine source says that the emperor was fighting along the walls and died defending the breach that the Ottomans had made. It is also said that a traitor opened a small gate and let the besiegers in.
first major Turkish defeat *...* At Lepanto, Malta, and later Vienna, they were reaching the limit of conquest: that is to say, the natural geopolitical limits of the Eastern Empire.

ERTOĞRUL GAZI TURBESI, p. 132
title of caliph *...* In 1055, the Selçuks began to rule at Baghdad as sultans, and the title of caliph became honorary, but remained in the Abbasid family. Two centuries later, in 1258, when the Mongols sacked Baghdad, one of the

Abbasids who survived the massacre of the family managed to flee to Egypt. In 1517, when the Ottoman sultan Selim the Grim conquered Egypt, he took the last of the Abbasids back to Constantinople.

Even though the Ottoman sultans thenceforth had the right, they never claimed the title of caliph until Abdül Hamid. Like the Latin word *imperator*, the word *sultan* means 'he who holds the power,' while the word *caliph* means 'successor' (of Mohammad). In the etymologies of these two words, we see the distinction between the two types of legitimacy we discussed in regard to Sunni and Shia. See p. 52.

My purpose is to obey... translated by Bernard Lewis, *Music of a Distant Drum: Classical Arabic, Persian, Turkish, and Hebrew Poems* (2011).

GREAT 'C' OF RECONQUISTA, p. 136
fleeting delusion... In Spanish *engaño*, like the delusions of the hero of Cervantes's novel *Don Quixote* (1604), many of whose adventures are a send-up of the old *chansons de geste*. This first great novel is a reflection of the fleeting dream of glory, reflected also in Calderón's *La Vida es sueño* (1635), or *Life Is a Dream*. 'The king dreams that he is king and lives with this delusion, ordering, / disposing, governing...' (*Sueña el rey que es rey, y vive con este engaño, mandando, / disponiendo, gobernando...*)
irredentist... a movement to recover territory perceived to have been lost, e.g., *Italia irredenta*.
modern capitalist system... We will now delve into Carlyle's dismal science of economics, which is 'dismal'—as he wrote—for 'find[ing] the secret of the Universe in supply and demand.'

PASSING OF GREEK MANUSCRIPTS, p. 138
Byzantine scholars... 'Without the help of Byzantine commentators and scribes, there is little we would know about the literature of ancient Greece' (Steven Runciman).

The dates on the map refer to the Ottoman conquests of Constantinople, Rhodes, Jerusalem, and Baghdad; and to the failed sieges of Vienna and Malta, which put a limit to their empire.

Florence 1438 refers to the Council of Florence, at which the Eastern and Western churches were technically reunited. At the same time, a chair was established to teach Greek in Florence for Gemisthos Plethon, who had come with the embassy from Constantinople. This visit of the Eastern emperor and patriarch to Florence is commemorated in Benozzo Gozzoli's painting *The Journey of the Magi*.

Venice 1495 refers to the founding of the Aldine Press with a Greek grammar. The press printed many first editions of the Greek texts, including Euclid's *Elements*, the book being handed across the peninsula of Greece from East to West. Latin translations of Euclid from Arabic had been available in the West since the 13th century, but it was not until the Renaissance that the text was known in the original Greek.

The development of Western science... In a letter, Einstein goes on to say, 'One has not to be astonished that the Chinese sages have not made those steps. The astonishing thing is that the discoveries were made at all' (quoted by Joseph Needham, in *Scientific Change*, A. C. Crombie, ed. [1963]).

Letters at this point... quoted in J. A. Symonds, *The Renaissance in Italy*.

CAPITAL FLOWS, pp. 140–41
created an inflation... Charles Gibson, *Spain in America* (1966). The best documentary sources for the 16th-century inflation, it is said, are the kitchen accounts of the Topkapi Palace.

declining ones... 'In 1566, the gold mint at Cairo—the only one in the Ottoman world producing coins from limited supplies of African gold—devalued its coinage by 30%.... The silver coins [became] "as light as the leaves of the almond tree and as worthless as drops of dew," according to a contemporary Ottoman historian' (Roger Crowley, *op. cit.*).

THE TURNING POINT, pp. 142–43
and then of the East... referring to the imposition of the West's fragmented nature on the defeated Ottoman Empire.
Spinoza... In a poem of 1920, Einstein wrote, 'How I love this noble man / More than I can say with words. / But I fear that he is left alone / With his bright shining halo.' (*Wie lieb ich diesen edlen Mann / Mehr als ich mit Worten sagen kann / Doch fürcht' ich dass er bleibt allein / Mit seinem strahlenen Heilegenschien.*)
greater good... These ideas were to be fully expanded and incorporated into Western liberal thinking with Locke, Hume, Bentham, Mill, and Robert Owen. In 1825, Owen attempted to put communism into practice in New Harmony, Indiana. It was the first such experiment since ancient times when Dionysus II, the tyrant of Syracuse, attempted to establish Plato's Republic in Sicily with the assistance of Plato himself. Both attempts failed.

FALL OF DAR AL' ISLAM, p. 146
zero-sum game... Geopolitics becomes a study at this time: geography did not become political until we ran out of it.
unleashed heretofore... Karl Marx, *The Communist Manifesto*, 1848.
Industrial Revolution... As there were four phases of the European expansion, there were three phases of the Industrial Revolution. The first, starting in the 18th century and continuing into the 19th, was powered by the steam engine, itself made possible by the ability to cast fine-grained steel and iron that could be precisely machined. The second, starting in 1870 and continuing into the 1960s, was based on scientific advances in electricity and chemistry that led to the inventions of Morse, Bell, and Edison. The third, starting in 1980 and based on the computer, is the Information Age. The first two were firmly in the control of the West; the third is open to the whole world.
quarterly in the stock market... If a company fails to meet Wall Street's quarterly projections, its share price generally falls.
limits of its conquests... the natural geopolitcal limits of the Eastern Empire.

CATHERINE AND POTEMKIN, p. 148
Potemkin... By contemporary standards, Potemkin was a giant, but since Catherine was the empress, I have chosen to represent him hierarchically here.
the Greek source... ΕΙΣ ΤΗΝ ΠΟΛΙΝ, phonetically *is-tan-pol[-in]*, or as Turkified, *is-tam-bul*. In the Byzantine Empire, Constantinople was referred to as 'the City,' as people living around any major city refer to it as simply 'the city.' Almost all old Greek place-names have been Turkified: Iznik for Nicea, or Izmir for Smyrna.
ceded the Khanate... The loss of the Crimea was a terrible blow to the Ottoman Empire. These were not just mere Christian lands conquered from infidels, but the lands of the khans of the Crimea, descended from Genghis and the Golden Horde, who had a more ancient claim than the Ottoman sultans to political legitimacy in Asia. Fearful of this, the Ottomans had the last khan, Sahin Giray, executed in 1787, the same year as Catherine and Potemkin's tour.

RUSSIAN BEAR, pp. 150–51
warm-water port... One of the reasons Putin supports the Assad regime in Syria is to keep the two Russian naval bases on the Mediterranean Sea, at Tartus and Latakia. The Syrian ports represent an option for the Russian Fleet on the far side of the Straits of Constantinople.

Under the terms of the Montreux Convention of 1936, free passage is granted to commercial freight of all nations in peacetime but Turkey has the right to bar transit of warships.

nothing more... 'What does all this Russian Pan-Slavic charlatanism amount to? The seizure of Constantinople and nothing more' (Friedrich Engels [1882]).

had to sail past... which is not an easy thing to do. The current flows westward out of the Black Sea, and for most of the year the wind is contrary. The only way to make the eastward passage was to wait at Troy for a favorable wind.

demanded the Straits... and would have gotten them under the terms of the secret Anglo-Russian-French Treaty of 1915.

GATES OF INDIA, p. 152
Jewel in the Crown... That is, India, which the British first secured by defeating the Nawab of Bengal and his French allies at Plassey in 1757 during the Seven Years' War, known in North America as the French and Indian War. Then, after losing her American colonies, she brought all of India under British Raj, or rule.

Gates of India... Admiral Jackie Fisher, the man who convinced the British government to convert the navy to oil, asserted that 'five strategic keys lock up the world.... These five keys belong to England.' They included the Straits of Malacca in the East. In regard to the Passage to India, the more proximate, more critical ones were the gates that Britain controlled or 'protected,' as well as the coastlines along either side of the crucial strategic passage.

'There is a striking similarity,' wrote Mackinder, 'between the Mediterranean of the Romans, with the legions along the Rhine frontier, and the Indian Ocean, with the British Army on the North-West Frontier of India, making the Indian Ocean a "closed sea."'

Iraq and Palestine... With the outbreak of war in 1914, the Ottoman Empire went from being a neutral power to an enemy and a dangerous one, with a port at the head of the Persian Gulf on the flank of the Passage to India. This seemed to justify the taking of Basra at the head of the Gulf. It was remarked that the gates of India were being extended farther and farther to the east. Certainly it justified the taking of Palestine as a Jewish 'homeland' to secure the eastern flank of the Suez Canal.

in an altered version... that of Spykman, the geostrategist known as the 'godfather of containment.' See note p. 242.

any sea power... It was Russia's loss of her fleet in the Russo-Japanese War of 1904—the first time a major world power was defeated by a 'backward' state—that led Mackinder to his theory. The bringing of the 'Great White Fleet' into the Pacific in 1907–9 demonstrated that the U.S. could command the Pacific against the growing Japanese threat, thus allowing Britain to safely bring her fleet back home to defend herself against the growing German threat.

central railway system... By the command of which, during the Russian Civil War of the early 1920s, the Red Army under Trotsky was able to defeat the fragmented Whites trying to strangle the newborn Soviet Union in its cradle.

crossing 1,500 miles of mountains... Rudyard Kipling, for one, seems to be quite aware of the improbability of a Russian invasion when he has one of his characters say, 'You could credit anything about Russia's designs on India... but a

little bit of sober fact is more than you can stand' (*Plain Tales from the Hills* [1899]).
oil had been known... Drilling at Baku began in 1846. Other Russian objects were to subdue Bukharan tribesmen, who for centuries had been slave-raiding along the border, and to secure markets for the nascent Russian industry.
Great Game... Named so by Major John Connelly, who died by being thrown down a well in Bukhara.

AFGHANISTAN, p. 154
surreptitiously surveying... In doing so, they discovered the highest mountain on earth, Everest, named in 1865 for the (then retired) surveyor general, Sir George Everest. The name of the second highest mountain, K2, was from the designation used by the Survey of India to refer to so-far unnamed peaks, signifying in this case 'Karakoram [Range] 2.'
buffer zone... To 19th-century European imperialists, this may have been a handy buffer zone, but historically this area was the epicenter of the Persian cultural zone—the birthplace of the poet Rumi, in the ancient Zoroastrian city of Balkh. See p. 118.
series of treaties... The northern border was established by the Joint Anglo-Russian Boundary Commission (1885–1888) and the Anglo-Russian Convention (1907). The southern boundary, the Durand Line, which divides Afghanistan from Pakistan (then British India), was negotiated in 1893 between the Emir of Afghanistan, Abdur Rahman Khan, and Henry Mortimer Durand, the foreign secretary of India. This line runs through Pashtun tribal areas and is 'one of the world's most dangerous borders' (Philip Walker, ForeignPolicy.com [June 24, 2011]).

The Joint Anglo-Russian Boundary Commission is the 'Border Commission' referred to in the article in the 1887 Paris *Trib* headlined, 'The Eastern Question, Again.' See p. 12.

POLITICAL FOOTBALL, p. 156
domestic politics on foreign policy... the main theme of Seton Watson's *Disraeli, Gladstone, and the Eastern Question* (1935).
and died for the cause... Byron died of fever at Missolonghi in 1824 without seeing action, frustrated by Greek internecine squabbling. He is remembered today in Greece as the Lafayette of their War of Independence.
an occasional massacre... Massacres were normal operating procedure with the Ottomans as with any of the raiding horse people off the steppes. Here from the *Independent Gazette* (Philadelphia) of August 1789: 'Vienna, May 13—They write from Croatia, that on the 12th of April, 1000 Turkish cavalry attacked a post of the Banant—five villages belonging to the Bosnians, which were under the Imperial [Hapsburg] protection, experienced the fury of the enemy; all men were immediately put to the sword—104 women and boys, 6000 horned cattle, 108 horses, and 507 goats were carried off, and three small towns all burnt to ashes.

'The enemy, after this, retired to the village of Pograzi, where they sold the booty to the best bidders—a Turk purchased two women and four children for 600 florins.'
alarmed Britain... The establishment in the Balkans of large Russian client states had alarmed Western powers. It is said that, at the news of the presence of Russian armies just outside Istanbul, Queen Victoria exclaimed, 'The Russians shall not have Constantinople!'

A music hall star wrote a popular song with the chorus: 'We don't want to fight but by jingo if we do, / We've got the men and got the money too. / We've fought the Bear before [in Crimea] and while we're Britons true / The

Russians shall not have Constantinople!' This is apparently when the word 'jingoism' enters the English language, meaning a belligerent form of nationalism. It is appropriate the word was coined in reference to the nationalistic struggles in the Balkans. See p. 78.

Conference of Berlin... at which the modern borders of the Balkans were drawn, and Romania, Serbia, and Montenegro became independent states. Austria was given a protectorate for Bosnia, with rights to annex if deemed necessary for strategic reasons. Britain got Cyprus.

Playing the role of 'honest broker,' Bismarck convened the conference to adjust various claims, but Disraeli was the center of gravity in Berlin. *Der alte Jude das ist der Mann* (The old Jew, he's the man), Bismarck exclaimed.

The object of the conference was to diminish Russian power and prevent the creation of a Greater Bulgaria, but it left most parties with seething resentments that eventually exploded in the First World War.

In the second Conference of Berlin in 1885, which is also called the Congo Conference, European powers met to adjust colonial claims in what is called the 'Scramble for Africa.' The lines remain more or less to this day.

SANDBOX OF EMPIRE, p. 158

disaster at al-Kut... where a British force under the command of General Townshend was besieged by an Ottoman army under the command of German general Baron von der Gotz. Some 23,000 British and Indian soldiers died in the attempt to relieve Townshend. The British paymaster, T. E. Lawrence, tried to bribe the Turks to let the besieged army escape. Townshend with 8,000 surviving troops surrendered in April 1916. The enlisted men were put to hard labor and half of them died. As an officer, Townshend spent the remainder of the war on one of the Prince's Islands near Istanbul. Kut was retaken by a stronger British force under the command of General Maude in February 1917. In March, Maude's army entered Baghdad.

The disaster at al-Kut traumatized the British. From that point on, especially after Gallipoli, there was no going back.

foreign minister... At a secret meeting in 1908 at Buchlau in Moravia hosted by the Austro–Hungarian diplomat Count Berchtold, Alois Aehrenthal duped the Russian foreign minister, Alexander Izvolsky, into agreeing to the annexation of Bosnia in return for a vague promise to support Russia's eventual control of the Straits. When the Austrians immediately announced the annexation and the trick was revealed, Izvolsky lost his position as foreign minister and was posted to Paris as ambassador. There, partly by bribing influential newspaper editors, he made sure that when the coming war did finally break out, the bellicose anti-German party of Raymond Poincaré was in office. Poincaré was elected president in February 1913.

Berchtold had been made Austro-Hungarian foreign minister in 1912. After the assassination of the archduke at Sarajevo in June 1914, he drafted the ultimatum to Serbia that, backed up by the 'blank check' from Germany, led to the outbreak of war in August.

would have gotten it... See note p. 234.

FULL STEAM AHEAD!, p. 160

muttering to himself... The Kaiser had always liked to take a *Spaziergang*, or stroll, around his gardens. Formerly in Germany, he would hold forth to his numerous suite, but here in exile at Doorn, Holland, he is just muttering to himself.

shriveled arm... A breech birth left him with a withered left arm about six inches shorter than his right arm. Historians have suggested that this disability affected his emotional development.

my uncle Bertie **...** King Edward VII, brother of his mother, Crown Princess Victoria ('Vickie'), daughter of Queen Victoria.

Baghdadbahn **...** The terminus of the Orient Express in Istanbul was Haydarpasha Station, a European-style railroad hotel. There—in the planned railway scheme only partly built by the outbreak of the War in 1914—a traveler changed to the Chemin de Fer d'Anatolie, which took him as far as Konya. At Konya he changed to the Baghdadbahn for Aleppo. At Aleppo he could continue on the main branch to Urfa, Nesibin, Mosul, Tikrit, Samara, Baghdad, Karbala, Najaf, and Basra, or change for the Haj spur to Damascus, Jerusalem, and Medina. Since the time of the Silk Road, Aleppo had been the junction with the road going south to Arabia and Egypt.

In order to be out of range of the guns of the Royal Navy, the main line of the Baghdadbahn was cut through the Taurus Mountains, the southern ramparts of the geopolitical fortress of Anatolia. In the same pass, that of the Cilician Gate, another German emperor, the Crusader Frederick Barbarossa, drowned while crossing a ditch.

by-product gasoline **...** Gasoline had been an almost useless by-product of the process of refining oil into kerosene to be used in lamps until Nikolaus Otto perfected the four-stroke internal-combustion engine, which Daimler and Benz used to power their automobiles, the first of which was sold in 1892.

heart of darkness **...** Dark rumors of atrocities coming out of the Congo had begun to make the imperial venture seem to Europeans less a *mission civilisatrice* than a moral embarrassment.

Full steam ahead! **...** V*olldampf voraus!,* the Kaiser's personal rallying cry. 'Mohammedan forces...my disposal': his letter *(Silvesterbrief)* to Chancellor von Bülow (1905); '...resolved by blood and iron!' (1912) quoted in John C. G. Röhl, *Kaiser Wilhem II* (2014).

ORIGIN OF THE WAR, p. 162

Lenin predicted **...** in *Imperialism, the Last Stage of Capitalism* (1914).

strange bedfellows **...** Shakespeare, *The Tempest.* England and France had been fighting over the inheritance of Eleanor of Aquitaine since the first years of the 13th century and throughout the Hundred Years' War 'in Flanders, in Artois, and Picardy.'

The rise of Germany in the center of Europe united these two former enemies against her. The Kaiser's failure to renew Bismarck's Reinsurance Treaty with Russia (1887) opened the way to the Franco-Russian Military Convention of 1892. The Reinsurance Treaty had been Bismarck's attempt to revive the Three Emperors' League (*Dreikaiserbund*), which had broken down with troubles in the Balkans over the Eastern Question, but after he was dismissed Germany drifted closer to Austria. The Kaiser felt that his personal relationship with Tsar Nicholas II would be sufficient to maintain the diplomatic relationship with Russia, but for Russia, drifting away from Germany inevitably meant drifting toward France.

After Fashoda (see text) and with a powerful Germany occupying Alsace and Lorraine, France was forced to align herself with Britain, which she did in the *Entente Cordiale* of 1904. What Bismarck most feared had come to pass: being one of two in a party of five.

The founder of modern Germany, he knew that his creation had upset the balance of power. In an attempt to ensure the peace of Europe, like a spider he spun webs of treaties. As Halford Mackinder wrote, 'No statesman ever adjusted war to policy with nicer judgment than Bismarck.... It was as though he had sent his sheep-dog round his flock to drive his sheep to him.' But, as in a Greek tragedy, all attempts to avert the doom prophesied by the oracle only work, in the end, to bring it on.

Bismarck predicted it: 'Jena [1806] came twenty years after the death of Frederick the Great [1786], the crash will come twenty years after my departure if things go on like this.' Bismarck died in 1897, twenty-one years before the surrender of Germany in 1918.

WHAT WAS THE CAUSE?, pp. 164–65
Dardanelles ... After the War, Winston Churchill wrote that when the *Goeben* arrived at the Dardanelles she brought with her 'more slaughter, more misery and ruin than has ever before been borne within the compass of a ship' (quoted in Robert K. Massie, *Castles of Steel* [2003]).
German victory ... 'Reports of German victories, skilfully exaggerated, have enormously influenced the following of Enver Pasha, and telegrams from Constantinople speak of war as inevitable' (*The New York Herald*, Sept. 4, 1914).

BUTCHER BLOCK, pp. 166–67
the Kaiser, or Hitler ... They had all been there before, or would be. Napoleon had made the first Western incursion into the Middle East when he invaded Egypt in 1795. The Kaiser abdicated in 1918 and watched the *dénouement* from exile in Holland, where he died in 1941. Lenin was cooking up trouble for the West by founding the Comintern in 1919 (see below).

Blaming the 'victors of Versailles' for the humiliation of Germany, Hitler would come to power in 1933. In 1918, he was hospitalized after a mustard gas attack when he learned of the capitulation, which he blamed on 'November criminals,' civilian leaders, and Marxists. In 1919, at the time the Great Powers were meeting in Paris, he was working as a *Reichswehr* intelligence agent in Munich assigned to infiltrate the socialist German Workers' Party (DAP).

Ho Chi Minh was in Paris, supposedly working as a pastry chef, when he petitioned the Peace Conference for the civil rights of the Vietnamese people in French Indochina. He was ignored.
starting the Cold War ... by founding the Third International (Comintern) in 1919. Two years later, in 1921, the same year that Britain was dividing up the Middle East at the Cairo Conference, the Bolsheviks convened the Congress of the Peoples of the East at Baku, the oil city on the Caspian Sea, to rally the nascent Third World against the Western 'imperialists.'
a 'homeland' ... The letter to Lord Rothschild, known as the Balfour Declaration, called only for a 'homeland.'

BREAKING OF SÈVRES, p. 168
breaking of Sykes-Picot ... a process that Isis continued in 2014, obliterating the century-old border between Iraq and Syria drawn in 1916 between what later became French and British 'mandates' under the League of Nations.
independent nation of Armenia ... The U.S. was asked to take a mandate for Armenia. Seeing the mandates as imperialism in modern dress, Wilson refused.

Mostly, though, Wilson went along with Lloyd George and Clemenceau at Paris in 1919 as long as they agreed to his League of Nations, which he believed would settle all issues afterward. But the treaty was rejected by the U.S. Senate, whose leader, Henry Cabot Lodge, saw acceptance of the League as a violation of the U.S. policy of avoiding 'permanent alliances' that George Washington had articulated in 1796 in his Farewell Address.
defying the Great Powers ... Abdül Aziz bin-Saud (Ibn Saud), the founder of modern Saudi

Arabia, also defied the Great Powers by seizing Mecca in 1925, ending 700 years of Hashemite rule by expelling Britain's client, Sharif Hussein bin Ali. The Hashemites claim direct descent from Mohammad. King Abdullah of Jordan is a great-great-grandson of Sharif Hussein.

ejected the invading... Atatürk's rapid expansion of Turkey to its present borders might be adduced as proof of Anatolia's geopolitical integrity.

MIGHTY CAESAR'S HEIRS, p. 170
Mighty Caesar... One of the many titles claimed by the Ottoman sultan. See p. 128.
deposed in 1922... It is appropriate that the sultan was deposed in the year 1922, when Atatürk's army drove the last of the invaders out of Turkey. In the following year, the Treaty of Lausanne ratified the existence of an independent Turkish state.
Byzantine Empire... Byzas was the name of the Greek colony that Constantine transformed into his new Rome, later Constantinople, later Istanbul.

In the 16th century under the Hapsburgs, the historical term 'Byzantine Empire' came into use, referring to what is also known as the Lower Roman Empire, that is, the empire that existed from the fall of Rome in the West (476) until the fall of of the Eastern Empire in 1453. In demoting it to 'Byzantine,' the Hapsburgs asserted a claim to being the true Roman emperors.
Napoleon III... was elected president of France by popular vote in 1848, staged a *coup d'état* in 1851, and made himself emperor in 1852.
ironically named... ironically because the last rulers bore the same names as the first. Romulus is the mythological founder of Rome; Augustus founded the Empire; Constantine the Eastern capital of Constantinople; Carl or *Carolus Magnus* (Charlemagne) refounded the Western Empire; Otto, the Holy Roman Empire; and Mehmet II, the Turkish version of the name Mohammad, conquered the city of Constantinople by virtue of which he and his successors could claim the title 'Mighty Caesar.' This may mean nothing more than that dynasties tend to lay claim to the status of a founder in the naming of princes, often to ironic ends.

YEARS BETWEEN THE WARS, p. 172
boxers in a ring... Roosevelt was president in the years between the wars but died before the Cold War began. Truman and Eisenhower were the first Cold War presidents. Stalin died in 1953, and his heirs continued the Cold War up until 1989.

RUSSIA AND THE U.S.: GEOPOLITICALLY, pp. 174–75
his novel Ada... in which he 'commingled granoblasticly' the two countries into an imaginary country with a Russian noble family owning vast tracts of Canada and the American Midwest who marry into a family of Irish-American investment bankers from New York.

RUSSIA AND THE U.S.: POLITICALLY, p. 176
Hegelian terms... Hegel does not use the term 'dialectic,' nor does Marx use the term 'communism.'
founders... of sociology... with Émile Durkheim (1858–1917) and Max Weber (1864–1920).
the haves and the have-nots... 'I saw society divided in two: those who owned nothing were united in one common desire, while those who owned something were united in common anguish. Between these two great classes, no bond or sympathy remained; everywhere the idea of an inevitable impending struggle had taken hold' (Alexis de Tocqueville).

logical fallacy... a phrase that is itself a logical fallacy: an oxymoron.

failed workers' state... Trotsky's name for a state where a revolution did occur, but which returned to being a bureaucratic tyranny. The world today is littered with such failed states.

Fifth International... The ideological concept of the continuing World Revolution against the globalized capitalist system. A history of the Internationals is the history of the dream of revolution—and its failure.

The First International was founded in 1864 as the International Workingmen's Association, but failed with the Paris Commune of 1871.

The Second International (1881), the largest in terms of members, succeeded the First, but was discredited when the Socialist parties sided with their particular national governments in 1914. For the workers the War was a nationalist cause that had nothing to do with their international, or rather supranational, cause.

The Third International (1919), or Comintern, was the Bolshevik project to spread the Revolution to the colonies, and after the Second World War, to the former colonies of the 'imperialist' powers.

The Fourth International was the movement founded by Leon Trotsky in exile to continue the Revolution, proclaiming essentially the same idea that Marx voiced at the end of *The Communist Manifesto* (1848): 'The Revolution is dead. Long live the Revolution!' Trotsky claimed in his book *The Revolution Betrayed* (1937) that the Soviet Union was a 'failed workers' state.' He positioned the intellectual Left as an antitotalitarian movement, from which position it slowly morphed into the Neo-Conservative movement that had—and continues to have—such influence on American foreign policy.

The Revolution never progressed to the workers' state imagined by Marxist ideology. Lenin wrote that the Revolution didn't spread to the West because the capitalists had created an 'aristocracy of labor,' buying off the workers with cheap imported goods—just as the 19th-century French author Brillat-Savarin wrote, the bankers had defeated the aristocracy 'with their money boxes and their chefs.'

Capitalism won. It continues to triumph because it has been able to include the workers in the system, to seduce them into thinking that they are part of it, even if they are not.

The Fifth International is the concept—and it is only a concept—that the World Revolution is still in the future, if ever.

PASSING OF THE BATON, pp. 178–79

leadership of the West... In 1899, Rudyard Kipling had urged this role on Theodore Roosevelt with his poem 'The White Man's Burden: The United States and the Philippine Islands.'

by Soviet definition, imperialist... Roosevelt had been insistent that French colonial rule not be re-established in Indochina after the Second World War. However, in an attempt to bolster a weak France against the Soviet threat creeping westward in Europe, Truman agreed to the transport of French troops and materials to suppress the incipient Viet Minh (League for the Independence of Viet Nam). Said Secretary of State Dean Acheson, 'France blackmailed the U.S. [into Vietnam].' Ho Chi Minh asked, 'The Statue of Liberty, is she standing on her head?'

'socialism in one country'... a theory of Stalin's (1924), later accepted as policy. It was a shift from the Marxist international revolution, and in opposition to Trotsky's theory of permanent revolution.

continuation of Potemkin's project... With the Comintern, the Bolsheviks easily stepped into the role of the tsarist Pan-Slavic movement,

no longer limited to the Balkans, but now extended to the whole world.
the last time... except in Libya in 2011–12, when Britain and France took the active role in enforcing a no-fly zone there.
stated principles... Self-determination was asserted by Woodrow Wilson in 1918 after he announced his Fourteen Points. Noninterference was established as a principle with the Peace of Westphalia in 1648.

Thomas Jefferson reaffirmed Washington's policy of 'no permanent alliances' in his inaugural address in 1801, using the term 'entangling alliances.' While stating that the U.S. would view any European interference in the New World as acts of aggression, the Monroe Doctrine (1823) affirmed that the U.S. would likewise not interfere in European affairs. It was not until after the Second World War that the U.S. diverged from these policies.
classic moral conflict... Cicero explored this conflict in his *On Duty* (*De Officiis*). Written in 44 BC, just before his assassination by order of Mark Antony, the book has had a profound influence on Western thought. 'Cicero himself seems to have regarded it as his spiritual testament and masterpiece' (Michael Grant).

A DELICATE BALANCE UPSET, pp. 180–81
Thucydides demonstrated... 'It was the rise of Athens and the fear that this inspired in Sparta that made war inevitable.' Halford Mackinder wrote, 'Have not all the great wars of the past in Europe come from the fact that one state [either] under Napoleon, Louis XIV, [or] Philip II became too powerful?'
former U.S. ambassador... Robert Oakley, quoted by Daniel Schorr, *Come to Think of It* (2008).
Benazir Bhutto... Benazir Bhutto, *Daughter of Destiny* (2008).

FATE POWER VACUUMS, p. 182
A millennium and a half before.... a balance of power had been established in the late 2nd millennium with what is called the brotherhood of kings. The oldest known treaty, the Treaty of Kadesh (1259 BC), between the Egyptian pharaoh Ramses II and the Hittite Hattusili III, dates from this period. A clay tablet written in cuneiform, it is preserved in the Istanbul Archaeological Museum. In 1970, Turkey presented a large replica to the UN in New York.

REVOLT OF ISLAM, p. 186
sword of oil... Daniel Yergin, *The Prize* (2008).
Revolt of Islam... The title of a long poem by Shelley. It has little to do with Islam, but much more to do with the disillusionment of European liberals following the Restoration, the attempted return to the *status quo ante* after the Congress of Vienna in 1815.
less interested in theology... Vali Nasr, *The Sunni Revival* (2006). Al-Afghani disguised his Shia origins when he moved to Constantinople by calling himself 'the Afghan.' In 1944, his remains were taken to Afghanistan and a mausoleum built for them in Kabul.
Recent actions... Quoted in Khursheed Kamal Aziz, *The Indian Khilafat Movement* (1972).

OIL FARM, pp. 188–89
in Russia and in the United States... Oil was discovered in Baku in 1846, and in Pennsylvania in 1859.
floated to victory... Quoted in Polk, *op. cit.*
failed in their objectives... Germany's objective was to seize the Caspian oil city of Baku, but was defeated before Stalingrad, now Volgograd (near Saray, the capital of the Golden Horde). This was the farthest reach of Western power into the Heartland. In the East, Japan briefly held the Dutch oil fields in Indonesia.

jugular vein of the West *...* Cyrus Vance, secretary of state under Bill Clinton, quoted in *Financial Times* (London), July 2012.
Kuwait's perceived overproduction *...* In late May 1990, the Iraqi dictator Saddam Hussein claimed that overproduction of oil by Kuwait and the United Arab Emirates was 'economic warfare' against Iraq.
U.S. demand *...* Daniel Yergin, *op. cit.*
new domestic supply *...* 'The new sources of American energy mean more supply has been added to global markets — almost the exact amount that has been taken off the market because of unrest at times in the Middle East and Africa over the last five years' (*New York Times*, Aug. 29, 2014).

With a decline in oil prices in 2014, 'the Saudis have taken the bold step of asserting their pivotal role in the oil market and subtly squeezing the finances of some of America's fledgling shale companies. Yet the falling price will deliver a de facto tax cut for American consumers and, if sustained, will hit both Russia and Iran at a time when Washington is trying to put pressure on both countries' (*Financial Times* [London], Oct. 7, 2014).

WORLD TRADERS AND RAIDERS, p. 190
new Red Apple *...* See note p. 227.
oil, globalization *...* Steve A. Yetiv, *The Petroleum Triangle: Oil, Globalization, and Terror* (2011).
provided a market *...* This is the economic system of mercantilism that was so resented by the American colonists, a resentment that eventually led to the revolt against Britain.
discovered in Iraq in 1927 *...* In the 'Red Line' Agreement of 1927, France and Britain agreed to cut the U.S. in on the newly discovered Iraqi oil fields at Mosul and Kirkuk in return for American support during the War.

legitimate booty *...* Ibn Khaldūn observes that the first caliphs 'removed the possessions' of the Persians and the Byzantines. To nomads, who live by raiding, booty is always legitimate. In the succession of states, hardy nomads naturally take booty from soft settled peoples.

GEOPOLITICS, p. 194
old newspaper *...* Paris *Herald Tribune*, Oct. 4, 1887. The title of this book is just *The Eastern Question* — not *The Eastern Question, Again* — but it does seem that the question is asked again and again.
Nicholas Spykman *...* A professor of international relations at Yale, Nicholas Spykman (1893–1943) sought in his writings to prevent another American withdrawal from world affairs after the Second World War, as had happened in 1919 with the rejection of the League of Nations. It is said that had the U.S. been a member, the League would not have failed and could possibly have stopped Hitler and averted war. The establishment of the United Nations under the auspices of the U.S. was a recognition of the earlier failure of the League. Spykman's ultimate object was a balance of power in the world, a proposition first recognized in modern times with the Peace of Utrecht in 1715, which ended the War of the Spanish Succession.
Rimlands *...* Spykman recasts Mackinder's dictum (see p. 26) as: 'He who rules the Rimlands rules Eurasia / He who rules Eurasia controls the destiny of the world.'
great border *...* of which the Mexican-American border and the Mediterranean Sea form the western end. The pressure is so intense in the Mediterranean from Africa to Sicily that the Italians have set up a search-and-rescue program to prevent the loss of life as happened with the shipwreck off Lampedusa when 300 people died. The Italians call this program

Mare Nostrum, the old Roman name for the Mediterranean. In 2014, this program was replaced by a new one named after the sea-god Triton.

The refugee children coming from Central America under a 2008 U.S. law to prevent child trafficking are another example of the pressure across this great border of the world.

DESERT & SOWN, pp. 196–97
haves and have-nots... de Tocqueville's 'haves and have-nots' of 1848. See note p. 239.
a Pentagon consultant... Thomas Barnett, *The Pentagon's New Map* (2004).
world systems... Wallerstein's 'world systems.'
four periods... typically driven by overpopulation in either desert or sown.

EAST & WEST, pp. 198–99
moving ever westward... with a sense that the world was at the same time always improving, a view that has been called the 'Whig interpretation of history.'
to some... Francis Fukuyama, *The End of History* (1992), though it seems that it was the German philosopher Hegel who first proposed such an idea.

A professor at Jena in 1806 and a witness of the battle, Hegel claimed that it represented the 'end of history' because Napoleon's victories would bring the 'universal homogeneous state,' in the words of Alexandre Kojèv. Fukuyama likewise saw the United States as the endpoint of humanity's socio-cultural evolution.
One theory... that of Seymour Martin Lipset, which holds that when per capita GDP rises to around $7,600, most countries have undergone a transition from autocracy to democracy. At the time of the Arab Spring in 2011, the GDPs of Tunisia and Egypt bracketed this figure. On the other hand, the new wealth of many Third World countries seems merely to spur corruption and undermine democracy, *pace* Lipset.
stability and chaos... In continuing to allow Vladimir Putin to rule, the Russian people have tacitly chosen his version of stability over the chaos that reigned under Yeltsin, when the so-called oligarchs seized control of the major industrial assets of the defunct Soviet state.
in accordance with the water's will... Bismarck used the same metaphor. See p. 14.

Maynard Keynes said that the workers permit the capitalists to rule over them only because the capitalists don't 'eat the whole economic pie,' but rather reinvest it, providing jobs.
state itself confounded... Shakespeare, Sonnet 64.
within its own boundaries... The concept of the modern state starts with the Peace of Westphalia of 1648, for which it is called the Westphalian state. Ratified by three treaties—the Peace of Münster, the Treaty of Münster, and the Treaty of Osnabrück—Westphalia marked the end of the Thirty Years' War and the recognition of the right of national states to be sovereign within their own boundaries, free from the interference of a supranational power such as the Hapsburg Holy Roman Empire or the Papacy, and introduced the concept of self-determination. See p. 142.

ORDER & FRAGMENTATION, p. 200
many different languages... In a letter home, the wife of the British ambassador to Constantinople, Lady Mary Wortley Montague, wrote in 1718, 'I live in a place that very well represents the Tower of Babel; in Pera [a suburb of Istanbul where the embassies are located] they speak Turkish, Greek, Hebrew, Armenian, Arabic, Persian, Russian, Slovonian, Walachian, German, Dutch, French, English, Italian, Hungarian; and what is worse there is [*sic*] ten of these lan-

guages spoke [*sic*] in my own family. My grooms are Arabs, my footmen French, English, and German, my nurse Armenian, my housemaids Russian, half a dozen other servants Greek, my steward Italian, my janissaries Turks. I live in the perpetual hearing of this medley of sounds, which produces a very extraordinary effect upon the people who are born here. They learn all these languages at the same time and without knowing any of them well enough to write or read in.'

    The present writer had a friend, the Egyptian novelist and poet Christian Ayoub, who was born in Alexandria, Egypt, in 1926, four years after the end of the Ottoman Empire. His father had been minister of justice under King Farouk, his great-aunt first Christian lady-in-waiting at the court. (Muslim women could not receive foreigners.) He spoke no language without an accent. Once when I asked him what language he had spoken growing up, he replied, 'We spoke Arabic to the shopkeepers, French to our parents, English to our nanny, and Italian to the servants.' I asked if the servants were Italian. 'Oh, no!' he replied. 'They were Greek!'

South Sudan... 'Instead of governing through strong institutions, many power brokers and generals in this nation still essentially command their own forces, their loyalties to the government often determined by their cut of national oil revenues. It is an extortion racket with bargaining ongoing on a regular basis, either with violence or the threat of violence as a form of negotiation' (Alex de Waal, exec. dir. of the World Peace Foundation, Tufts University, quoted in *N.Y. Times*, Jan. 1, 2014).

most dangerous... 'The World's Most Dangerous Borders,' Philip Walker, *op. cit.*

Peace in this World... See p. 128.

is not unaware... even if later pulling back from this forward position.

PERSIA/IRAN, p. 202

thrones are shattered... Goethe, *East-Western Divan*.

his son... the Shah who was overthrown in 1979 by the Ayatollah's Islamic Revolution.

has been called... by a British MI6 agent who took part in the operation, in his memoirs, quoted by Polk, *op. cit.*

possession of a nuclear weapon... '[A] growing number of countries seek to acquire weapons of mass destruction. This is logical: if you have the bomb, no one will touch you' (Vladimir Putin, *N.Y. Times*, Sept. 11, 2013).

SYRIA/ISIS/ISRAEL, p. 204

a Greater Syria... existed only in the minds of British and French diplomats at the moment of its being broken up in 1919–21. It comprised almost the whole area covered under Sykes-Picot, whose architects drew it on the map merely to divide it. The twelfth of Wilson's Fourteen Points claims only the autonomous development of the nations under the rule of the Ottoman Empire and does not mention a 'Syria' per se in any shape or size. This was the land that Prince Faisal expected to rule over as an independent Arab state, according to British promises.

    In an adjustment to Sykes-Picot, the San Remo Conference (1920) provisionally divided the Middle East into mandates of the League of Nations. France was given a mandate for Syria in return for letting Britain keep Jerusalem and Mosul, plus 50 percent of Iraqi oil revenues. In the battle of Maysalun in July 1920, Faisal and his Arabs were defeated by the French on the road to Damascus, and he fled to England. At the Cairo Conference (1921), Faisal became king of Iraq and his brother Abdullah king of Trans-Jordan, now Jordan. Faisal's grandson Faisal II was overthrown and killed by a mob in

1958, opening the way for the Baath party and the eventual rise of Saddam Hussein.

Isis... On May 14, 2014, the U.S. State Department announced its decision to refer to the Islamic State of Iraq and the Levant as 'ISIL.' However, the second 'S' stands for *al-Shaam*, the Levant, or Greater Syria in Arabic. Properly, it is called al-Dawlet al-Islamiyah, or al-Dawlah. Derogatorily it is, apparently, Da'ash.

In 2014, its leader took the name Abu Bakr, after the first caliph (573–634). He proclaimed a new caliphate on June 29, 2014. At the same time, Isis removed 'Iraq and al-Shaam' from its name, and began to call itself simply the 'Islamic State.' Analysts have observed that dropping the regional reference reflects a widening of its scope to the global *jihad* and the establishment of a universal caliphate.

It may be said that Isis survives only because it serves interests larger than itself. For instance, Turkey has the second largest army in NATO and could easily wipe Isis off the map, if it served Turkish interests.

Islamic rebel state... David Motadel of Cambridge University characterizes the classic Islamic rebel state as one whose 'leaders were religious authorities, most of them assuming the title of "commander of the faithful." Their states were theocratically organized. Islam helped unite fractured tribal societies, as Ibn Khaldūn observed, and served as a source of absolute, divine authority to enhance social discipline and political order, and to legitimize war' (*N.Y. Times*, Sept. 23, 2014).

As precursors of Isis, Motadel cites the Wahhabi of Saudi Arabia in the 18th century, the anticolonial forces in North Africa led by Abd al-Qadir in the 1830s and 1840s, the Mahdist state in Sudan in the 1880s and 1890s, as well as the Caucasian imamate that was eventually defeated by tsarist troops. We might add the Dervish State of Somalia that held off the British until suppressed by air power in 1920.

However well organized, these Islamic rebel states have always been unstable and never truly functional, Motadel points out; yet the original Muslims under Mohammad and the caliphs, as well as later under the Ottoman sultans, could also be said to have begun as Islamic rebel states.

the river of Egypt... or the 'Brook of Egypt' in old translations. In Paris in 1919, when Lloyd George was asked what the border of the proposed Palestine mandate should be, without pause he replied, 'From Dan to Barsheeba': that is, the northern and southern limits of David's kingdom (Margaret Macmillan, *Paris 1919*).

trash can of history... свалка истории (Svalka istorii), or 'trash can of history,' a phrase made famous by Trotsky's use of it when the Mensheviks walked out of the Second Congress of Soviets in October 1917, thereby relinquishing power to the Bolsheviks: 'You are pitiful, isolated individuals! You are bankrupts. Your role is played out. Go where you belong from now on, into the trash can of history!'

UKRAINE, 2014, p. 206

In 1699... In the same year, with the Treaty of Carlowitz, the Ottomans made their first major concessions, giving up Croatia and Hungary.

Cossacks... Under the tsars, the Cossacks protected the frontiers and put down rebellions. They were used as well against the Jewish population in the Pale of Settlement. The Soviets almost annihilated them. In 1996, the Cossacks' leader Alexander Demin came to Boris Yeltsin's support after which they were given some of their lands back. Today they are employed as auxiliary policemen.

wide borderland... The present writer had a friend, Eleanor Perenyi, who lived in the late

1930s on her Hungarian husband's estate near Uzgorod on the western slope of the Carpathians in what is now Ukraine. Before the War, Uzgorod had been Hungarian; Versailles made it Czechoslovakian; for a time when she lived there it was Ruthenian. In 1939, the Germans occupied it. After the war it was Soviet, then after 1991, Ukrainian.

In 1946, Mrs. Perenyi published a memoir of her life there titled *More Was Lost*, a reference to the Hungarian saying 'more was lost at Mohács.'

DREAMS FROM MY FATHERS, pp. 210–11
They are unconquerable ... 'An Afghani along the road says, "I am for anyone who is against the enemies of Islam. The Taliban are the people. They do not want to fight, but the country has been occupied by Jews and Christians, so their struggle is just."'There is no military solution to the insurgency, as NATO's failure to defeat the Taliban shows. Their leadership is headquartered in Pakistan, which makes them unconquerable.' (*Economist*, Nov. 29, 2014).
a revolutionary situation... 'Whenever there exists a power that considers the international order or the manner of legitimizing it oppressive, relations between it and other powers will be revolutionary' (Henry Kissinger, *Metternich, Castlereagh, and the Problems of Peace, 1812-22* [1957]). From earliest to latest, Dr. Kissinger's writings have focused on the question of order.
Concert of Europe... considered to have maintained peace from 1815 until 1914, with exceptions such as the Crimean War as well as the Franco-Prussian War, the crucible in which modern Germany was forged. It was a system of open congresses, such as the two in Berlin that drew the lines in the Balkans and Africa. It was supplanted by the system of secret treaties that led Europe into war in 1914.
the revolution is permanent... Trotsky 'continued to advocate, insistently and unswervingly, the idea of the "permanency" of the Russian revolution, which argues that after the revolution has begun it cannot come to an end until it effects the overthrow of capitalism and establishes the socialist system throughout the world' (Sverchkov's memoirs, quoted in Trotsky, *My Life* [1930]).
frenzy of history... *Ibid.* Revolutions occur at moments in history when inchoate feelings of resentment, outrage, anger, and fury inspire people to a frenzy. 'A riot is the language of the unheard' (Martin Luther King).

OXBOWS IN TIME, p. 212
one of those old newspapers... *The Independent Gazette* (Philadelphia), August 1789.

ACKNOWLEDGMENTS

The author wishes to acknowledge
the help of the following:
George Bradley
for carefully reading the various drafts
and making many very useful suggestions;
Keith Goldsmith
for his continued support;
David Jernigan
for putting the project
in its historiographic context;
Ann LaFarge
for correcting stylistic inelegancies
and 'docking prolixities';
Pat & Lew Leibowitz and *Patrick Murphy*
for their encouragement;
John McGhee
for his excellent copy editing;
Andreas Mink
for geopolitical conversations,
wielding the editorial ax,
and reordering the argument;
Dennis O'Brien
for lending me Labberton's
Historical Atlas;
Sue Siskin
for teaching me watercolors;
my brother and sister-in-law
Bryan Danforth and *Marina Caillaud*
my sister *Alexandra*
and my mother and father
for their interest and encouragement.